COLLECTOR'S GUIDE TO

COLLECTOR'S GUIDE TO
BUYING ANTIQUE
SILVER

Rachael Feild

LITTLE, BROWN AND COMPANY

BUYING ANTIQUE SILVER

A LITTLE, BROWN Book

This edition published in 2001 by
Little, Brown and Company (UK)

First published in 1988 Little, Brown and Company (UK)
Copyright © 1988 Rachael Feild

A CIP catalogue record for this book is available
from the British Library

ISBN 0-316-85839-0

Production by Omnipress
Printed in the Czech Republic

Little, Brown and Company (UK)
Brettenham House
Lancaster Place
London WC2E 7EN

Contents

Acknowledgements

The author would like to thank the following for their generosity
in giving their time and help in providing illustrations and
photographs:
Sotheby's, New Bond Street, London W1.
Phillips Blenstock House, New Bond Street, London W1.
Edward Donohoe.
Brand Inglis.
John Culme.
The author is particularly grateful to Mary Cooke of Mary Cooke
Antiques Ltd and William Price of J. H. Bourdon Smith Ltd for
their patience, time and trouble in the correction and compilation
of this book.

The History of English Silver: an introduction

In the days of Queen Elizabeth I, as the history books relate, England stood alone, bravely defending herself from the might of the great Spanish Armada with her gallant little fleet. There were many reasons for the Spaniards' desire to defeat the English and sink their ships, and one of them was revenge. The Spanish galleons running the gauntlet up the English Channel to the Spanish Netherlands were full of gold and silver bullion, and England had none. England's famous brave sea-captains were pirates to a man, and their chief aim was to capture as many Spanish treasure ships as possible, wherever they might be found.

It was no mean feat for Sir Francis Drake to sail round the world in his ship the *Pelican*, which was scarcely larger than an off-shore trawler. He took five ships and 164 men, and his voyage, which took him round the ferocious Cape of Good Hope, lasted three years. But his mission was not, truth to tell, to drive the Spaniards from the seven seas, but to find their source of bullion and seize as much treasure as he could find, to replenish the empty coffers of his queen. This he accomplished apparently without too much difficulty. Sailing up the coast of Chile, the ship's log records that 'we went to a certain port called Tarapaca; where, being landed, we found by the sea side a Spaniard lying asleep, who had lying by him 13 bars of silver, which weighed 4,000 ducats Spanish. We took the silver and left the man.'

During his long voyage in that year of grace 1577, he also plundered one Spanish ship of 25,000 pesos of pure fine gold and from another took 27 wedges of silver, each one weighing about 20 lb. He also captured the *Cacafuego* and took from her holds 13 chests full of plate, fourscore pound weight of gold and 20 tons of silver. And it is to those early English buccaneers that we owe the name 'plate' by which all silver and gold is known in England today. *Plata* is the Spanish for silver – the River Plate was named after it, long before Argentina was given its name. As for the word 'sterling' by which all assayed plate is known, it probably owes its origins to the main source of silver in Europe before the days of the Spanish treasure ships – Saxony, the Hartz mountains, Bohemia and Transylvania, from which came the word *esterlins*. But until the Spanish began to bring tons of silver bullion into Europe, gold was more common as a precious metal, brought in from the more accessible African Gold Coast, and mined in small quantities all over Europe. Even the British Isles had gold mines – in Cornwall, Wales, Scotland and Ireland. The craft of the goldsmith is more ancient than that of the silversmith, and when the Goldsmiths' Company admitted silversmiths into their guild, the silversmiths too officially assumed the title of 'goldsmith', which even today remains their proper title.

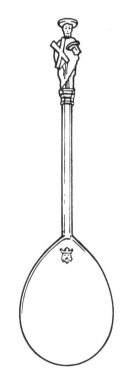

16th-century apostle spoon of St Andrew with an early London hallmark in the bowl.

Silver gilt salver on a trumpet foot. The border is chased with formal acanthus leaves. London 1655. 13 in (33 cm) diameter.

The mark of the leopard

Great quantities of gold, silver gilt and silver plate, displayed with ostentation, were always an outward and visible sign of wealth and power. Not only did such displays demonstrate wealth – they were instantly convertible into coinage. Right up to the reign of William and Mary, which began in 1689, any wealthy lord or baron, finding himself short of ready cash, could take a massive piece of silver plate to a 'goldsmith banker' and have it turned into coinage. In times of plenty he could with equal ease convert the contents of his moneybags into a splendid loving cup or goblet.

Pure, unadulterated silver is a very soft metal, too soft to endure, either as coinage or as an artefact. From ancient times, therefore, silver has been alloyed with a very small amount of base metal – usually copper, with which it has an affinity – to make it more durable and more easily workable. This very fact, however, has made it a simple matter for silver to be adulterated, for 'short weight' to be given.

Metallurgy is a complicated subject, classed in those early days as a 'mystery' and closely related to alchemy. Although silver had been used as a currency in England since Anglo-Saxon times, there had been little precise knowledge of the metal, or control over the amount of pure silver used in the coinage of the realm. In Europe, where there were great deposits of metallic ores in Saxony, the Hartz mountains, the Tyrol and Bohemia, knowledge of mining and metallurgy were considerable, and in the twelfth century Henry II called in experts from Saxony to improve the English currency and establish a standard of purity of silver coin. The proportions established at that time have remained constant from that day to this, with a few rare periods of change – for the worse under Henry VIII, who debased the English coinage, and for the better under William III, when a higher standard of silver was introduced. The proportions finally laid down in 1238 were 92.5 parts of pure silver to 7.5 parts of copper alloy. This 'sterling' silver was to be the legal standard for all English coinage.

There was still no control over silver used for anything other than coinage, however, a fact which must have made the value of silver a contentious affair. The Crown had frequent cause to raise money in taxes, and the variable amounts of pure silver in ingots or in decorative or ceremonial pieces that from time to time had to be melted down for coinage continued to present problems – the more so since at that time the coiner and the silversmith were one and the same person, known as 'the moneyer'. In 1300, having expelled from England all the recognised moneylenders, who up until then had maintained some control over the purity of gold and silver coinage, Edward I introduced a statute to control the standard of all 'sterling' silver for whatever use. In that year the marking of all plate with a 'halle' or 'head' mark became law. The mark, a leopard's head, was struck on all 'sterling' silver which had been officially assayed and found up to standard.

It was, in fact, the head of a lion when it was first struck – a lion with a shaggy mane and beard, with a ducal crown upon its head. It could never originally have been a leopard because, according to the language of old heraldry, 'the thicknesse of a Lyon's mane is a testimony of his generous birth and by the same he is distinguished from the degenerate and bastard race of Leopards begotten between the adulterous Lyoness and the Parde'. The 'parde' was a panther. Ancient heraldic language, a mixture of Old French, Anglo-Saxon and Latin, was the cause of the confusion. A lion was 'leo' and appeared in coats of arms in a number of poses: 'couchant', 'sejant', 'passant'. The arms of the King of England from the time of Henry II onwards was of three lions 'passant guardant' or 'partant' – 'regarding as he passes'. Thus the King's mark was a 'leo part', heraldic shorthand for a lion passant guardant, and so was called a 'leopart' in the statute of 1363 when Edward III reinforced the laws by ordering a maker's mark to be struck in addition to the King's mark. The 'leo' continued to be recognisable as a lion, less shaggy but still crowned, until the 1820s, when he lost his crown and became to all intents and purposes one of the 'degenerate and bastard race of Leopards' that he is today.

Church and Crown – ceremonial plate

Up until the sixteenth century, much of the silver plate in England belonged to the Church and was used, as it was on the Continent, for embellishing altars and side chapels, for candle-

Hallmarks on the stem of a 17th-century trefid spoon, c.1690, probably West Country.

Late Elizabethan seal-top spoon by a provincial silversmith, c.1590.

Steeple cups were made from about 1600 up to the Civil War. Very English in design, made at a time when there was very little Continental influence on shapes and patterns of gold and silver.

Triangular trencher salt and a simple rounded shape which later developed into a capstan salt. Both patterns were made in the first decade of the 17th century.

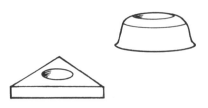

sticks, crosses, crucifixes, ewers, basins, alms dishes and all the panoply of the Roman Catholic faith. During the Reformation, vast quantities of elaborately wrought gold, silver gilt and silver plate were forcibly removed from the Church to the Treasury to finance the wars and weddings of Henry VIII. But even all the Church's riches were not enough to pay for all the battles England had to fight for economic, religious and political reasons as a result of Henry VIII's break with the Pope and the Holy Roman Empire. He debased the coinage by increasing the amount of copper in 'sterling', and when Queen Elizabeth came to the throne, England's economy lay in ruins at her feet.

Most Church plate before about 1535 has vanished. What 'Roman Catholic' plate survived the Reformation was looted during the Civil War from 1643 onwards. But from what can be gleaned from surviving plate, the most important items in both secular and ecclesiastical ceremonial pieces were the great cups and chalices. In churches and cathedrals they were of massive size and beautifully wrought, as were the ewers, basins and alms dishes. From about 1565, however, most of the grand chalices were exchanged for simpler, smaller cups and covers, more modest and fitting to the newly established Protestant Church of England.

The two most prized possessions of a rich lord's household were the standing salt and the loving cup. The ceremonial loving cup, sometimes known as the 'cup of assay' was one of the grandest pieces of all. It was from this cup that the lord's personal Taster sipped, to ensure that the wine had not been poisoned – a very real fear in those days of accession and succession. Often these cups were inset with turquoise, believed to turn pale in the presence of poison, or crystal, which supposedly went cloudy. And they were given names which have the same ring to them as those given to the great bells – 'Chantepleure', 'Bennesonne' or a resounding pun such as 'Godezere' for 'God is Here', by which one cup was known.

Salt was scarce and expensive, and to display a large container of fine salt was another measure of wealth. In Tudor times, the grand standing salt was placed at a strategic position on the banqueting table. Those who sat above it were deemed to be of first rank; those below the salt were members of the household and retainers. Frequently these magnificent salts incorporated rock crystal and semi-precious stones, set in beautifully wrought gold, silver gilt or silver. Standing salts were ornate, important pieces, measuring between 12 and 17 in tall. The earliest were often shaped like an hourglass, but by about 1569 they tended to be more cylindrical or square. Wonderfully intricate galleons called 'nefs', often with mother-of-pearl or shells for the hull, and finely beaten silver or gold for sails and rigging, were also made as vessels for salt, although few of those which have survived were made in England, but came from the German city of craftsmen, Augsburg.

Times changed, and with them customs. By the end of the sixteenth century the grand standing salt had been supplemented by individual trencher salts, and the centrepiece of the table began to vary. In some households the salt became more and more ornamental until it was purely decorative. In others, more practical uses were found, and bell-shaped salts were made with three compartments to hold spices. There were spoons but no forks – guests at banquets ate with their fingers, washed clean of grease by serving boys who went slowly down the length of the table with ewers of scented rosewater and highly decorated basins. The central boss of the basin was raised, and often engraved or embellished with the nobleman's coat of arms, or embossed with scenes from classical mythology. The ewers, too, were remarkable pieces of workmanship, with elaborate cast handles in the shape of tritons, mermaids or heroic warriors, standing on richly ornamented stems, their bases fitting over the central boss of the accompanying basin.

All these pieces were reserved for the Court, the rich and the privileged until Queen Elizabeth came to the throne and Spanish ships began to flood Europe with gold and silver bullion. It was nearly twenty years before England's debased coinage was restored to the proper sterling standard, but by then England had begun to grow rich again. There was plenty of silver for all manner of domestic items, and as William Harrison noted in 1586, even a farmer's silver would have consisted of 'a silver salt, a bowl for wine, if not a whole ne(a)st, and a dozen spoons to finish up the sute'.

Double bell standing salt, with separate compartment above for spices.

Top and bottom *Two Charles I slip-top spoons, London 1624 and 1629.* Centre *Charles II Puritan spoon, provincial c.1665.*

Yet though England had plenty of silver for fashioning into decorative objects of all kinds, she had lost a great deal of skill in both craftsmanship and design. The church and the monasteries had fostered both with their constant demand for richly decorative plate. After the Reformation, the numbers of goldsmiths and silversmiths dwindled as they were reduced to relying on the commissions of a few rich patrons and little more. Moreover, in the past inspiration for design and decoration had come from the ornate work of Continental craftsmen, from whom England was now virtually cut off. Much of the silver that was made from the end of the sixteenth century until the end of James I's reign tends to be rather stilted and repetitive, as though the goldsmiths and silversmiths, lacking new inspiration, continued to make new versions of earlier designs, using a limited range of techniques and decorating their work with simple methods, some of which were also used on contemporary pewter.

Fine octagonal coffee pot with a faceted curved spout, engraved with contemporary armorials. London 1717. 9½ in (24 cm) high.

The raising stake and the sinking block

Early surviving English domestic silver bears little relation to the massive plate made on the Continent, and its simple lines and decoration run parallel to pewter as befitted its secondary role as display plate – more humble than that of gold. Most of the grand ceremonial silver made for the Church and the Crown up to the end of the Elizabethan period was either gilded or 'parcel gilt', a term which is simply a corruption of 'partially gilded'. Silver also served a functional purpose in those early days, and very ordinary objects such as graters and saucepans, as well as massive objects like fire dogs, fire grates, shovels and tongs, were made in silver. This was not purely an outrageous display of wealth – metals of all kinds were scarce in England and silver was very good natured and cleaner than wrought iron, with a higher melting point than pewter, the most common and most available metal of the period.

Few special tools were required for working silver, and methods used by those early silversmiths may seem primitive and laborious, yet they have changed very little in many respects in the long years between the sixteenth century and today. In the eighteenth and nineteenth centuries methods of mass-production were harnessed to an ever-growing market for cheaper, lower-quality articles of every kind, but handmade silver is still made with almost the same tools and expertise as those used by silversmiths in England from time immemorial. Blocks of silver were hammered into sheet and then cut to an approximate size suitable for making the piece required. The sheet metal was then worked on in a sinking block – no more than a depression hollowed out from a block of wood, made in several sizes. The sheet metal was steadily hammered from the rim to the centre, until it fitted the shallow curve of the sinking block. Hammering, however, changes the structure of the metal, making it brittle and liable to crack. In consequence it was frequently annealed – heated and quenched – so that it remained malleable.

Shallow bowls, porringers, bleeding cups and the like were then shaped over a sand-filled leather 'saddle', but beakers, mugs, jugs and pots had to be 'raised' over a raising stake or block. This was similar to an anvil, and made of iron. This time the hammering began at the base of the bowl, slowly drawing it out and shaping it, still with frequent annealing to keep the metal workable, until it was gradually elongated and drawn out into the shape of the body of a pot. Each time the silversmith reached the rim, he hammered it down all round, strengthening the edge of the metal. Foot rims were made separately and soldered on to the base with a silver/brass alloy after the vessel had been planished. The planishing hammer was heavy and flat-faced, and great skill was required to beat and flatten all the marks made by hammering on the sinking block and the raising stake. The most difficult pieces to make were those with plain surfaces, where every mark was visible on the finished piece – salvers, waiters and trays, for example, with no surface decoration.

Handles, finials and spouts were cast separately and soldered on to the finished body. Spouts were generally cast in two halves and soldered together, after which a hole of exactly the right size had to be cut in the vessel, and the spout soldered in with great precision. Decoration was simple in those early days, and for the most part the techniques were similar to those used for pewter: punching, stamping and embossing, also known as repoussé, when simple shapes were pushed out from the back to form surface patterns. Chasing, which achieves a sharper definition, raises the metal in shapes on the surface, or adds more detail and a crisper line to embossing. A technique known as 'flat chasing' was also used, which produced results similar to engraving, although not as sharp. No metal is removed, but the silversmith uses punches to impress the design on the surface. Flat chasing tends to be less fluid than engraving, and the lines are more angular than the swirls and curves of engraving.

There were other ways of making simple shapes of hollow ware: sheet silver could be curved round into a cylindrical shape and the edges soldered together. After that, it was shaped on a raising stake before the base was soldered on. With this method, it was often necessary to strengthen the rim with silver wire to prevent the metal from splitting, denting or bending. Another technique, usually associated with much later periods, was spinning. In fact, spinning is almost as ancient as wood-turning and very similar in technique, except that whereas the turner shaves the wood away as the lathe spins, the silversmith presses a flat disk of sheet silver against a hardwood block which has been turned to the desired shape.

Dutch influence and the first flowering

From about 1600 to 1625 it seems that English silversmiths worked mainly in sheet metal and used very little cast work, with the exception of spouts, handles and finials. Decoration was limited to embossing and chasing – there was some engraving, though much fine silver was sent to Holland and thence to Germany to be engraved by the master engravers of Augsburg. During this period, less and less silver bullion came into Europe, as the mercantile power of Spain ebbed with the fortunes of trade and war. In England, the inauguration of the East India Company in 1600 meant that silver bullion no longer remained in England but flowed out again to pay the merchants of the East, who considered that 'white metal' was more valuable than gold.

For a brief time, from 1625 to 1643, Charles I and his Catholic queen, Henrietta Maria, restored some of the broken links between England and the Continent, and the design and quality of English wrought plate improved. It is almost as though a new generation of silversmiths was at work, eschewing the earlier fashions for silver gilt and highly decorated work in favour of very plain styles, embellished with oddly old-fashioned engravings of coats of arms, or with bands of matting as surface decoration. The workmanship was superb, since plain surfaces required a far higher degree of technical skill than those which were embossed and chased. Side by side with this plain, rich style went small dishes, beakers and porringers, made from rather thin

Two common constructions of a tankard. Top *The body is made from a cylinder of sheet silver, with the base soldered in before the foot rim was applied.* Above *The body is beaten up from a single sheet, with an integral base, and the foot rim then applied. With the cylindrical sheet construction, a mouth wire was added. In both cases, the flange to the lid was also applied.*

metal, sometimes lacking the fine attention to detail and finish which marks the work of highly proficient craftsmen. It may be that this period has been badly misjudged, and that what has survived was deemed too small and insignificant to be taken and melted down during the Civil War, but certainly the majority of pieces which have come down to us today are small porringers, bowls and beakers, mainly decorated with simple punched designs.

Before the standard of the Roundheads was ever raised and the country flung into turmoil and Civil War, the Crown caused havoc among the noble families of England, levying illegal taxes, demanding loans from the rich and alienating Parliament, which in turn levied even larger taxes from wealthy guilds and institutions. In order to raise the money, both domestic and ceremonial plate was melted down to pay these taxes – in 1643–44 alone there was a crushing levy of £10,000 a week on the City of London and many guilds were forced to sell their plate to avoid prosecution or worse. Lost among all this splendour is almost all the superb work of a Dutchman, Christian van Vianen, nephew of Paul van Vianen, Court silversmith to the Emperor Rudolph II in Prague, who was working in Utrecht. Christian van Vianen came to England in about 1628, probably at the instigation of Charles I, and made, among other great pieces, the new plate for the Chapel of the Order of the Garter at St George's Chapel, Windsor. His 'auricular' style, so-called because of its similarities to the curves and undulations of a human ear, is astonishing in its fluidity of design, pre-dating rococo by a hundred years, though many of his designs were based on the sinuous shapes of shells and fishes and not on 'rocaille'. Sadly, few traces of his work survive in England. The 17 pieces of plate at Windsor were looted in 1642, and have vanished. Christian van Vianen left England before the Commonwealth, but returned in 1660, and English silver after that date bears considerable evidence of his influence.

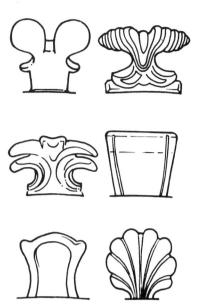

Tankard thumb-pieces. Top *Twin cusp, ram's horn or corkscrew, 1640–1710.* Centre *Scrolled, upright, 1690–1780.* Bottom *Pierced chair and shell-shaped, 1760–1890.*

Restoration silver and the beginning of change

England's economy was at a low ebb after the Civil War – there was precious little bullion in the Treasury, and very little decorative silver seems to have been made during the Commonwealth. What has survived is purely practical – candlesticks, punch bowls, tankards and pocket boxes, with plain lines and little ornament or decoration. But with the Restoration of Charles II to the throne of England and the return of luxury and frivolity at Court, all things became more extravagant, and life was richer and more expansive. When the Court moved back to London from The Hague, Charles II brought with him a train of skilled craftsmen and customs from the Netherlands. For here, in the melting-pot of Europe, there was silver bullion and design derived from the Spanish, as well as workers and craftsmen who had already left France with the growing persecution of Protestants in Catholic countries. The Spaniards had lost their supremacy at sea, and Holland was now the major maritime power, with fleets of ships bringing new ideas, new skills and new materials back to Europe from the Far East.

Charles II tankard chased with stiff leaves, with a leaf-wrapped bud finial and an openwork lattice thumbpiece. London 1677. 7¼ in (18.5 cm) high.

Silver bullion flowed into Europe again after a lean period between about 1625 and 1660, although it was a while before England was rich enough again to use gold and silver for anything but trade. The first, most marked change in design was the adoption by English silversmiths of the fluid, naturalistic representations of flowers, foliage and fruit, richly and deeply embossed and chased. In flavour, the Carolean style was almost a return to the rich Baroque of earlier periods, with beautifully wrought dishes, salvers and display plate. Some of the most flamboyant work is to be found in the silver wall sconces of the period, richly embossed and chased, with ornate cast candle-branches to hold the candles which reflected in mirrored sconces and turned silver to gold with their yellow light.

From about 1667 onwards it is evident too that some silver-smiths were using the technique of 'cut card work' often attributed to the Huguenots, who did not arrive in England until later in the century. This is a method of applying layers of cut sheet silver over the surface and soldering it on, to produce decoration in relief without weakening the vessel with embossing and chasing, or making cast decoration. Cut card work was lavishly used towards the end of the century, often built up in several layers. But then, Huguenots from France had begun to seek sanctuary in England years before the cruel revocation of the Edict of Nantes in 1685 drove them out of France by the thousand. Pierre Harache, for example, was admitted to the Goldsmiths' Company in 1682, despite the threat of 'aliens, journeymen and foreigners' to London craftsmen. Later, their attitude was far less lenient.

England was at war with the Dutch off and on throughout the reign of Charles II. His Catholic queen and his wavering towards the Church of Rome kept most of the persecuted Huguenots away from England, and it was not until William of Orange succeeded to the throne in 1689 that there was peace between the Dutch and the English, and large numbers of Huguenots fled to England, at last an avowedly Protestant country. It was a fearful loss of talent and craftsmanship for France: in 1685 alone it has been estimated that about 50,000 families fled, representing about 500,000 souls in all.

The grumbles and complaints from the guilds in England which had been growing ever since the flight of the first Huguenots in 1678 rose to a howl, and English craftsmen blocked their entry into the guilds. The Goldsmiths' Company refused to assay their work, and since it was illegal to sell any unmarked plate, the only way a 'foreign' goldsmith or silversmith could make a living was to persuade a willing freeman of the guild to take his work on his behalf for assay and touch. Pierre Harache was one of the few to gain admission. Other Huguenot goldsmiths were forced to find other ways round this denial of freedom to work in the City of London – Peter Archambo, another famous silversmith, actually became a member of the Butchers' Company in order to gain the right to work.

The Huguenot influence

From 1688 onwards there was a surge in the acquisition of gold and silver plate by the rich in England. Massive pieces of furniture were covered in sheet silver, pictures and mirrors were framed in elaborate silver gilt frames, sets of 12 or 24 wall sconces were commissioned for state rooms and banqueting halls. Andirons, grates and fire tools were richly embellished with cast silver ornament – a fashion which had been prevalent during Elizabethan times and was now revived.

Largesse by monarchs was not new, but William III's generosity seems excessive, and one suspects that this new, foreign king of England gave favours deliberately to those members of the Court on whose loyalty he depended. It was his habit to give his Grooms of the Stole and Gentlemen of the Bedchamber – confidential posts in the Royal household – massive quantities of gold and silver plate when they left his service or rose to higher

Wall sconces in the late 17th century harked back in design to those made during the Restoration, and were usually made in long sets to light state rooms.

positions. These perquisites were worth a small fortune: Robert Harley, later Earl of Oxford, was given no less than 8,000 oz of plate when he was made Speaker of the House of Commons, and a further 1,000 oz when he became Principal Secretary of State.

Yet with all this generosity to the Royal Household, in 1721 St James's Palace had 28 wall sconces, 14 looking-glass sconces and 10 embossed sconces wrought with 'pictures'. Kensington Palace had 24, Hampton Court 18 and Windsor no less than 50. Such a staggering amount of silver does no more than hint at the outward visible signs of wealth in England at the beginning of the eighteenth century. It was at this time that the English silversmiths began to complain that they had to work up plate more extravagantly because of the new fashions brought in by the foreigners. Whether they liked it or not, they began to raise their own standards of workmanship. From the surviving wall sconces dating from the end of the seventeenth century it can be seen that English silversmiths still tended to work in thinnish sheet silver, with rather careless, imperfectly finished embossing, of which the 'boyes and crownes' found on the carved backs of Carolean cane-backed chairs was a common design, still being made as late as 1702.

The Huguenots, on the other hand, with their expertise and knowledge of casting and finishing, made richer, heavier pieces, engraved with designs taken from French pattern books, far more elegant than the sparse engraving done by English craftsmen. Engraving, even of coats of arms, had been little used in England during most of the seventeenth century because the fashion had been mainly for heavily embossed and chased surfaces. After the Restoration, when plain surfaces returned, English engravers took their patterns from long outdated, stiff forms of cartouche, dating back to the beginning of the century.

Huguenot workmanship during the same period is almost instantly recognisable by the high quality of cast work, the far heavier, more lavish pieces they made, and a distinct outline and silhouette which differs considerably from the simple forms of English craftsmen. In general, these French silversmiths did not adopt the rich, Baroque, lavish style of Paris and the French Court, but a simpler, less ornate version. The majority of them came from provincial towns and cities, many of them from regions nearer to Germany, Austria and Switzerland than the heartland of French culture. But their designs were more rounded than English work, more generous in form, and hinted at a more voluptuous excellence than the reluctant standard of finish and detail of the London silversmiths. Gradually the conservative taste of English patrons was weaned away to more elegant styles by the virtuoso use of cut card work and strapwork which, in the hands of the Huguenots, was as different as a French carbonade of beef from a spit-roasted piece of scorched raw meat. The ingredients were the same, but the results were quite stunningly different.

As well as their skills and techniques, the Huguenots brought with them items unfamiliar to the English table. Ewers and basins had been relegated to the sideboard once forks were in general use in England, but the more fastidious French were still using scented water to wash their fingers between courses, or at the end of banquets after the guests had been offered fruit or deliciously sticky sweets and confectionery. Helmet-shaped ewers and highly decorative basins were still *de rigueur* in France, and soon made their appearance in more elegant households in England. Designs had the flavour of grand Elizabethan plate, with dolphins, conches, tritons, shells, marine monsters and a frilled leaf reminiscent of a certain kind of seaweed, quite different from the English stiff, stylised leaf of cut card work. In shape, these fashionable ewers were like the helmets of classical warriors, wide-mouthed vessels on elaborately decorated stems.

Another innovation which came to the English table at the end of the seventeenth century was the tureen or 'terrine' for soups and ragouts – meats cooked in rich wine sauces. The French 'ragoo' was quite new to English cuisine, and was served in massive, luxuriously designed tureens with much cast applied decoration, resembling smaller covered versions of the vast wine coolers of the period. They were individual, important pieces, not included in silver table services until the mid-eighteenth century.

One object with which the 'foreign' silversmiths were not very familiar with was the traditional English tankard. Beer-drinking in France was uncommon, particularly among the silver-owning classes, and most of the tankards made in England until the beginning of the eighteenth century were the work of English silversmiths, following the traditional shape, although decorated increasingly with cut card work or strapwork, with plain foot rims and stepped lids. When the second generation of Huguenot silversmiths – boys at the time of the flight from France, who had served their apprenticeship under Huguenot masters – began to make tankards as part of their necessary stock in trade, the

Impressive ewers of silver and silver gilt were imported into England from Augsburg and Nuremberg during the first decades of the 17th century.

An 18th-century camp canteen – two beakers fitting together to hold knives, forks, spice box, marrow scoop and nutmeg grater-corkscrew. The handles are all detachable and when assembled it fits into a mahogany case. James Smith I. London c.1725. Beaker 3¾in (9.5cm) high.

difference was very clear. The bodies of the tankards were round-bellied, the handles more generous and sweeping, the lids almost always domed and surmounted by a decorative cast finial – beautiful as objects, but awkward to drink from.

Huguenot work was nearly always more expensive than the work of English silversmiths. The cost of fashioning was charged according to the weight of metal, and was calculated by the ounce, so the plainer the style, the lower the cost. With the imposition of a higher standard for sterling silver at the end of the seventeenth century, more expensive because of the increased content of pure silver, English silversmiths tended to offset the extra cost with even simpler designs and consequent lower charges for fashioning, or by using relatively thin metal and keeping cast ornament to a minimum.

Getting and spending – the higher standard

There was still no difference in the sterling silver used for coinage and the silver used for fashioning wrought plate, nor any control over the immense spending and profligate displays of wealth during the last decade of the seventeeth century. Parliament was finding it difficult to supply the Mint with enough silver for coinage, and blamed the shortage on the excessive amount of work carried out by the silversmiths. In 1697, all measures of taxation having completely failed to deter the noble houses from amassing yet more gold and silver, depleting the nation's supplies of raw silver in massively decorative plate, Parliament passed an act to bring in a higher standard of silver content for wrought plate, thereby making it more expensive. All coinage in circulation was called in and re-minted into new money, with milled coins to prevent the ancient practice of 'cutting coin'. A handsome bounty was offered to anyone who surrendered their wrought plate – a gesture which further deprived posterity of much fine early English plate. Inevitably the opportunity to grow

Covered sugar bowl and bullet-shaped teapot with a straight tapering spout engraved with elaborate contemporary cartouche. Teapot London 1722. Sugar bowl 1745.

rich with very little effort appealed to many a wealthy patron, who sent his family silver to London and the Mint.

The new, higher standard altered the proportion of pure silver to copper alloy for wrought plate from 92.5 per cent to 95.8 per cent pure silver. The higher standard is known today as the 'Britannia Standard', for new marks were also introduced. Sterling silver was no longer struck with the traditional 'leopard's head crowned' but with a figure of Britannia and a 'lion's head erased' – another heraldic term meaning a lion's head in profile, with the neck ending in a jagged edge. This remained the assay mark for higher standard sterling silver until 1720, when it was no longer legally enforceable.

The period of Britannia Standard silver, which lasted from 1697 to 1720, is one of the most interesting in the long history of English plate. There were two distinct streams of influence, one of which originated in France, the other in the Netherlands. When William III came to England, like Charles II before him, he brought with him highly esteemed artists and craftsmen. Among the most influential was Daniel Marot, a cosmopolitan architect and designer who came originally from Paris and had fled to Holland along with so many talented Huguenots. Marot's influence can be seen in the elegantly proportioned architecture, interiors and furniture of this period in England. The most recognisable style in silver which owed its origins to the Netherlands was a far more disciplined, better-proportioned shape, ornamented with lobed fluting – a style which had its roots in the lobes and fluid lines of Christian van Vianen's work. The English silversmiths took to this design easily, since it used sheet metal and the gadroons and lobes were embossed – a traditional technique.

In most surviving examples – on loving cups and punch bowls, porringers and wine cups – the weakness of the English silversmiths' skill in casting solid silver can be seen. The handles are cast in simple S-scrolls, sometimes embellished with leaf shapes, and tend to be too weak and ungenerous for the objects themselves. The English craftsman had lost, too, the swinging, flowing lines which had so distinguished them from Continental silversmiths. And although their technical skill in chasing and flat chasing was remarkable, as can be seen in the short period of 'chinoiserie' decoration, the general standard of engraving was still relatively poor.

The fashion for 'chinoiserie' and Chinese porcelain which swept the country proved to be a huge drain on currency and coin. In 1717 alone, three million ounces of sterling silver left England by way of the East India Company to pay the merchants. And since the Chinese insisted on payment in silver bullion, yet again silver coin and wrought plate were melted and cast into ingots, thus defeating the object of the higher 'Britannia Standard'. The Dutch East India Company was also in need of silver and English merchants did a brisk trade across the Channel, exporting silver bullion and importing gold in exchange. This unexpected drain on England's coinage and silver supplies may have been a major factor in the decision to return to the old

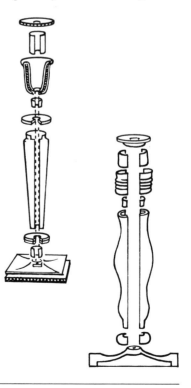

Two 18th-century methods of candlestick construction.
Left *Sheet silver stamped and embossed, joined with collars and loaded or filled with pitch with a central rod for stability.*
Right *The stem is cast in two halves and soldered vertically with the other parts cast separately and soldered together.*

Cast table candlestick by specialist candlestick maker James Gould, with detachable nozzle. London 1738. 6¾ in (17 cm) high.

Charles II cluster column candlesticks in embossed and chased sheet silver, c.1670. 7¼ in (18 cm) high.

sterling standard, since the higher standard had failed to deter merchants and noblemen from using wrought plate as currency for trade. Whatever the reason, in 1720 the Britannia Standard was abandoned, although Huguenot silversmiths continued to use higher-standard silver for about another decade or so.

A marriage of excellence – Queen Anne silver

By about 1700 it was no longer possible for the Goldsmiths' Company to keep the Huguenots out. They may even have damaged their own relationship with wealthy patrons by doing so. It mattered little to a rich nobleman that a silversmith's commissions were not assayed or hallmarked in London, for they would never be seen there, nor offered for sale. If he wanted his old-fashioned plate refashioned in a new style and returned in profuse evidence of his wealth and modishness, no one could prevent it. And if the rich, heavy style of Huguenot silversmiths appealed to him more than the plainer, more simple work of London makers, he was free to commission them, registered or not, for his private work.

The Huguenots were proud of their origins, and even after they had been admitted to the Goldsmiths' Company many of them, perhaps out of defiance, continued to strike their marks incorporating the French fleur-de-lys surmounted by a crown. A few English silversmiths began to learn and master the style and techniques of the 'foreigners' – among them George Garthorne, who was rewarded by the patronage of Queen Anne, for whom he executed numerous commissions. But in lesser ways the Huguenots had already influenced a far wider sphere of design and craftsmanship, and techniques introduced by them had already been adopted wholesale by English makers. Most radical of all the changes during the last two decades of the seventeenth century was the design and construction of that essential household item, the candlestick.

The pattern of English candlesticks up to the middle of the seventeenth century was a fluted column or cluster-column, embossed in sheet silver, usually with a square base and a decorative embossed and chased drip pan set low on the stem, of a type which was also common in Scandinavia at the same period. The candlesticks from the early 1680s owed nothing to this pattern, in either design or construction. They were considerably smaller, measuring only about six or seven inches, and were cast in solid metal, with square bases, simple baluster stems and plain spool-shaped nozzles. The first recorded candlesticks of this type were made by Pierre Harache in 1683 – undoubtedly of Huguenot origins. There seems to have been no dissent over this change, for English silversmiths began to make cast candlesticks to this pattern at almost the same time, and by 1685 variations on the simple theme had become common.

While the French-influenced designs tended to be more curved and rounded, the English silversmiths gradually returned to an earlier love of plain, pure flat surfaces, with the judicious use of simplified versions of the more ornate applied decoration so loved by the Huguenots. Fluting and gadrooning were used with more restraint by English craftsmen, generally on the lower part of the body of vessels and cups. The elaborate cut card work was simplified into a particularly delightful variation of lanceolate leaves with central beaded ribs, and the crinkly leaf of the French helmet-shaped jugs was adapted into a purer form like a calyx cupping the rounded bases of coffee pots, two-handled cups and covers, and tureens. Gradually, as their expertise improved, the English silversmiths reduced the amount of decoration and concentrated more and more on plain, polygonal shapes – a remarkably sophisticated form requiring a high degree of technical proficiency. Surfaces were left free of any ornament except for beautifully engraved cartouches in wonderfully free-flowing lines, with none of the old-fashioned stiffness of the previous period. The accent was on pure form and reflecting surfaces – neatly stepped, reeded bases and rims, and plain, perfectly proportioned finials were the only decoration.

French cuisine began to infiltrate plain English cooking, and sauces and melted butter became *de rigueur* for all manner of dishes. Sauce and butter boats seem to have been made and used in England from about 1720 onwards. Early patterns were double-lipped, with curved handles on either side, and their sides were often scalloped and shaped in an extremely impractical manner. Between 1725 and 1730 a more practical version appeared, looking a little like a truncated helmet jug, but with a single lip, a deeper body and a cast handle, and standing on a plain spreading foot.

Wax jack or taper stand with coiled taper, by Robert Hennell, London 1797. 6½ in (16.5 cm) high.

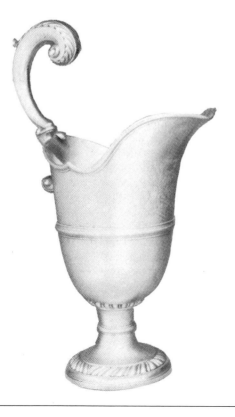

Helmet-shaped ewer with leaf-capped flying scroll handle, engraved with the royal coat of arms under the lip. John Hugh le Sage. London 1748. 17 in (43 cm) high.

Georgian silver – rich and heavy

Many changes took place in England under George I, the first of the Hanoverian kings, whose brief reign between 1714 and 1727 is so often amalgamated with the Queen Anne period in the decorative arts. His Court came from Germany and had Prussian connections, and the King himself spoke no English. He imposed his own way of life on the noblemen of England, bringing customs which were unknown to the unsophisticated, uproarious banquets and ceremonial occasions. Although forks had been used in England for almost a century, it was still not considered essential to provide them for guests, who usually brought their own sets of cutlery in beautiful leather or shagreen cases. Yet by the 1720s the custom of dining *à la Berline* had been adopted by all grand households, and services of knives, forks and spoons were laid at individual place settings. Matching sets of plates, bowls and glasses were provided, and servants handed each course, one at a time, to the guests as they lounged in wide-seated dining chairs round a single, long dining table. In some households where money was temporarily short, a last plundering of the sideboard silver, melted down, provided enough for a bare two sets of forks and spoons – one of silver, one of silver gilt.

From this period onwards, the work of Huguenot silversmiths can no longer be separated from that of the London craftsmen, although some of them retained their heavy, French style and were favoured by royal commissions – Philip Rollos worked for George I, while his son the Prince of Wales preferred Pierre Platel. But in general the work of the London silversmiths had risen to such a peak of perfection that it equalled, if not surpassed, that of the Huguenots in everything but intricate cast ornament.

Surviving English silver dating from between 1688 and 1720 shows that there were many different versions of domestic articles being made. There was the old, traditional floral embossing which originated in the Carolean period – wrought sheet silver in a style which suited the old manorial houses with low ceilings, beams and high dining halls. All manner of simple, traditional objects were made to this pattern, from porringers and two-handled cups and covers to candlesticks and, far grander, toilet sets in silver gilt. Then, as the English virtuosity for working with plain surfaces asserted itself, there were undecorated, faceted, octagonal, hexagonal and circular shapes with simple stepped mouldings and well-proportioned cast finials. Parallel with these English lines were the rounder, heavier, more luxurious shapes of the Huguenot silversmiths, with applied strapwork and cut card work, and cast decoration – seen at its best in helmet-shaped jugs and ceremonial pieces, and less happily in tankards with domed lids and finials instead of the plain, flat stepped lids and lines of English-made pieces.

By 1720 only lobes and gadroons remained to show the strong earlier styles. Some English silversmiths, becoming more confident and sophisticated, took the plain straight fluting and gave it a swirl, particularly on lids and covers, ending in a small flame finial. The severe, angular cut corners of salvers and bases of

Heavy cast candlestick with lobed and fluted stem, spool-shaped sconce with corded border and detachable nozzle by Ebenezer Coker. London 1766. 10 in (25.5 cm) high.

candlesticks were dimpled into concave curves, or softened into octafoil shapes. But the next decade saw a pure, expansive style of architecture based on classical Palladian forms, and silver began to reflect this influence with simple shapes overlaid with extravagant applied cast ornament, sometimes on angular shapes, sometimes on more rounded forms.

Reluctant rococo

Between 1730 and 1750 there was a true merging of the Huguenot and English streams of influence into a single, individual style. The restrained forms of traditional English taste were enriched with heavy cast handles, feet and finials of superb workmanship, and embellished with cast and applied ornament. This was the age of some of England's greatest silversmiths – second-generation Huguenots, many of them, thoroughly absorbed into their adoptive country – Paul de Lamerie, Paul Crespin, Nicholas Sprimont, David Willaume among them, setting the style for others to follow.

It was inevitable, then, that when the French Court goldsmith Juste Aurèle Meissonier introduced a completely revolutionary concept in design the leading masters in England should interpret it for their rich patrons. In the work of Paul de Lamerie from the late 1720s can be seen the embryo eccentricities of the rococo style, so fashionable in France, yet so reluctantly accepted in England. This writhing, curling style, based on 'rocaille' – rocks, shells, waves and underwater fronds – was too alien, too foreign for English taste, and was never really successfully integrated into the calmer, more ordered symmetrical design of English architecture, furniture and silver.

The nearest the English came to accepting this bizarre fashion was in the symmetrical shell bases to candlesticks and ornate

Soup tureen in full rococo taste with heavy cast decoration on the body and the cover embossed and chased with leaves, rocaille, vegetables and fish. William Cripps, London 1750/51. 18 in (46 cm) wide, 5,000 g.

cast borders of dishes and stands for tureens and salvers. Sauce boats lent themselves to shapes of shells with high, elaborately decorated flying-scroll handles, and individual salts, too, were quite properly in the shape of shells, since salt came from the sea. And there were shell-shaped butter dishes and sweetmeat dishes, often piled on a centrepiece which sometimes curled and broke like a wave over rocks. The sinuous, asymmetrical, flowing shapes of rococo are most evident in the cartouches surrounding armorials on important pieces of the period.

By the mid-eighteenth century, England's silversmiths finally found their individual voice and style, and heavy cast ornament gave way to lighter, less bold relief and more delicate strapwork, no longer confined to the stiff leaf of the acanthus and palm but incorporating classical medallions and intricate patterns derived from Greece and Rome. Handles were more elaborate than the simple S-scroll of earlier periods and curved instead in a double C-scroll, decorated with frilled leaves or richly cast ornament. Subdued rococo influence can be seen in the curved spouts of coffee and chocolate pots with 'animalier' heads, and on finials and handles of tureens and vegetable dishes, cast in forms appropriate to their contents – dolphins for fish, artichoke finials, turtles for turtle soup. Applied ornament was heavy with swags and masks, and feet were massive lion's paws or scrolled shells, sometimes combined with grotesque masks of classicial gods and goddesses.

The inspired designs of the silversmiths were now regarded as beautiful objects in their own right and not as potential bankable assets, and the goldsmiths and silversmiths wrought intricately decorative pieces, safe in the knowledge that they would be greatly admired and sought-after. In the world of finance, all the institutions of a capitalist society were established in the mid-eighteenth century: banks, limited companies, stocks, shares, promissory notes and even insurance companies. And as the wealth of the country increased, an increasing number of self-made men with great fortunes began to follow the lead of their fashionable friends whose roots were deep in history and tradition.

The age of excellence

The period between 1750 and 1770 is the richest, the purest, the most recognisable in all the uneven history of English design. This was a time when the most strongly held belief was that everything could be improved, made better and more beautiful – even nature. In the grounds and gardens of England, the old stilted parterres were uprooted as 'Capability' Brown landscaped the countryside, levelling hills and diverting rivers to flow into mirror lakes which would reflect the perfect proportions of houses that stood like temples to aestheticism. Huddled hamlets were swept away to make room for parkland, and even the animals were chosen as part of the design – red deer, pale cattle, brood mares and their foals.

The trendsetters in this new excellence were the brothers Adam who, inspired by the newly excavated ruins of Pompeii and the ancient splendours of Rome, monopolised the entire field of English taste. They were by no means the sole instigators of the neo-classical style which swept the country. Josiah Wedgwood was largely responsible for domesticating the classical vase shape at his new factory at Etruria, and from the 1760s onwards the bibles of all designers of the day were the *Museum Florentinum*, the *Antiquities of Herculaneum* and the works of Pergolesi.

Other factors were at work too, changing the entrenched traditional taste of the rich and powerful. Feminine influence had been growing steadily, and as the shape and style of life and architecture changed, whole wings of houses were devoted to the ladies of the household. Boucher, Fragonard and Watteau set the style for boudoirs and bedrooms. Pale colours, blonde woods, chintz and calico gave a totally different flavour to these feminine rooms, in contrast to the rest of the house where the gentlemen still preferred good solid mahogany. Angelica Kaufman has been credited with far more painted panels and pictures than she ever produced, but she was copied again and again by lesser artists, even though she was more or less dismissed by the critics of the day.

The second half of the eighteenth century was by no means the first time that women had ventured into silversmithing. In many

The change in style to one of simplicity and plain surfaces, with armorials virtually without any elaborate cartouche, is summed up by this large salver with an engraved shield suspended by ribbons, and an applied feather edge and shell border. London 1769. 15 in (38 cm) diameter.

Right *Classic Adam-style sauce tureen with boat-shaped body and loop handles, on pedestal base and with urn-shaped finial. John Robins. London 1786. 9½in (24cm) wide.*

Elegant but lightweight ladle by Hester Bateman with feather-edged stem and shell bowl. 1774.

ways it was well suited to the creative talents and nimble fingers of female hands. As more and more middle-class women wanted silver teapots and coffee pots, tea caddies and tableware, it was only right that it should be a woman who catered deftly to their needs. Hester Bateman was entered at the Goldsmiths' Hall in 1761 and her work in shaping such everyday domestic things, handled to a great extent by the women of the house, has been an enduring influence.

After the 'Marlborough Wars' the broad band of middle-class households had grown more prosperous, more secure, more concerned with their surroundings and the image they reflected. Coinciding with the lighter, less ponderous lines imposed by neo-classicism, silver was once again devoid of heavy cast ornament, based on a vase shape with elegant upswept handles, often oval, always beautifully porportioned. Demand grew and the London silversmiths prospered, unchallenged by foreign intervention and influence, in competition with no one. The great provincial cities of Birmingham and Sheffield, which were to play such an important role in the last three decades of the eighteenth century, had not yet been granted their own Assay Offices.

Adam silver and the neo-classical style

The two most active members of the Adam family were Robert and John, but they were all remarkable entrepreneurs. Seeing great possibilities in the new neo-classical 'look', they set about designing interiors, ceilings, mouldings, panels, fireplaces, grates, fire tools and fenders, all with the same unifying proportions and themes, based on the tripod, the urn, the medallion, serpents, classical figures and battle trophies. Unlike James Wyatt, another talented contemporary architect who designed his own silver, neither of the Adam brothers is recorded as the originator of 'Adam' silver designs, but they worked in close co-operation with Boulton and Fothergill of Birmingham, and later with the Sheffield silversmiths who made the bulk of highly fashionable 'Adam' silver for a wider market.

Matthew Boulton was another great entrepreneur and, with the gifted jeweller and silversmith John Fothergill as partner, executed many commissions for the Adam brothers. Such was their eye to the general market that Robert and John tried to lure both Matthew Boulton and Josiah Wedgwood away from the Midlands to exhibit their work in the Adam 'design centre' in the Adelphi, near the Strand in London. But both these hard-headed businessmen preferred to remain independent. Apart from any other considerations, by the early 1770s piracy was rife. Most of Boulton's newest and most fashionable designs had to be sent to London or Chester for assay, where unscrupulous agents copied pieces before returning them – a serious matter for a man close to the source of original design for exclusive patrons.

There had been a revolution in England. Fine furniture, damasks, silks, richly draped curtains and handsome furnishings were no longer reserved for the privileged few. Ever since Thomas Chippendale had published his *Director* in 1754, with designs for every single item of household furniture and furnishings, the provinces had ceased to be provincial. Hundreds of daily papers in the Home Counties and the shires informed the ladies of York and Birmingham, Bath and Exeter, of the latest fashions. *Household Furniture in Genteel Taste for the Year 1760*, published by Robert Sayer, was less expensive and more obtainable than Chippendale's *Director*, and provincial craftsmen began to make 'London-style' furniture, metalwork, glass and china for the first and greatest consumer boom in England.

The rise of Sheffield and Birmingham

From about 1765, when the first neo-classical candlesticks appeared, combining an acanthus-decorated base with a tapering, fluted column, cast in solid silver, it became apparent that this design could be simplified and made by machine, using stamped sheet silver which could then be 'loaded' or filled with pitch to add weight and stability. The Corinthian column candlestick, like the Adam firegrate, has been reproduced by the million ever since. Sheet silver, while solving the problem of using less to produce more, also dictated to a certain extent the patterns and shapes which could be made. The original baluster design of Adam's classical candlestick, for example, became a plain, straight-sided column, better suited to the new methods of manufacture. Sheets of silver were rolled in 'flatting mills' and no longer hammered out by hand. New die-stamping methods enabled raised patterns to be stamped out on sheet silver and not embossed. Simple rim and edge patterns were made in similar fashion, and beading and gadrooning was executed with one blow of a crisp steel stamp, made in the steel town of Sheffield.

The growing industrialisation of Sheffield and Birmingham, with their mass-production techniques, began to threaten the livelihoods of the London silversmiths. When the new industrial magnates of the Midlands, led by Boulton and Wedgwood, petitioned for Assay Offices to be opened in Birmingham and

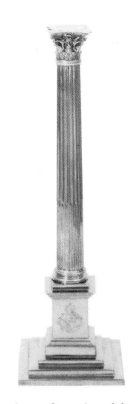

Imposing early version of the Corinthian column candlestick with cast stepped square bases rising to plinths engraved with contemporary armorials. Peter Werritzer. London 1760. 15 in (38.5 cm) high.

Sheffield, their appeals were met with hostility. Tentative experiments with 'fused plate' had proved successful and Boulton himself had been among the first to take it up and begin to manufacture what is known as 'Sheffield plate' on a considerable scale.

The steady swing of the fashion pendulum had at last been set in motion. As the styles originating with the rich and exclusive became available to the mass market, new designs took their place for the privileged few. By about 1775 virtually no classical candlesticks were being made in London and the bulk of neo-classical design had been taken over by Sheffield – less expensive, less exclusive, more available to the general public, in London and in the provinces. At that time too, Sheffield began to make large quantities of fused plate – but until the mid-1770s, Matthew Boulton's Soho Works in Birmingham was the largest producer in England, and many of the techniques of manufacture which were later used in Sheffield were developed by Matthew Boulton in Birmingham.

Heavy-lidded opulence – the Regency period

Classical inspiration can, it seems, always be relied upon to breathe new life into seemingly exhausted ideas. At the end of the eighteenth century, Thomas Hope found a source of entirely new classical themes, based more on Egyptian than Greek or Roman,

Left *Silver gilt ecuelle and cover applied with a band of alternating anthemions and shells with a bud finial, 1821. 11¾ in (30 cm) wide over handles.* Right *Silver gilt salver with gadroon, shell and foliate border, 1818. 9½ in (24 cm) diameter. Both by Rundell, Bridge & Rundell.*

but embracing the heavy, voluptuously decadent life of the last Roman Emperors, and fresh impetus was given to designers and makers of opulent silver for the rich. Once again, heavy cast ornament returned, at first still based on shapes of urns with upswept handles, richly gadrooned and lobed, with lions' masks in high relief, formal acanthus leaf and shell decoration, and lotus and palmate designs. Candlesticks assumed an elegantly curving shape, with inverted baluster stems and vase-shaped sockets – and incorporated all the features which could not be imitated in Sheffield fused plate.

It is inevitable that a rich, heavy style, once accepted, will become overblown and too ornate, just as simple lines gradually fade to the ghost of their pure shapes. Early Regency silver is stunning in its richness, yet by 1820 the severity afforded by the sheer weight of metal was beginning to be overburdened with too much ornament. Slowly and remorselessly through the first three decades of the nineteenth century, too many swirls and swags, bulges and curves obliterated the underlying shapes. In their desire to produce new designs, the silversmiths added all manner of extras, harking back to French rococo, merging it with arabesques and themes from earlier periods, and even adding Chinese and Japanese motifs to the overloaded shape, until it became so swamped with decoration that the original lines were no longer visible.

Elaborately decorated silver tea kettle and stand with elements of rococo, chinoiserie and earlier styles, demonstrating the Victorian love of decoration. London c.1864.

Very fine cake basket chased with flowers and foliage, engraved with a rococo cartouche, by E., E. J. & W. Barnard. London 1832. 13½in (34cm) wide.

A factor which did not help to curb this over-enthusiastic rush of ornament was the increasing use of mechanical means to produce the effects of embossing and chasing. By the mid-nineteenth century, patterns were die-stamped on to thin spun silver to make a wealth of trinkets and small objects. These techniques also proved an inexpensive method of making cheap imitations of rather florid styles from earlier periods. Of grand silver, some quite remarkable craftsmanship and skill is apparent on grandiose table centrepieces, challenge cups, race cups and, more functional but every bit as ornate, wine coolers, tureens, presentation tankards and loving cups. The massive, classical theme of Regency silver, so elegantly interpreted by Paul Storr, was revived by the artist and sculptor John Flaxman. He worked, as Paul Storr had done before him, in association with Rundell, Bridge and Rundell, and massive pieces of incredible intricacy were produced. Among them was the famous Shield of Achilles, three feet across and weighing 20,808 grams. When it was put on display in the showrooms of Rundell, Bridge and Rundell, 'the narrow thoroughfare outside the shop was jammed in the afternoon with fashionable carriages and the bustle of pedestrian traffic eager to see the treasures laid out within'.

Machine-made parodies and High Victorian splendour

Not all Victorian silver deserves to be relegated to dusty cupboards and ignored by any means. Some very fine interpretations of the 'Queen Anne style' were made during this period, as well as some excellent copies and variations of Georgian silver. But it is our great misfortune that many fine pieces of plain early silver in pure Queen Anne and early Georgian designs were devalued and virtually destroyed by 'late embossing' and 'improving'. With their mania for decoration, the Victorians defaced plain silver surfaces with embossed flowers, leaves and unsuitable, anachronistic embellishment, which in many cases caused the silver to become stretched and weakened. In addition, many a newly dubbed knight of the 'sauce and pickle peerage', with plenty of new money to splash around, bought plate which had been disposed of by older families fallen on hard times, and proudly had their brand new armorials engraved on it, thus reducing its value and, often, its unsullied charm.

But once again, a technical revolution arrived which caused the makers of original handmade silver to branch out into genuinely creative work again. The invention of electroplating and electrotyping in 1840 meant that there was virtually no shape or design which could not be made cheaply, and in quantity – often miserable parodies of the periods which they claimed to reproduce. The great silversmiths of the day turned away from riotously embossed surfaces and returned to heavy applied ornament, or richly cast solid silver plate. In particular, wine jugs, flagons, ewers and wine coolers were among the most original and imposing pieces, returning not to the Adam helmet shape, but back to an almost medieval interpretation of classical themes. Twining tendrils of vines, festoons of grapes, classical masks and caryatid handles, together with a subtle use of matting on plain surfaces are typical of the lustrous, heavy silver plate made in the second half of the nineteenth century. Back into fashionable favour too came dolphins, tritons and shells,

Early Queen Anne tea canister which has been later embossed with 19th-century flowers and scrolls.

Far left *Milk jug with entwined serpent handle, engraved with a crest, by Robert and Samuel Hennell, London 1803. 5¼ in (13.5 cm) high.* Left *George III salver in Regency style by Robert Garrard, London 1814. 7¾ in (19.5 cm) diameter.*

probably in response to the Prince Regent's lavish 'Dolphin Suite' at Brighton Pavilion.

The Victorian passion for thinly veiled female figures was also very much in evidence. Singly, or in threes and fours, they supported table centrepieces, candelabra, dessert dishes and candlesticks. Perched saucily, naked to the waist and disguised as mermaids, they leaned on salt cellars or leapt from sauce boats – unwieldy handles and quite impractical. Cherubs and infant Bacchus figures were also much loved, though their coyness owed more to *The Water Babies* than to classical mythology.

Light, Liberty and Art Nouveau

Out of all this orchestrated chaos, the disciplinary note struck by William Morris and his followers was like a tuning fork, bringing harmony to discord, with a return to pure proportions and understated decoration based on natural forms. Craftsmanship threatened to become an end in itself, such was the reverence for traditional techniques and materials – to such an extent that 'arty crafty' became a perjorative term. But the Arts and Crafts Movement was in the vanguard of an entirely new attitude to design, badly needed in those days of shoddy, mass-produced, machine-made goods.

Victorian ewer and matching beakers decorated with fern fronds, by Martin & Hall, London 1875/6. Beakers 4½ in (11.5 cm) high.

Today, only the clichés have been handed down in fabric and textile design, but Arthur Lazenby's Liberty's department store in Regent Street probably had as much influence on the taste of the general public as Chippendale's *Director* had in the mid-eighteenth century. Here, under one roof and within the financial reach of every forward-looking citizen of taste were to be found textiles, furniture, lighting, glass, silver and metalwork, based on the new dictates of the Arts and Crafts movement, led by the hands of genuinely creative artists and designers. Their inspiration stemmed from the Pre-Raphaelite movement, and their use of materials owed its origins to medieval England. Enamelled jewels were inset into hand-hammered silver, goblets took their form from medieval paintings of chalices – design was rooted in tradition but in their hands never quite became pastiche.

As the longest reign in England's history came to an end and the Edwardian era began, these new shoots of creative growth struggled to remain alive in the rich, exclusive world of the privileged before the First World War. But there was a lamentable return to the great days of Empire, and nostalgia sent the wheel of progress into reverse. Precious little advance was made in the world of design, and those who did produce new themes and new ideas found recognition abroad, and not in England. The Edwardian craftsman excelled where he married new industrial techniques with traditional shapes and designs. While the Victorian period was to a great extent decadent, with shoddy versions of earlier styles piled one upon another, the Edwardian era was without doubt the finest for excellent reproductions. These were by no means cheap and nasty – extremely expensive copies of early silversmiths' work were made to satisfy the

Silver tazza by Aspreys, London 1938. 7½ in (19 cm) high.

Wine cup with loop handle by Omar Ramsden.

demand for fine quality pieces of ready-made history. The American market played a considerable part in this latterday restoration of old styles: Europe was invaded by culture-hungry transatlantic visitors, all yearning for silver made in pre-Colonial style. They returned home with perfect reproductions, bought in Bond Street or Regent Street, of the culture from which they had sprung.

After the First World War the English, too, preferred the traditional to the modern: Georgian preferably, to set off the fine pieces of reproduction Hepplewhite and Sheraton furniture in their post-war Georgian revival brick-built houses. There was precious little genuine creative talent, but Omar Ramsden, drawing from the inspiration of ancient Celtic culture, was a lone voice crying in the smugly satisfied wilderness of the 1920s. Apart from such rare exceptions, the shape of silver remained entrenched in classic, traditional pieces, made in silver plate, fused plate and electroplate, until the 1950s. And then it was the Scandinavian designers like Georg Jensen who introduced a new style, made not in silver, but in its poor relation, stainless steel. But the lines were so pure and original that it was from this source that many modern silversmiths took their cue. Base metal and precious metal came together again, as in the early days of silversmithing in England, when the shape of pewter and silver plate ran so close together.

*Victorian lidded wine jug
in electroplated silver.
Elkington & Co.
11¾in (30cm) high.*

Sheffield Plate 1745–1840

It was not a new idea to coat the surface of metals with a layer of silver. For decades, cutlers and steelworkers had coated the surface of steel by 'charging' it with silver leaf, not just for decorative purposes but for purely practical reasons. Steel corrodes and stains very easily, and a layer of silver protected the surface, particularly of knife blades, sword blades and other cutting edges. The steel surface was heated and a layer of silver leaf was applied and burnished on with a steel tool under great pressure. Sometimes surfaces were 'charged' with as many as 30 to 60 separate layers of silver leaf, a method known generally in the trade as 'French plating'.

In about 1779, another process, more durable and less costly, was developed in England, which could be used on brass as well as steel. The metal was heated to red heat, and dipped first in sal ammoniac and then in molten tin. While the metal was still hot, it was covered with a layer of paper-thin silver foil, which was pressed against the molten tin and the flat parts beaten down with a cloth-covered hammer. After that, a soldering iron was passed over the surface, melting the tin again, and forming a solder which united steel with silver. This method, known as 'close plating', was used on snuffer blades, skewers, cheese scoops, fish slices, pickle forks and knife blades as late as 1809, when it was superseded by mechanically produced rolled silver foil, particularly for cutlery. Intricate parts of items made in fused plate or 'Sheffield plate', such as taps for tea urns, were also invariably close plated.

The credit for discovering a method of fusing a layer of silver on to a sheet of copper before it was made up into finished items is generally given to Thomas Bolsover or Boulsover, a scale-maker – that is to say a knife-handle-maker. At first the process was used on sheets of copper, but in 1745 it was found that a considerable thickness of silver could be fused with a copper ingot, using a flux of mercury, after which the combined metals could be rolled out to any thickness without distorting the silver covering. To begin with, only very small items were made, such as buckles and buttons, but soon larger objects were being made with great success, among them small pocket boxes. As the use of fused plate became more ambitious, the copper core was alloyed with brass in the proportions of 1:5 because the brass gave extra strength and rigidity.

Fused plate was coated with silver on one side only from about the mid-1760s, and its manufacture into finished objects caused considerable problems. Fused plate was, however, extremely suitable for making hollow ware, and from as early as the 1750s the plating trade had begun to make copies of silversmiths' designs for teapots and coffee pots, water jugs and canisters. But the limitations imposed by this one-sided silver dictated both the design and the methods of manufacture. Exposed edges, for example, showed the copper core, and silver solder was used to cover it, but it was a method which was not lasting. In 1758 Joseph Hancock developed what is known as a single-lapped edge to fused plate, where the surface coating of silver was drawn over the exposed edge to cover it. Hancock, also a cutler, was the first person to exploit the wider implications of fused plate, and the first man to venture into production of domestic tableware with this cheaper version of sterling silver. He took over Thomas Bolsover's works in 1762, expanding it and taking on more workers to meet the demand of the middle classes, who longed for real silver but could not afford it.

By this time, fused plate was coated with silver on both sides, opening up a whole new range of articles which could be made, including bowls and dishes, salvers, trays, soup and sauce tureens. Hollow ware continued to be made with single-faced fused plate, since the insides of lidded jugs and pots could not be seen. The insides were tinned to prevent liquids coming into contact with the copper, which could release a poisonous chemical, particularly with acid liquids. As the range of articles made in fused plate grew, more problems were encountered in copying current silver designs. The silversmiths were using pierced decoration, which proved impossible to make in fused plate at that time. Piercing was done with a fretsaw which, used on fused

Venison dish and cover with a monogram engraved on a sweated-in panel of silver, Sheffield c.1815. 25 in (63.5 cm) wide.

plate, broke the surface of silver and exposed the copper core. It was eventually found that, under great pressure, fly-punches, used with specially cut punches would break through the surface, burring the edges and hiding the copper.

In the 1760s another Sheffield craftsman, Benjamin Huntsman, a clock-maker, developed a method for making steel dies which, used together with the weight of a drop-hammer, would stamp the metal into high relief. In the 1770s, with further improvements, the process of die-sinking was developed, when sheet metal was hammered into a cast, made in two halves, then soldered together. Shapes of feet, finials and applied decoration were stamped out, filled with a lead-tin alloy to make them more solid and then applied to the body.

Die-stamping made it possible to mass-produce individual parts which could then be assembled, and soon many parts were interchangeable – the bases of jugs, for example might be the same as those used on candlesticks. Swage blocks produced ready-patterned silver-plated ribbon in gadroons, beads and other simple repetitive motifs, but soon die-stamping replaced the swage block, and longer strips of decorative edging could be produced at one blow of the hammer. Lids of hollow ware joined the list of die-stamped parts, as well as spouts for teapots and coffee pots, but these were not entirely successful until die-sinking and expensive cast steel dies produced a crisp, sharp result. Cast steel dies were used in Sheffield from about 1793 onwards, for sterling silver as well as fused plate.

Another technical advance, developed originally for a more satisfactory edging to fused plate, was the use of plated silver wire from about 1768 onwards. Plated copper wire was drawn and then beaten flat and fixed to the raw edge of fused plate and soldered with the edges lapped over, so that the copper core was completely hidden. Silver wire had greater possibilities, however, and from the 1770s it was used for making small wire baskets and elaborate epergnes – sugar bowls and dessert bowls were made with glass liners, and the wire was often decorated with thin ribbons of stamped leaves, flowers and decorative patterns. These wire baskets were almost exclusively the work of fused plate makers, although there are some rare pieces made in sterling silver, worked up from sheet, then pierced and cut with a fretsaw.

That great eighteenth-century magnate, Matthew Boulton, had been among the first to realise the possibilities of fused plate, and sought the advice of Joseph Hancock who had already harnessed horse power for the production of fused plate to supply to a growing number of manufacturers. Boulton was hampered at his Birmingham Soho Works by lack of water-power for the new machinery needed for production of fused plate. Once he too had harnessed horse power to his machines, it was possible to make and roll thicker ingots into larger sheets of prepared metal, and larger items such as candlesticks and stands for silver soup tureens were added to his production list. Soon after 1773, Boulton's famous partnership with James Watt began, and steam power was introduced into the Soho Manufactory. Many of the techniques of mass-production which were later used in Sheffield were originally developed by Matthew Boulton.

Engraved decoration was impossible on fused plate, for it exposed the copper beneath, and flat chasing was used as a substitute, particularly by the Sheffield makers. The method differed slightly from chasing on silver, in that the pattern was accomplished with a series of short lines or dots, and not in a continuous line, as in silver. This can usually best be seen from the back of the surface, where the pattern shows in a series of broken lines. Chasing was used continuously from the 1780s onwards, on teapots, coffee pots, sugar basins, tea urns, coasters, salts, mustard pots and canisters.

As fused plate became more and more socially acceptable – even the master silversmiths of the day ordered stands for tureens and dishes of great magnificence to be made in 'Sheffield plate' – serious problems arose from commissions which stipulated engraved armorials on tableware. Flat chasing was not fine enough for such exact work, and at first no expense was spared, and a very thick-gauge silver coating was used for the entire piece. This was a costly business for prestigious patrons, but it was soon ingeniously hurdled by using bands of applied sterling silver on which the coat of arms was engraved. Then, from about 1790, panels of sterling silver were inserted into the fused plate, with

Tea tray with ornate applied border of shells, flowers and foliage, flat chased with flowers and rococo scrolls and engraved with armorials in the centre. Attributed to Gainsford & Nicholson of Sheffield, c.1820. 28¾ in (73 cm) wide over handles.

the join dextrously hidden by an engraved cartouche border – a method which, again, can most easily be seen on the reverse side.

Strangely, in spite of all the running battles between the provincial silversmiths and plate makers and the jealous London Assay Office, there was no restriction on the makers of fused plate regarding the amount of solid silver incorporated into their detail and design, providing the applied parts came within a long list of small items which did not have to be separately assayed. Neither was any tax levied on embellishments falling into this category. So, from 1770 onwards, as well as using applied panels of sterling silver for armorials, bands of applied bright cut engraved decoration were incorporated into fused plate when the expense of using thick gauge silver plating was not justified by the article or the commission.

By the 1800s, the Sheffield platers adopted an even more economical method of engraving on fused plate. A thin plate of sterling silver was soldered on to the surface, just thick enough to allow engraving. By about 1810 there were further economies: four thicknesses of silver leaf were 'sweated on' to the surface and then engraved. All these methods can be seen in genuine old Sheffield plate – the inset silver panel, the sterling silver overlay, and the sweated-on silver leaf which is the least easy to detect. If, however, the piece becomes heavily tarnished, the engraved panel shows quite distinctly as a different colour.

In a way, these penny-pinching devices were an abuse of the latitude which the Sheffield platers already enjoyed. There was no duty on Sheffield plate, although the duty on sterling silver climbed steadily, until in 1784 the price of Sheffield plate was one-third the price of sterling silver. When the duty on sterling rose to one shilling an ounce in 1797 the silversmiths complained bitterly and demanded that a duty of threepence an ounce should be levied on fused plate, a plea that was heard without sympathy. In 1804 duty on sterling rose to one shilling and threepence, and in 1815 to one shilling and sixpence. The Sheffield platers happily went on embellishing their wares with the judicious addition of untaxed sterling silver. Not only that, but by 1810 the ratio of silver to copper core which, in its early years, had been at least 1:10, went down to 1:20 and in the 1840s sank as low as 1:50. Admittedly the fortunes of fused plate suffered a setback during the Napoleonic Wars (1798–1815), when there was a dire shortage of copper, every ounce of which was needed to make brass for ordnance and cannon. But the fortunes of Sheffield did not waver. They returned to traditional close plating methods over steel, marking their wares with spurious 'hallmarks' – a practice which had long been illegal for makers of fused plate.

Here, too, makers of fused plate seem to have been treated leniently. A poorly worded piece of legislation required maker's marks to be registered by law from 1772, but until the following year, when the Birmingham and Sheffield Assay Offices were set up, many of the plate makers openly stamped fake 'hallmarks' on their wares. In 1773 this practice was officially declared illegal but, undeterred, the plate makers adapted their marks so that to the uninitiated they could still be mistaken for hallmarks. A further act in 1784 tried to enforce legal controls over the plate makers, and declared that all makers must register their marks at Sheffield, whether they worked in that town or in Birmingham. Curiously, this order was never actually enacted as a legal obligation, and of the hundreds of workshops and plate makers who were active at that time, only 77 Birmingham makers registered their marks, and even fewer from Sheffield – a bare total of 55.

At the end of the Napoleonic Wars, a mass of cheap plated goods was imported from France, poorly finished, of very thin gauge, and distinguished by an almost pinkish colour as a result of the use of spun copper which imparted an unpleasant tone to the fused silver. Because of these imports, English plate makers were permitted to strike the mark of a crown – the Sheffield town mark – on fine-quality fused plate. It was also specified that all fused plate should bear one mark only, so that it was instantly distinguishable from sterling silver with its separate marks. But even those honest plate makers who had dutifully registered their marks now found that the single mark, which had to be struck on finished articles, was so heavy and ugly that it often damaged fine pieces. Disgusted, the upright plate makers ceased to mark their products at all and joined the majority of renegades who had never registered their marks at all.

Regulations for electroplating, which was invented in 1840, were more severe, but to those who are ignorant of the twists and turns in the history of Sheffield plate, it should be noted that any piece stamped with the words 'Sheffield Plated' is almost certainly electroplate. The records of genuine old Sheffield plate show that these words were never used by the makers of fused plate.

Repairs
and Restoration

The amount of repair and restoration legally permitted on any English silver is very clearly defined, yet within these limits there are still many danger areas which can reduce the value of a piece of silver.

These days, most antique silver is cherished and cared for, but it was originally made to be used, and many pieces have been victim to considerable hard wear and rough handling. Hinges of tankard lids may have been twisted and bent, feet of salvers and sauceboats badly knocked about, foot rims bent, and bodies of everyday objects dented and bruised. It is perfectly in order for feet to be removed, straightened out and resoldered, for hinge pins to be replaced and hinges mended and a normal amount of maintenance work to be done.

Deep scratches may be buffed out a little, as long as the thickness of silver removed is very small and the patina is not totally destroyed, and dents may be beaten out. If, however, past owners have attempted to remove dents without the proper process of heating or annealing, the metal may often show small hair-cracks under a microscope which are the collector's greatest nightmare. Often these tiny cracks occur on hollow ware – mugs, jugs and tankards – which will make them leaky and unserviceable. Great attention should be paid to the parts of a vessel which have been beaten out into a curve, where the metal is thinner and the likelihood of denting most dangerous. No reputable dealer would consider selling such a piece, however delightful or rare, without stating its condition. But there are always bargain-hunters who fall for a wonderful 'find', only to discover when they get it home that it is too badly damaged to use, and worth much less than they paid for it.

Transposed marks have fooled many an experienced buyer – full sets of hallmarks cut from a small piece, such as a spoon, and set into the edge of a foot rim, for example, or into an ornate Victorian version of an eighteenth-century original pattern or design, or let in to the base of a good but recent reproduction coffee pot or teapot. Be very wary of worn hallmarks in positions where they would be unlikely to have much wear – the bases of coffee pots is a typical example.

Many a sharp-eyed but innocent beginner, spotting a let-in hallmark, has been talked into believing that this is an example of the historic 'duty dodger's' work, but do not be deceived. It is illegal for any piece of 'duty dodger's' silver to be sold unless it has been hallmarked again after proper assay – and the marks may well be very recent indeed.

Electroplating has been used by many an unscrupulous dealer as well as genuine owners restoring their silver to mint condition out of sheer ignorance. Hair-cracks are extremely difficult to repair invisibly, and not infrequently the piece may have been electroplated after the cracks have been mended to conceal the repair. The colour of the silver will be harsher and have less sheen – electroplating deposits a layer of pure silver on the surface, which lacks the bloom of genuine sterling silver with its small percentage of copper alloy. Again, this is most common on hollow ware, and the insides may have been deliberately stained to look as though it has been in daily use for tea or coffee for generations – in fact the staining conceals the repairs which may well be otherwise extremely visible on the inside.

Electrotyping has also led to considerable quantities of table-ware in particular being reproduced from a single genuine piece, well hallmarked so that the electrotyped copies appear to be completely genuine. Incomplete sets of table silver are obviously far less valuable than full sets of a dozen, and the odd missing pieces may have been 'cast up' from the originals. The discriminating buyer will quickly recognise the rather grainy, gritty outline of the hallmarks which have been reproduced rather than struck. An additional clue is the fact that the hallmarks will be positioned in identical fashion to the original piece from which the facsimile has been taken.

With candlesticks, too, 'cast up' copies to make pairs or fours are not unknown. A cast is made from a genuine candlestick and a new copy taken from it. The copy will be slightly larger than the original all round, and again the hallmarks will be in identical positions to the genuine one. No two sets of hallmarks are ever in precisely the same position on pairs or sets – each one was struck separately by hand, with small variations in the placing of each mark.

Early English silver, dating from before the Queen Anne period, was often made from relatively thin sheet silver, and the construction was less sturdy than in later periods. Handles, foot rims and finials may have parted from the bodies of porringers, two-handled cups and small bowls. Here again, it is perfectly in order for a skilled silversmith to repair the damage and resolder the parts which may have come loose, but on no account may he make new handles or finials unless they are hallmarked with the date they were made and added. Recently a silversmith was taken to court for replacing a finial on a Commonwealth porringer with a copy of the original which had not been assayed or hallmarked. He was charged with 'improper alteration' to a hallmarked piece, as well as contravening the Trades Description Act with a false description.

The advice to beginners in the field of silver is the same as for any other collector of antiques – find a dealer who is both reputable and friendly, and rely on his judgement until your own is sound enough to cast off into the wider, more difficult seas of saleroom and auction on your own.

'Old Sheffield Plate'

This is a misnomer for a process described in full in the relevant chapter, and called throughout this publication 'fused plate' to distinguish it from electroplate. The dangers of buying are immense, but the rewards are great: it is possible to harvest virtually identical patterns as sterling silver in fused plate at a fraction of the cost, but each piece should be in fine condition, and again the advice of a knowledgeable dealer is of prime importance.

Recently a patent preparation has come on to the market which has caused a great deal of grief to uninformed buyers: an instant rub-on solution of silver nitrate gives a convincing coating of silver to old fused plate which has worn down badly to show the copper core beneath. This perfidiously applied silver surface will come off at once with one good rub with silver-cleaning wadding – although it is unlikely that any prospective buyer of fused plate will set off with a tin in their pocket. But a moistened handkerchief rubbed vigorously over the surface will almost certainly show that this treatment has been carried out. So, too, will a good wash in warm soapy water, but by this time it may well be too late and money will irrevocably have changed hands, and proof of unfair trade practices be hard to establish.

Cleaning and care

The great eighteenth-century silversmith Paul de Lamerie prescribes the use of 'warm water, soap and sponge and a dry soft linen cloth'. He also advises that all silver should be kept in a dry atmosphere, since damp will tarnish and stain. If silver is put away for any length of time, it should be wrapped in tissue paper – black if possible, to exclude the light and further prevent tarnishing, white if there is no alternative. Newsprint may stain silver unless it is well used and the chemicals in the print have worn off.

If a piece of silver has become so badly tarnished that it is actually stained, Paul de Lamerie recommends that straight-sided pieces should be rubbed with a damp cloth from top to bottom, but 'basins, ewers and salvers should be rubbed round-wise and not across'. This is because silver, like wood, has a grain which forms during the making, annealing and beating. Most modern patent silver-cleaners do an efficient job because they actually remove a minute layer of the surface when they are applied. Therefore they should be used very, very sparingly, and frequent rubbing with a soft chamois leather cloth kept specially for the purpose will keep silver clean and shining, and give it a soft bloom which patent preparations actually remove.

Badly stained insides of teapots and coffee pots can be cleaned with a weak solution of washing soda and water, poured ready-mixed to the brim and left to stand overnight. A remarkably efficient old wives' recipe for cleaning badly tarnished silver is to fill a bowl with skimmed milk and allow the piece to soak completely covered for a few seconds. Take it out and leave it to dry without rinsing. Then, when it is completely dry, rub it with a soft cotton or linen rag and finish off with a soft chamois leather.

Fused plate should never be cleaned with any patent preparations because the silver coating will gradually be removed, and with each cleaning the piece will be slowly devalued. It should be kept in a dry atmosphere and rubbed up frequently with nothing more than a clean, dry chamois leather or a soft yellow duster.

Value and Price

Silver objects are an oddity in the antique market, because silver itself is a precious metal and has a value of its own as bullion. But, except for a very brief period in recent years, it is virtually unknown for the bullion price of silver to exceed the price of wrought silver – pieces made into decorative and useful articles. On that one rare occasion, the price of silver bullion was artificially raised to a grossly inflated price, and regrettably dealers and owners of heavyweight objects had them melted down for the value of the silver alone. Many early Victorian pieces, not greatly admired at that time, went into the melting pot, never to be seen again.

If the sad day arrives when 'the family silver' has to be sold and it is not of very great aesthetic value – cigarette cases, silver-backed hairbrushes and the like are prime candidates for this unfortunate knacker's yard – often the buyer or dealer will tell the sorrowing owners that all he can do is offer 'the melt price'. This is a fixed rate per gram or ounce (Troy weight) but it does not represent the actual weight of the object itself. Firstly, silver is an alloy containing a small amount of copper (7·5% in sterling silver) and secondly, in the making of the object a certain amount of solder may have been used during the fashioning. Another point to bear in mind is that in many cases, particularly when it was made at the end of the nineteenth century, silver was of no great weight, and even the family teapot is worth very little when it comes to the final weigh-in. All dealers, however, who buy silver for scrap or for its melt price, are kept informed daily of the going rate, which is fixed, and you are perfectly entitled to ask for confirmation that the price offered is indeed the going rate for the week.

Armorials and Cartouches

Heraldic colours.

Purpure
purple

Sable
black

Vert
green

Gules
red

Azure
blue

Heraldry is an ancient and wonderful part of English heritage, but it is a difficult subject to absorb quickly. It is important, however, that anyone who is really interested in collecting silver should know a little about the basic terms they will encounter. A full set of armorials consists of the coat of arms, the cartouche which surrounds it, its supporters (for a noble house – for example the lion and unicorn of the Royal Coat of Arms), the mantling, and any appropriate coronet where the bearer of arms is a member of the peerage. As a general rule, the more important pieces of family plate were engraved with full armorials, and lesser pieces with the family crest. The crest is a device which has its place on the upper part of a helmet which surmounts a coat of arms.

The mantling was originally a term used for the plumes or cloth attached to the helmet, a functional addition to protect the helmet from stains and rust, and not originally a decorative device. Peers have mantling of particular colours, depending on their standing, as they also have coronets which mark out their degree and rank.

Coats of arms were devised as instant visual symbols for retainers and armed forces on the battlefield, and colours played a vital part in their distinction. Since colours cannot be engraved on silver or metal, a series of cross-hatching and dots represented the basic colours of heraldry when depicted on silver or engraved in black and white. Up to the beginning of the eighteenth century, English engravers were not skilled enough to master this extremely fine work, and the heraldic symbols on a coat of arms engraved without the detailed cross-hatching and armorials of earlier periods can be easily distinguished from later, more detailed engraving.

The style of the cartouche engraved on a piece of silver gives an instant clue to the period in which it was made. Armorials engraved at a later date on early silver, however beautifully, do not, as might be supposed, enhance the piece, but considerably reduce its value.

Coronets.

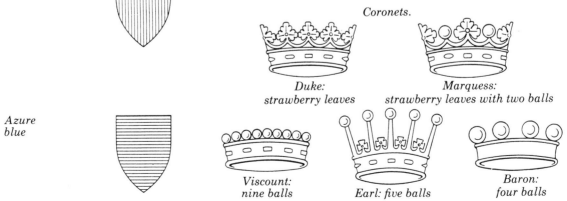

Duke:
strawberry leaves

Marquess:
strawberry leaves with two balls

Viscount:
nine balls

Earl: five balls

Baron:
four balls

c.1650

c.1710

c.1740

c.1745

c.1780

c.1825

Changing styles of cartouche.

Assay and Hallmark

*Figure of Britannia.
Britannia Standard
1697–c.1720.*

*Figure of Hibernia.
Dublin town
mark from 1731.*

Sovereign's head duty marks.

George III 1784–86

George III 1786–1820

George IV 1820–30

William IV 1830–37

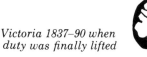

*Victoria 1837–90 when
duty was finally lifted*

The craft of goldsmithing is so ancient that its vocabulary is as archaic as that used in heraldry – a long-forgotten mixture of Old English, Old French and Medieval Latin. The permitted amount of copper to be alloyed with silver, laid down in 1238 and made law in 1290, was 92.5 parts of pure silver to 7.5 parts of copper, and that word 'alloy' whispers its ancient Old French origins – *a la loi*, or 'according to law'. 'Assay' means simply to test or try, still to be found in the modern French form 'essayer'. 'Halle' is the Old English word for 'head', while the word 'sterling' is lost in the obscurity of Medieval Latin, Old English and Old French. It is from such arcane roots that the Goldsmiths' Company grew. In 1180 a guild is mentioned, although it had yet to be granted the King's licence. In 1267, almost thirty years after the 'sterling' standard had been laid down, there was certainly a guild of goldsmiths, for they are recorded as having fought a pitched battle with the Tailors' Guild near London Bridge – an event involving some five hundred freemen of London, several of whom were actually killed during the affray.

The Guild of Goldsmiths was incorporated by letters patent in 1327, during the reign of Edward III. By a further act of 1363, all sterling silver had to be marked with the maker's mark, as well as being assayed and found to be 'alloy de bon esterling'. The 'tuche' or 'touch' was the earliest way of assaying silver and gold for purity and it was an extraordinary mixture of instinct and science. Alloys in varying proportions were made up, including the correct ratio for sterling silver, and made into needles. These needles were 'streaked' on a touchstone and the streaks compared with the silver to be assayed. The touchstone itself was basanite, a black flinty slate on to whose soft, abrasive surface particles of metal would cling. Some instructions for assay by the touch advise that the surface of the touchstone and the streaks should be licked with the tongue, when the impurities would be dissolved and the true nature of the alloy seen. A more scientific method was to wash the 'streaked' touchstone in aqua fortis which dissolved the alloyed metals, leaving only pure gold or silver on the surface.

Assay by touch was better for gold than silver, and a different method of assay was recorded in 1300, which remained unchanged for centuries. This was 'assay by the cupel'. About ten to twenty grains were scraped from various parts of the piece being assayed, and carefully enfolded in a thin sheet of lead, which was then heated to a bright red heat. The impurities alloyed themselves to the lead and left a small pinhead or button of pure metal. The difference in weight of the silver taken before and after the alloy showed the amount of alloy present. If the metal was found to be below standard, the entire object was crushed and returned to the maker.

In 1477 yet another statute imposed heavy penalties on the Goldsmiths' Company for any malpractice or default by the Keeper of the Touch in the Assay Office, and also made the Company directly responsible for 'aliens and straungers' working in and around the City of London. It therefore became vital that any defaulting Warden of the Touch should be instantly identifiable in order that he might be brought to book. The Warden of the Touch was elected annually, on 19 May, St Dunstan's Day, patron saint of goldsmiths, and his name inscribed in the record books. If the date of assay was known the Warden could be identified – and on 17 December 1478 the date letter was incorporated into the assay marks, using a 20-year span of letters in alphabetical order, omitting the letters I, V, W, X, Y and Z. After its rather hasty introduction the date letter series coincided with the annual appointment of the Warden. The surrounding shield was not incorporated into the date letter mark until 1560–61, the year that Queen Elizabeth I issued new coinage, secure at last on her throne since the death in in 1560 of the French king, Francis II, husband of Mary Queen of Scots.

A further mark had been added during the reign of Henry VIII – that of the full figure of the Royal lion, crowned and 'passant guardant', which was struck from 1544 onwards. Whether this mark was originally imposed by the King himself on the debased silver of his reign will probably never be established. But some hint that this was so can be drawn from the goldsmiths' defiant declaration that same year that they would not 'work any worse silver than upright sterling'. The goldsmiths stripped the lion passant of its crown in 1550, and a new lion passant guardant was struck in 1575 when a statue of Queen Elizabeth firmly re-established the sterling standard. This became the legal mark for all silver assayed in the provinces or in London, and the leopard's head became the town mark for the City of London. York, Exeter and Norwich were among the old and important trading towns and ports which had Assay Offices and town marks of their own as early as the Tudor period. There were also Assay Offices at Barnstaple and Taunton – odd places, until it is realised that there were quite important silver mines in Somerset.

In 1696 William III passed an act calling in all money in circulation to implement his plans for the Great Recoinage. New coins were issued with milled edges to prevent any clipping of coin, and silver for wrought plate had to be made to the higher standard of 95.8 pure silver to 4.2 copper alloy in order to distinguish it from coinage. A lion's head erased replaced the leopard's head crowned, and the figure of Britannia was struck instead of the lion passant guardant. The higher Britannia Standard remained in force until 1720, when it became no longer compulsory. The sterling standard was reintroduced, together with its mark of the lion passant guardant.

At the same time as the sterling standard was restored, a duty of sixpence per ounce on wrought plate was imposed – an extremely unpopular tax which was greatly resented by gold-

Date letters showing changing type face for each year.

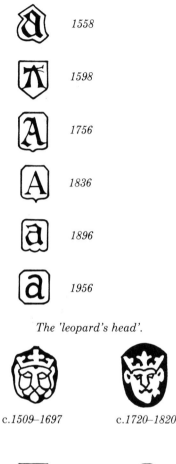

a	*1558*
Ⱥ	*1598*
A	*1756*
A	*1836*
a	*1896*
a	*1956*

The 'leopard's head'.

c.1509–1697	*c.1720–1820*
1820 to the present day	*Lion's head erased. Britannia Standard silver 1697–c.1720.*

The lion passant.

1562–1668	*1669–97*
1720–1821	*1821 to the present day*

Barnstaple

Taunton

Birmingham

Sheffield

Edinburgh

smiths and silversmiths. The duty was collected at the Assay Office and no piece could be struck before tax had been paid. Duty dodging was rife – some silversmiths avoided the Assay Office completely, working only for patrons whose commissions would not be on public sale, and simply striking their own marks four times in a rough approximation of the positions of the Assay Office marks. Others took small finished pieces to be assayed and marked, and paid duty on them. Back in their workshops, they cut the marked silver out and incorporated it into far larger, more costly pieces on which they paid no duty. The Assay Office was well aware of this particular dodge, but attempts at regulation were singularly unsuccessful. In 1739, all goldsmiths and silversmiths were ordered to register entirely new marks so that old silver returned to the makers for refashioning could not have the marks removed and re-used, but even this did not deter determined duty dodgers. For a while the Assay Office took to striking each mark separately and as far apart as possible, in an effort to make it impossible for them to be cut out. This, too, was ineffective, and in 1757 the Government stepped in with a flat-rate duty fee of £2 for every maker and trader in precious metals.

In 1784, duty of sixpence an ounce was again levied on individual items of wrought plate, and the mark of the sovereign's head was struck on each dutiable object when payment had been made. From 1 December 1784, when the duty mark was introduced, until 1786, the head of George III was struck facing to the left. After that date the King's head faced to the right until 1837, when Queen Victoria's head once again faced to the left. Duty was levied until 1890, when it was finally lifted and the duty mark of the sovereign's head ceased to be struck.

One of a pair of Queen Anne lidded jugs finely engraved with a contemporary cartouche and armorials. Seth Lofthouse. London 1713.

Sideboard dishes

Signs of authenticity

1. Hallmarks on surface of dish indicate early date – from c.1685 marks struck under rim.
2. Relatively light in weight compared with eighteenth-century versions.
3. Border wire applied and soldered with silver/brass solder, distinctly yellowish in colour.
4. Decoration raised by embossing, chasing and repoussé, and not cast.
5. Flowing, naturalistic representations of fruit, flowers, unlike more stylised work of Continental makers.
6. From c.1697 Britannia Standard marks.
7. Provincial town marks on Britannia Standard only after c.1701.
8. In silver gilt, with original gilding still intact.
9. No gilding on underside.
10. Armorials, cartouche correct style for period.

Likely restoration and repair
11. Hallmarks on underside of rim distorted, or in centre of base – may indicate original piece was plain dish, correct date, with embossing, chasing added later.
12. Gilding too bright and strident – regilded at later date.
13. Thinner gauge in centre of dish – armorials or deep scratches buffed out.
14. Cartouches in later style – engraved at later date, thereby reducing value.
15. Embossing weakens silver, sometimes wearing small holes which may have been repaired. Examine closely and hold up to light to detect any small splits, cracks, which reduce value.
16. Gilding on underside as well as surface may indicate later gilding, after c.1780, or manufacture after that date.

A glimpse of the magnificence customarily displayed on the sideboards of great houses still remains, although many of the finest pieces are in museums. Only a person of royal blood was allowed five 'stages' to his sideboard. Nobles of highest rank had four, and so down the scale to a single stage for knights bannerets and families of good blood who were not ennobled.

Richly decorated plates such as these might occasionally be brought to the table for a dish of rare fruits but little else. Large, plain dishes of similar form to alms dishes were used as 'voyders' on to which the remains of a banquet were scraped before being removed to the kitchens. In lesser households, there were simpler versions of sideboard dishes, their more shallowly embossed rims often echoing the treatment of the stiff acanthus leaf of the same period.

Sideboard dishes and dessert dishes do not have a central boss, indicating that they were not originally made with ewers. At this period, so rich it is definitely Baroque in flavour, the remarkable talents of English silversmiths in embossed and chased work are plain for all to see. The modelled naturalistic flowers and fruits appear to stand out in high relief because of the matted surface that surrounds them.

Construction and materials

These remarkably lavish and handsome dishes were made from fairly thick gauge silver, hammered up from blocks of metal into sheet and then painstakingly embossed, to raise the main patterns of fruit, flowers and leaves on the reverse side, before being rested on a block of pitch or bag of sand while the detail and crisp definition was added with a series of metal punches and tools, in a technique known as repoussé chasing. Border wires were made separately, sometimes corded or patterned with simple punches in a 'piecrust' pattern, and soldered on with silver/brass solder. These dishes are far lighter in weight than their appearance suggests.

Once all the work had been completed, the silver was fire-gilded, using an amalgam of gold and mercury, painted on to the surface and then heated so that the mercury vaporised and the gold coating partly fused to the silver surface.

Decoration

The main themes for these dishes were fruit, flowers, mythological beasts and heraldic animals. The centres were usually left plain, and engraved with armorials. These should be in contemporary style, with appropriate cartouches for the period, matching the date of the hallmarks as nearly as possible. In the case of seventeenth-century silver, the loss of value for armorials engraved a very short period after the plate or dish was made is relatively small – the greatest damage is when eighteenth- or nineteenth-century coats of arms or crests have been added.

Reproductions

In the last quarter of the nineteenth century, services for dessert, usually including a tazza or comport standing on a single foot and several accompanying dishes either on a pedestal or on four small feet, were made, generally in silver gilt.

In the 1900s many well-known silversmiths also made great dishes based on Carolean designs, although the fruit and flowers are distinctly sinuous, the tendrils too twining, and the centres often swirled into shapes more reminiscent of Art Nouveau than the seventeenth century. These dishes, too, may well be lighter in weight than the eighteenth-century versions, since spun silver and rolled silver were used; the lightness in weight should not deceive, any more than the unlikely use of columbine and eglantine among the flowers.

Variations

Less ornate and more serviceable dishes with finely decorated rims were made up to the end of the seventeenth century, as well as plain, wide-rimmed deeper dishes known as chargers, in silver and in silver gilt, upon which slices of meat cut from the spit-roasted joint were offered to guests as they sat at table.

There was a revival in popularity of Carolean silver during the Regency period, although the decoration was more lavish. Two of the greatest exponents of silver gilt in the Carolean manner were William Pitts and Edward Cornelius Farrell, both working in the early nineteenth century.

Price bands

17th-century, £4,000–£8,000. Georgian, heavy cast decoration, £20,000+.

Early 19th-century, heavy quality, £3,800–£7,000+. Victorian, £2,000–£3,500.

Pairs more than double.

Far left *Charles II silver gilt dish, with armorials of slightly later date. Probably London c.1670.*

Left *George III silver gilt fluted dish in Britannia Standard silver by Edward Cornelius Farrell. London 1818. 10 in (25.5 cm) diameter.*

Caudle cups and porringers

Signs of authenticity

1. Hallmarks in full scattered on base, or in roughly straight line near rim of body, to one side of handle.
2. Full set of hallmarks on cover to c.1725, after which only maker's mark and lion passant guardant may be found.
3. Britannia Standard marks c.1697–c.1720.
4. Lids loose without inner flange to c.1670.
5. Exceptional to find early porringers in sizes other than about 3–3½ in (7.5–9 cm) or 7–7½ in (18–19 cm).
6. Foot rims not applied, but bossed out from body to c.1680. Occasionally found with spreading foot, but should date from before c.1660.
7. Applied cast foot rims on larger porringers from c.1680.
8. Engraved, chased armorials contemporary with hallmarks.
9. All decoration embossed, chased to c.1680, including early stiff acanthus leaf and palm. Simple cut card work from that date, but not common before c.1700.

Likely restoration and repair
10. Applied foot rims before c.1680 suspicious – heavy soldering may indicate base and hallmarks have been added.
11. Handles may have pulled away causing damage to body.
12. Hallmarks on covers may not accord with those on base, indicating 'marriage'.
13. Splits around bossed-out base common – may have been repaired.
14. Fine splits in decorative chasing can be seen when held to light.
15. Britannia Standard marks may be found to c.1735.
16. Larger sizes from 8 in (20 cm) to 9 in (23 cm) of much later date.

Two-handled cups such as these are called variously posset pots, caudle cups and porringers. Possets and caudles were made with cream or milk curdled with white wine. The curds floated to the top and were carefully skimmed off, leaving a clear liquid below. Both curds and whey were considered particularly nourishing to nursing mothers – caudle cups were often given to wives after the birth of their first child, sometimes engraved with the initials of the father and mother, with the surname initial above and the first names of husband and wife below.

Early versions with ring handles, made before the Civil War, are rare survivals. Mostly caudle cups are somewhat pot-bellied, made from fairly thin sheet metal with two cast handles in S-scrolls or in the shape of rather skinny caryatids. From the Restoration onwards, designs became more elaborate, with lobes and gadroons marking the Dutch influence of the notable silversmith Christian van Vianen. Daffodils, poppies, dragons, and heraldic and mythical beasts such as the wyvern were popular subjects, with the tulip marking patriotic Dutch influence from the accession of the Dutch king, William, to the English throne in 1689 to the end of the century.

Many posset pots and caudle cups originally had covers which, when turned upside down on the table, acted as small spoon trays after the curds had been skimmed off.

Construction and materials

There is no particular evidence that the larger-sized versions of these vessels were made for caudles and the smaller ones for possets. As they were traditionally given as presents to celebrate the birth of a child in every household which could afford silver, it is more likely that the size was governed by expense rather than use. For all their rich decoration, caudle cups did not contain a great quantity of metal, except for the handles which were almost invariably cast. The simplest, often decorated with no more than punched work and pricked with initials, had handles made from thick silver wire. Undoubtedly made throughout the seventeenth century, in general those that have survived date from the Restoration onwards. By about 1705 they had largely been replaced by slightly more grand two-handled cups and covers.

Decoration

Apart from a very brief period of 'chinoiserie' from the late 1670s to the 1680s, early caudle cups and posset pots were embossed and chased with typical Stuart flowers and animals until Dutch influence showed itself in lobes, gadroons and a more flaring mouth from c.1690. The patriotic tulip had a brief popularity before it was replaced by more formal decoration of acanthus and palm leaf round slightly raised bases, although the typical caryatid handle continued to be used, as well as a plainer, S-scroll cast handle, sometimes with gadrooning, during the later period. Armorials were plain, with little cross-hatching or detail, the most typical being flanked by crossed plumes.

Variations

It is likely that an earlier custom of using small bridal cups during the pre-Reformation marriage ceremony was continued in some areas of the British Isles, and that some of the plain, simple, small two-handled cups were intended for this purpose and engraved with the initials of the newly wedded husband and wife. Some churches kept such cups specifically for the purpose, and during the Catholics' long struggle to retain their rituals and beliefs, such cups may have been used clandestinely.

Charles II silver gilt porringer and cover, engraved with later armorials, with caryatid scroll handles. London 1678. 7 in (18 cm) high.

Simple porringer engraved with initials of a married couple, with scrolling handles. 1730. 3½ in (9 cm) high.

Reproductions

Some caudle cups and porringers in Carolean style were made by eminent makers during the early 1900s in Britannia Standard silver, marked accordingly, but they tend to be much larger than authentic pieces. Anything resembling the early period in style but with hallmarks later than about 1720 should be examined with great care. Early pieces were handed down from generation to generation, receiving some very hard ware, and in many cases have become so battered as to be unsaleable. But judicious matching of bases from later, less important pieces with repaired bodies can result in a convincing 'Carolean' piece to the uninitiated.

Elaborate presentation porringer and cover in 17th-century taste by R. & S. Garrard. London 1901. 9¾ in (25 cm) high.

Price bands

17th-century prime condition with covers, armorials etc., £10,000 + .
Without covers, simple decoration, £600–£2,000.

Chinoiserie decoration, £3,000–£5,000 + .

Queen Anne, early Georgian, £600–£1,200.

19th-century reproductions, £500–£1,000.

Two-handled cups and covers

1. Correct marks for period, struck on base or near rim of cup, to one side of handle.
2. Britannia Standard marks to *c.*1720 but also used in later periods.
3. Sovereign's head duty mark indicates date from 1784 to 1890.
4. Appropriate cartouche for period.
5. Crest only on lid – must accord with armorials on body.
6. Rare to find solid cast handles – commonly cast in two parts and soldered together.
7. Plain or reeded girdles made separately and applied.
8. Pronounced short stem from *c.*1715 onwards.
9. Marks on cover or lid from *c.*1725 correct if limited to maker's mark and sterling mark of lion passant.
10. Marks must accord on body and lid in style and identity.

Likely restoration and repair
11. Foot and stem may have been squashed, distorted – check for signs of refashioning and repair.
12. Handles pulled or twisted – weakening of body will show with minute cracks radiating out from join.
13. Later engraving of armorials, crests – lessens value.
14. Stem too pronounced and signs of heavy solder on base may indicate replacement of damaged part or clumsy restoration.
15. Faintly metallic, blue, cold colour may indicate extensive repairs and later plating.
16. Bright gilding over entire body may indicate later gold plating to conceal repairs, weaknesses.

After a short period from about 1690 to 1700 when the shape of the two-handled cup was little more than a slight development of the Carolean caudle cup, a sleeker, more elegant and altogether grander version took their place. Raised on circular feet, sometimes embellished with gadrooning, the size of two-handled cups and covers grew until they measured as much as 10 in and more, and could be said to have replaced the tall standing cups and covers that were an essential part of a rich man's panoply in Tudor times.

One can only guess at their purpose and contents, but many and various were the beverages consumed in the early years of the eighteenth century – wine, beer, cider, caudles, possets and strange mixtures consisting of a strong alcoholic base flavoured with spices, herbs and fruits. When not in use at a grand celebration banquet, these cups would have formed part of the display plate which, after the Restoration, was both grand and profligate.

By the middle of the eighteenth century, two-handled cups and covers stood on a decorative, extended foot rim which gradually lengthened into a stem or pedestal base with the classical influence of the vase shape so fashionable at the time. The grandly ceremonial cup and cover had by then become ideal for trophies and race cups and, in the form of the Warwick vase, it survived as such with great splendour into Victorian times.

Construction and materials

The finest examples of these grand pieces were made during the period of higher Britannia Standard silver – between 1697 and 1720, while the form was still pure and well proportioned. Simple girdles, either reeded or plain, were applied to a body of considerable thickness of silver, and the leaf-capped handles were cast, generally in two parts, the outer band being soldered on to the curving underside.

The foot and short stem, which ended in a cup shape, were made separately and also soldered on to the main body of the vessel. Finials were also cast and generally joined to the cover with an extra thickness of metal, either plain or decorative.

Early cups of this form were sometimes decorated round the base with cut card work in symmetrical leaf shapes forming a calyx which was usually repeated on the lid.

Decoration

The progression from the harp-shaped handle so favoured by Huguenots to a simpler leaf-capped S-scroll coincided with an altered position of the applied girdle. It could be said that until the 1730s the English silversmiths were more successful with plain, undecorated shapes. After that period, although they had to a great extent mastered the difficult technique of cast strapwork decoration, their ambitious attempts to equal the work of Huguenot craftsmen often just missed the right proportions, or used a double C-scroll handle with extra decorative work around the joins which spoiled the simple grandeur of their work.

By about 1730 the rich geometric strapwork became more ornamental, with classical portrait medallions alternating with a more ornate leaf shape.

Variations

Basic, simple versions two-handled cups continued to be made from about 1700 right through to the 1760s with little variation. At the other end of the scale, interpretations of the gadrooned style were lavishly mixed with chased leaf motifs cupping the base of a more rounded body and deep collet foot. This style was popular during the Regency, after the wearisome shape of the vase had invaded almost every object of domestic and display plate.

Simple Queen Anne two-handled cup with harp-shaped handles and applied reeded girdle. 1704. 5½in (14cm) high.

George II cup and cover with leaf-capped scroll handles and baluster finial. London 1727. 10in (25.5cm) high.

Reproductions

If anything, the Victorian versions of these handsome cups were better-proportioned than the English silversmiths' early attempts to emulate the Huguenot designs – except that they were presentation cups and far larger than the originals, which seldom exceeded 10–12in (25.5–30.5cm). This example is a yachting trophy, and although the craftsmanship of the cast and applied strapwork is excellent, it is too widely spaced, and the applied girdle is set just a little too high. It is of monumental proportions, measuring 17in (43cm) and weighing 3414g. Except for the most lavish early-eighteenth-century examples, the weight was in the region of 1865–2250g.

Tumbler cups and beakers

It is quite possible that William Harrison, writing in 1586 and remarking that even a farmer's silver consisted of 'a bowl for wine, if not a whole ne(a)st', refers to a nest of tumbler cups which stacked one inside the other and were carried about while attending cock fights, foot races, hunting or racing, or as an essential piece of equipment on the tediously lengthy journeys over pitted and pot-holed roads. At least until the eighteenth century most daily life and entertainment took place outdoors, and even inside, household essentials were often portable.

Tumbler cups are very practical drinking vessels since they can be jogged and jostled without falling over. The alternative drinking vessel before the days of glass was a beaker. Often made in horn, sometimes silver-mounted, or in sheet silver, these are rarely decorated with more than a single band of formal engraving, or with initials or, for grander households, with a crest or coat of arms. Both beakers and tumbler cups were often made in pairs in the first half of the eighteenth century, either fitting inside each other or rim-to-rim, forming a container in which sets of cutlery, spice boxes and corkscrews were kept as part of the large array of travelling necessities including shaving gear and toilet sets.

The only period in which straight-sided beakers were decorated with bands of embossed leaves and flowers was during the reign of Charles II. Early, slightly flaring beakers on a decorated foot rim were taller and slimmer than those made in the eighteenth century. Pairs of beakers which screwed together in the form of a barrel date from the last quarter of the eighteenth century onwards and formed part of the tippling man's travelling essentials, particularly for sporting events, when they accompanied a flask.

Signs of authenticity

1. Beakers made in three parts – body, foot rim and mouth wire.
2. Tumbler cups beaten up from thick gauge silver with the weight in the base and no foot rim or mouth wire.
3. Seams visible as vertical hairline on beakers.
4. Hallmarks on tumbler cups in roughly straight line near rim or on base.
5. Hallmarks on beakers generally on underside of base until late eighteenth century, when they are found in a line near the rim.
6. Pairs of tumbler cups screwing together generally marked on sides near base.
7. No embossing, chasing on tumbler cups – engraving usually only of armorials.
8. Any armorials, engraving consistent with date of piece.

Likely restoration and repair
9. Small vertical splits running from rim down into body will show when breathed upon.
10. Heavily soldered underneath round foot rim may indicate base has been tampered with.
11. Tumbler cups much harder to repair, restore. Check rim for dents, hammer marks.
12. Check armorials for authenticity – most likely cause of reduced value if engraved at later date.
13. Beakers may be late-embossed – typical Victorian motifs relatively easy to recognise.

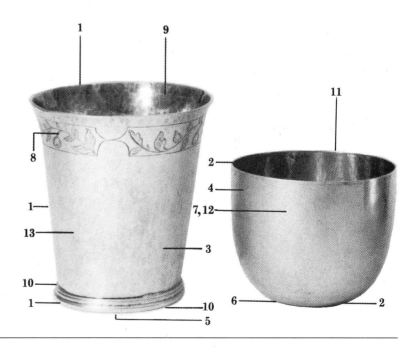

Construction and materials

Beakers, which are straight-sided with a slightly flaring line, are made from sheet metal, the main body simply curved into a cylindrical shape and seamed, with the foot wire or foot rim added. This is generally plain, with incised lines of reeding added by turning on a lathe. From the Georgian period the mouth wire was treated in similar fashion, with one or two lines of reeding added for extra strength. Tumbler cups, on the other hand, which are raised from a thick gauge metal, are extremely unlikely to show any signs of splitting. The nature of silver when hammered up makes it almost impervious to denting or bending. It is the weight of metal in the base that causes tumbler cups to return to an upright position when knocked or jogged which gave these cups the name 'tumbler'.

Decoration
On beakers, the most common decoration is a single band of hatched arabesques or stylised foliage and flowers, or occasionally initials, until the beginning of the eighteenth century when they were engraved with contemporary armorials. For a brief period between *c.*1665 and 1695 broad bands of typically Stuart flowers were embossed and chased, but otherwise beakers were plain and functional.

Tumbler cups were seldom decorated with anything other than cyphers, crests or armorials, except if part of travelling sets, when the decoration may be more elaborate – but the cups themselves in this case are half-way between a beaker and a tumbler and do not always have the very thick, rounded bases of true tumblers.

Reproductions

The most elegant versions of small drinking beakers made during the nineteenth century were sets of silver or silver gilt beakers decorated with a simple band of matting – a style which was briefly current during the latter half of the seventeenth century but has not been recorded as having been used to decorate beakers at that period. Other, far more obvious versions are the over-decorated embossed and chased small tumblers, sometimes made as an alternative to christening mugs, and the pairs of barrel-shaped beakers that screw together which were part of the sporting man's paraphernalia, still made to order by silversmiths today.

Victorian silver gilt beaker with an engraved crest and motto above a broad band of matting. E. & J. Barnard. London 1862. 5 in (12.5 cm) high.

Variations

Completely plain, straightforward silver beakers were made for a variety of purposes, including children's drinking cups, right through to the nineteenth century and later. In general, however, mugs were more common by the late eighteenth century, although there was a revival of small silver beakers with lavish decoration in the second half of the nineteenth century. Plain, straight-sided silver containers made during the nineteenth and early twentieth centuries may originally have been cases for glass bottles which were part of lavishly fitted 'dressing cases', and can be distinguished by an absence of foot rim or mouth wire.

Plain slightly flaring Georgian beaker with applied reeded foot rim. London 1777.

A squat Charles II tumbler cup engraved with contemporary armorials and chased with baroque flowers and foliage. York 1673. 2¼ in (6 cm) high.

Price bands

Tumblers:
Early 18th-century, £500–£800.
Rare inscriptions, decoration, £1,800+.

Beakers:
17th-century, £400–£800.
Georgian, £350–£600.
Victorian, £60–£400.

Pairs more than double.

Candlesticks 1685–1735

Signs of authenticity

1. Hallmarks on underside, generally on angles of cut corners on square-based, clustered together on round-based candlesticks.
2. Pairs more valuable than singles – hallmark positions should differ slightly.
3. Cast in solid metal, not sheet, in three parts: base, stem and sconce.
4. Stem usually cast in two halves and soldered together vertically – seam visible when breathed on.
5. Mark of sterling lion passant guardant should appear on sconce, Britannia Standard marks at appropriate period.
6. Plain spool-shaped sconces without detachable nozzles until *c.*1730.
7. Height should be between 6 in (15 cm) and 7 in (18 cm) for this period.
8. Absence of vertical seam down stem does not necessarily indicate lack of authenticity – French silversmiths of the period cast stems in one piece with hollow centres.
9. Very roughly finished undersides to bases.

Likely restoration and repair
10. Hallmarks identically positioned on both bases of a pair – may indicate that a second has been cast up from the original.
11. Heavy soldering on underside where stem joins base – may indicate 'marriage' of two damaged candlesticks of similar but not identical pattern.
12. Poor-quality casting resulting in cracks, patches on metal reduces value.
13. Dents, score-marks round rim of sconce where wax has been levered, scraped out reduces value.
14. Examine pairs closely – patterns often remarkably similar.

Silver candlesticks dating from before the Restoration are of sheet metal, square-based, with a drip pan set low on the column, with some repoussé decoration on bases and drip pans. Another form first made during the Commonwealth was a trumpet-shaped candlestick, of which a few rare pairs dating from about 1653 survive. A third type, which has much in common with those made in Scandinavia and Northern Europe at the same period, has square, columnar stems or clusters of columns bound with girdles, often with gadroon decoration on the square bases.

By 1690 there had been a revolution in the construction and design of candlesticks. From this date they were cast in solid silver and no longer made in sheet metal. The first surviving and recorded pair of candlesticks made with this technique are by Pierre Harache, dated 1683, and can therefore be attributed to the Huguenot skill in casting techniques.

In most houses, the day ended at sunset and except for a candle to light people to bed, the lighting in kitchens and outhouses would have been dips or rushlights. In 1724 John Hervey, first Earl of Bristol, ordered a 'silver hanging candlestick for the nursery', but this was a wealthy household. A Gloucestershire baronet at about the same period had only two pillar candlesticks, six square candlesticks, two hand candlesticks and another half-dozen around the house in brass, and seven in the dairy, where work began before dawn.

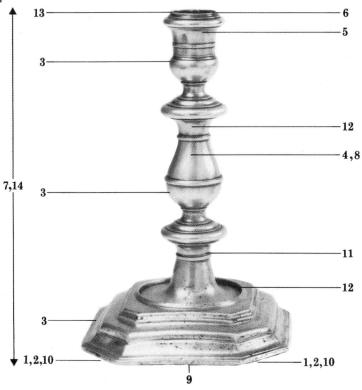

Construction and materials

It has been surmised by some that Britannia Standard silver was softer than sterling silver and was therefore not so durable or easy to work in intricate shapes. The only sign of this possible softness in candlesticks is that they could be turned crisply with ring decoration which is less pronounced after the 1720s.

Candlesticks of the basic baluster stem pattern were cast in several pieces: generally the base in one piece, and the stem and sconce either in one hollow core-cast section, when the base of the candle-socket will show signs of having been filled with silver solder, or in two halves vertically and then soldered together down the seams with silver/brass solder. Occasionally the sconce was cast separately and a seam between the base of the spool-shaped sconce and the top of the stem will be visible. The bottom of the stem was formed in the shape of a threaded screw which fitted into a hole in the base section or with a rivet soldered to the join to increase stability.

Decoration

The first pattern of cast candlesticks had a stem in a series of knops, decorated with ring turning, standing on a square or cut-corner base with stepped moulding, the flare of the stem encircled by a small raised band. The only decoration was a crest engraved at the base of the stem. Later the shape changed to baluster or inverted baluster form, briefly from c.1700 matched with circular bases and then, c.1710, changing to octagonal bases with faceted stems and cushion knops.

Variations

Candlesticks with octagonal or hexagonal faceted stems are variations on the classic baluster shape, and are sometimes a little taller than the average size of 6–7 in (15–18 cm).

Round-based candlesticks have been noted in journals and inventories as 'desk' candlesticks, and in view of the fact that writing furniture and early card and games tables of this period have circular dished slides or dished lobes with circular depressions, it can be conjectured that this was one purpose for round-based candlesticks at this early period.

Above *One of a pair with inverted baluster stems and twin knops, with banded spool-shaped sconces, by specialist candlestick maker James Gould. London 1731. 7 in (18 cm) high.*

Reproductions

It is perhaps curious that these admirably proportioned and designed early baluster cast candlesticks have been reproduced so seldom. Not until the 1920s, when Americans wanted copies of early English 'Queen Anne', were some few copies made – generally in sterling standard and not Britannia Standard, and often a little taller than the original small size.

Reproduction of a pattern known as trumpet-based, originally made in the first half of the 17th century. This pair has detachable nozzles, which the originals would not have had. T. Bradbury & Son. Sheffield 1907. 7 in (18 cm) high.

Price bands

Pairs:
Early baluster, fully marked, £7,500–£10,000.
George I baluster, £5,000–£8,000.
Faceted, octafoil, £6,000–£10,000.
Pleated bases, £2,500–£5,500.

Reproductions, £350–£500.

Singles less than half, genuine sets of four rare, £20,000 + .

Left *Typical pattern by James Gould with tapering faceted stems, lobed shoulder knops and deep spool-shaped sconces with detachable nozzles. London 1738. 6¾ in (17 cm) high.*

Candlesticks 1735–1765

Signs of authenticity

1. Pairs genuinely matching in design, hallmark, date.
2. Detachable nozzles of same date, maker, style as rest of candlestick – many have been replaced.
3. Vertical seam down stem where two halves cast separately and soldered together.
4. Some stems cast in one piece with hollow centres – different method of joining base to stem underneath.
5. Undersides left rough and not turned, cleaned off.
6. Hallmarks scattered on underside, either at corners or one on each of four sides.
7. Crests must be consistent with date of piece.
8. Detachable nozzles must bear at least two hallmarks – sterling lion passant and maker's mark.
9. Sconce should also be hallmarked with maker's mark and sterling lion passant although marks may be badly rubbed.
10. Height 7½–9 in (19–23 cm).

Likely restoration and repair
11. Join between stem and base may be additionally soldered on underside – indicates damage, repair.
12. Hallmarks in identical positions on undersides of both candlesticks of a pair – one has been cast off from the other. Genuine pairs have different positioning of hallmarks.
13. Marks on detachable nozzle not according with rest of piece indicates replacement, with consequent loss of value.
14. Height over 9 in (23 cm) usually indicates later reproduction.
15. Marks on outer rim of base indicates loaded candlesticks made of sheet metal, probably in nineteenth century.

The fact that the first group of cast candlesticks were made without nozzles or drip pans suggests one of two things – either that the French-born makers had assumed that England had fine wax candles, or that the imported tallow, much of which came from Russia, produced better-quality candles than those of later dates.

The second group of cast candlesticks were slightly taller than their predecessors, measuring from about 7½ in to 9 in, and most of them were made with detachable nozzles for saving the dripping wax and making the removal of candle stubs easier. As they developed, their lines changed to a pleated square-shaped base, sometimes so curved that it was almost round, with knopped and lobed faceted stems of baluster form.

From the end of the 1730s the rococo shell motif decoration is clearly evident, although in a subdued and disciplined form, and the flared nozzles often repeat the shell motif. The transition from the wavy, stepped pleated bases to the shell can be easily seen, together with the change from circular, pleated nozzles to more square shapes, in sympathy with the squarer form of the bases. This pattern of candlestick was made throughout this period, with slight variations in proportion and detail, and was still being made well into the 1770s.

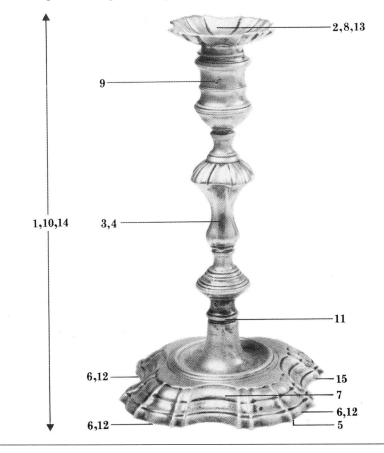

Construction and materials

Except for a few of the early versions of these highly popular patterns which were made during the Britannia Standard period, cast candlesticks of this period should bear the new version of the sterling lion passant and, if London-made, one of four slightly different 'leopard's heads' which changed in 1724, 1726, 1728, 1736 and 1739, the latter of a bold design which continued until 1750.

In the main the sconce continued to be plain, spool-shaped, with a slightly vase-shaped curve in shell-based patterns. Detachable nozzles were flared and pleated until the shell-based design, when they had small shells at the lobes to match the bases. Shell-based candlesticks made after c.1765 may have additional corded bands on the sconces, but these are rarely found before that date.

Decoration
The basic design elements of the shell-based candlestick varied very little – it is the proportions and quality of crispness in the casting and chasing that makes the difference between a good example and a mediocre one. The repetition of the shell motif on the shoulder knop, the slight upcurving shape of the stem itself, the tight integration of the shells on the base are a matter for the eye alone to judge. Sometimes the bases splay out too far in an almost collapsed form, the shoulder knop is too heavy for the stem, or the sconces have not developed from the rather heavy spool shapes of earlier designs.

Variations

During the period from c.1735 to 1750 some candlesticks were made in a far more rococo style, ornately cast and chased. The other variation in rococo style were candlesticks with figures or half-figures as stems, usually holding up the sconce with one or both arms above their heads. These candlesticks often stood on a three-cornered swirling base. Highly decorative but also very alien to the English taste, both these patterns sat uneasily in the pure lines of the period which followed, and many of them were discarded, often damaged.

Reproductions

Variations of the shell-based candlestick were made in fused plate, and in loaded sheet silver from the 1840s onwards, but they were taller, measuring as much as 10 in (25.5 cm), and had stockier bases because sheet metal needed an inset wooden base. Copies of the 'figure candlesticks' were made in great numbers, but incorporating the Victorian ideals of feminine grace and with full-length figures rather than the demi-figures which owed their design to classical models.

Price bands

Pairs:
Pleated bases, £2,500–£3,200.
Shell base, £1,200–£3,000.
Rococo, £3,500–£6,000.
Figures, £3,500–£7,000.

Reproductions, £450–£1,000.

Fours more than double.

Above *One of a cast silver pair in the form of caryatids, a pattern copied often in the 19th century. Pairs should always face to the left and right. These are by specialist candlestick maker John Cafe. London 1749. 8¼ in (22 cm) high.*

Left *One of a set of four with slightly squarer bases, deeper sconces with detachable nozzles. London 1743/4. 7¾ in (19.5 cm) high.*

Above *Early shell-based pattern with crests engraved on small panels on the bases, and detachable nozzles. London 1751/2. 8¼ in (22 cm) high.*

Candlesticks 1765–1795

1. In cast silver, hallmarked on underside of base and sconce – detachable nozzle with maker's mark and sterling lion passant.
2. From 1784 marks must include duty mark of sovereign's head. From this period sconce may be unmarked.
3. From *c.*1772 onwards almost all fused plate unmarked.
4. Birmingham Assay Office established 1773 with town mark an anchor.
5. Sheffield Assay Office established same year with town mark a crown.
6. Matthew Boulton making both fused plate and sterling silver *c.*1765 onwards in almost identical designs and patterns – silver to 1773 marked with Chester or London mark.
7. Loaded candlesticks marked only on outer rim of base and detachable nozzle.
8. Height 9½–11 in (24–28 cm).

Likely restoration and repair
9. Cast candlesticks must follow rules of earlier periods – pairs genuine and not matching singles or cast off from one original.
10. Fused plate considerably thinner gauge than sheet silver – can be seen from edge on underside.
11. Blurred detail indicates blunted dies, usually of later date since quality was vital during fashionable period.
12. Signs of solder around thin, slender parts indicate damage, repair.
13. 'Fire-stain' marks or patches of blemish may indicate splitting and cracking of sheet silver heated and repaired with solder, causing original metal to distort.
14. Edges of sheet silver round base may be split, dented, frilled with wear and use – lowers value.

Candlesticks were becoming increasingly part of an overall theme in interior design by the 1750s and 1760s, when there was a return to heavy, simple cast silver with gadrooned decoration. Candlesticks were frequently made from this period onwards in 'long sets' – a dozen or two dozen of the same pattern to be used on the long mahogany tables and side tables of the period.

It was in the neo-classical Adam period that candlesticks were designed specifically as part of the overall grand design. The bases of early Adam period candlesticks were still square, but by 1765 classical columns with Corinthian capitals were being made. Soon after, as the urn, the vase and the column virtually took over as the main ingredients of any design, candlesticks were round-based, with tapering elongated vase-shaped stems and vase-shaped sconces, with stiff acanthus leaf decoration.

The first candlesticks in stamped embossed sheet silver were made in London, and then in Birmingham and Sheffield in both fused plate and sheet silver. Few neo-classical candlesticks were made in London after 1775, when London makers began to make richer, more decorated silver, with inverted baluster stems cupped with a calyx of acanthus leaves and more elaborate designs which harked back to the days of rococo.

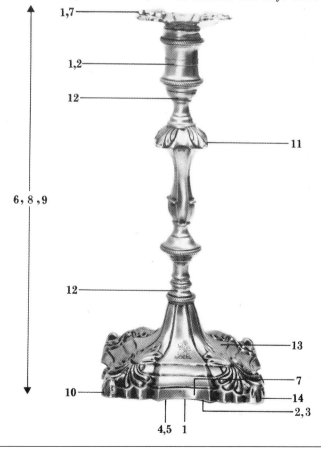

Construction and materials

This period can be extremely confusing, since three quite different types of candlesticks were being made: cast, loaded sheet silver and fused plate. Moreover, the bulk of fused plate was being made by Matthew Boulton's manufactory in Birmingham and not in Sheffield until after c.1775, when both die-stamped loaded sheet silver and fused plate were made in that town. Methods of die-stamping and die-sinking produced each candlestick in a multitude of parts, and many of them had seams running vertically which do not necessarily line up on the finished piece.

Early fused plate was overlapped so that the raw edges did not show and the edge was turned over the wooden or pitch base after it had been loaded. Sheet silver was seldom turned over – the gauge of metal was thicker and many had a metal base-plate with holes through which the pitch was poured before the base was covered in green baize cloth.

Decoration

Candlesticks before the arrival of the neo-classical form are among the most attractive, with swirl bases and corded or gadrooned bands round knops, shoulder and sconce, and with faceted stems which accord better with the square bases than the slightly earlier rounded versions. Engraved armorials, crests or initials are found on cast candlesticks of the period – die-stamped and die-sunk patterns either had high stepped bases or decorations of ram's heads, swags or stiff leaves which left little room for engraving.

Reproductions

This early group of neo-classical patterns has been the basis for many later designs. Contemporary copies in fused plate of swirl-based and square-based early neo-classical patterns can hardly be called reproduction. Often the size will give away the late origins of such late period candlesticks – the contemporary height was between $9\frac{1}{2}$ and $11\frac{1}{2}$ in (24 and 29 cm), and sometimes even taller. Later copies tend to have been scaled down from the original height to an average of 10–11 in (25.5–28 cm).

Cluster column candlestick in electroplate by Richard Hood and Son, late 19th century. 13 in (33 cm) high.

Variations

Many of the designs and patterns made in London in sheet silver from about 1765 onwards were copied almost identically in fused plate. The plate makers achieved remarkable results with this new and difficult material. One could almost say that the plate makers' designs were purer than those of the silversmiths, since the material dictated the form of the object and excess ornament was discarded and the results are extremely elegant.

Square, swirl-based with gadrooned decoration, faceted stems. Banded spool-shaped sconces. London 1768. $11\frac{1}{2}$ in (29 cm) high.

Early Sheffield fused plate cluster column candlestick in a pattern also made extensively in silver. c.1765. $11\frac{1}{2}$ in (29 cm) high.

Price bands

Pairs:
Cast square base, £2,500–£4,500.
Cast swirl base, £3,200–£4,750.

Sheet silver, loaded
Classical column, £1,800–£3,500;
Cluster column, £1,000–£1,800.

Fused plate, same patterns, £500–£900.

Reproductions, £280–£600.

Sets of four nearly double.

Candlesticks 1795–1895

By the end of the eighteenth century the manufacture of candles took a great leap forward from the archaic materials and methods used down the centuries. Candles were expensive and generally used by the more wealthy except for dire necessity. In poorer households where brass candlesticks were more common, a device for ejecting or pushing up stubs was incorporated into candlestick design.

At the end of the eighteenth century, self-consuming candle wick greatly reduced the pools of candle grease and continual use of various devices to trim the wicks as they burned and blackened. But as late as 1851, the formula for candles in England was mainly tallow or animal fat and suet, mostly mutton with a leavening of ox, deer and other beasts. Beeswax and spermaceti were for the Church and the very rich in England – on the Continent these ingredients were more common, particularly in Catholic countries where religious institutions kept bees for that specific purpose.

In 1854 paraffin wax ousted the tallow candle. The change is marked in candlestick design by the fact that from this date detachable nozzles were often made as cylindrical sleeves. The size of candlesticks reached their highest point since there was no longer a risk of the entire column becoming clotted with rivulets of melted wax.

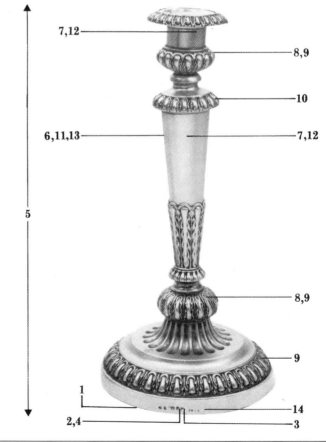

Construction and materials

The majority of neo-classical candlesticks were made in Sheffield from 1775 onwards, in silver and in fused plate. The most popular patterns continued to have square bases until about 1810 when circular-based near-copies of the inverted baluster began to be made in quantity. Methods of manufacture had been simplified, and fewer and fewer separate parts were stamped out as techniques adapted to styles. From c.1840 onwards the invention of electro-plating drastically reduced the demand for fused plate. Rich, heavy cast candlesticks with more than a hint of rococo revival were also made during this period by such great masters as Rundell, Bridge and Rundell and later by Paul Storr of Storr & Mortimer.

Decoration

Some rich, plain classical column candlesticks were made as early as the 1760s, unadorned but for armorials or crests. Die-stamping and die-sinking encouraged an abundance of swags, rams' heads, wreaths, urns and stiff formal leaves in late interpretations of the heavier classical styles of earlier periods.

The shape of sconces, particularly on round-based versions of neo-classical forms, became too bulbous to be called truly vase-shaped, and in many cases the original proportions were lost in the rich mixtures of lobes, gadroons, festoons and exuberant embellishment.

Reproductions

The period from c.1900 yielded a large number of well-made near-copies of many earlier styles, of which the classic columnar candlestick was the most popular. In general, the difference in size will provide the first clue – reproduction column candlesticks were made from as small as $5\frac{1}{2}$ in (14 cm). Many from this period onwards were made as dressing-table lights and wired for electricity. It is as well to check that there are no signs of holes and repairs in the bases where the cord originally went.

Standard reproduction pattern by the Goldsmiths and Silversmiths. London 1897.

Variations

During the whole of this period, patterns based on earlier eighteenth-century candlesticks were made, but a sharp and educated eye can tell by the slightly dumpier sconces, the rather heavier curves and less pleasing proportions that they were made at a later date. Comparison of styles, from books or from the pieces themselves, will enable the buyer to distinguish variations in patterns. It is more satisfactory to attempt to date the piece by eye and then to check the hallmarks than to reverse the procedure. Mistakes are easily made when relying solely on hallmarks.

Above *Fine example of crisp die-stamped decoration in the neo-classical manner by William Hutton. London 1909. $11\frac{3}{4}$ in (30 cm) high.*

Price bands

Pairs:
Sheet silver, loaded
Round-based, £800–£1,200.
Adam-style, £750–£950.
Corinthian column, £550–£750.

Fused plate, same patterns, £300–450.

Victorian rococo, £600–£850.

Sets of four less than double.

Left *Adam-style classical pattern with die-stamped rams' heads, swagged Corinthian columns. London 1895. $11\frac{1}{4}$ in (28.5 cm) high.*

Tapersticks

Miniature candlesticks, usually made to the same pattern as table candlesticks, are known as tapersticks, and were made from the beginning of the eighteenth century until about the 1760s. There has been considerable puzzlement about just what the function of these small candlesticks was, but one of them was certainly for the use of gentlemen smokers. A picture by Benjamin Ferrers who died in 1732 is a portrait of Sir Thomas Saunders Sebright, Bart. with a group of his friends, smoking the long clay pipes of the period, with a taperstick in the centre of the table in the smoking parlour.

It is hard to imagine a world without matches or some form of instant flame. The only way of striking a light was with a tinder box and flint, or to use a small pair of tongs to lift a piece of glowing ember from the fire. For all sorts of purposes a small candlestick with an inexpensive length of candle must have been something of a necessity. For melting sealing wax with which the increasingly literate society of the day sealed documents and letters, for lighting long tapers with which the candles in a 'hanging candlestick' or chandelier were lit, and for a host of activities which today we cannot guess at, tapersticks performed a vital function.

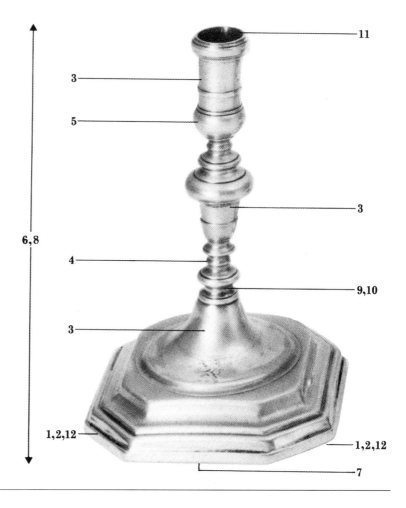

Construction and materials

Almost all tapersticks are made of cast silver, since the custom of smoking clay pipes ended among the gentlemen of fashionable society in the 1760s when they took to snuff. A few were made in fused plate, for tobacco-smoking lingered on in the middle classes for another decade or two before snuff became fashionable.

From the 1730s onwards, an alternative taper holder was made, known as a wax jack or taper stand, consisting of a straight central rod on a circular foot, with a device for holding and nipping the fairly expensive turpentine-wax taper which was coiled around the rod.

Smaller versions of the 'figure candlestick' were also used as tapersticks – but whatever the pattern, the height seldom exceeded 4–5½ in (10–14 cm), although the tapersticks made around 1760 and later may be as tall as 6½–7 in (16.5–19 cm).

Decoration
The patterns followed the candlesticks of the same period so closely as to lead to the belief that they were made by the same makers and supplied to households 'en suite' with the candlesticks they required. It is unlikely that they were originally made in pairs, and the existence of more than one made to identical patterns probably means little more than that several households were supplied with singles in the same pattern, but made by different makers.

Variations

There are other small versions of candlesticks which may be encountered, but which are not true tapersticks at all. Small candleholders were made as part of a writing set, in plain styles and intended to be used for sealing wax. Sometimes a handbell formed part of the inkstandish equipment, sometimes a candlestick. Short 'desk candlesticks' and 'chimney candlesticks' were made up to the 1740s, but the nozzles make it evident that these were made to hold candles and not tapers, which were far slimmer. At the beginning of the nineteenth century there was also a vogue for dwarf ornamental candlesticks, possibly for desks or dressing tables.

Reproductions

It is possible to find find reproductions of 'Queen Anne' tapersticks made in the 1900s and 1920s, although it is likely that most of these went to America, almost in the nature of expensive souvenirs in the great trans-Atlantic treasure hunt for antiques of the period. A few Victorian examples of the figure-type taperstick may also be found, but are instantly recognisable from the subject of the figure which is likely to be slightly whimsy, with children or peasants seen through the romantic eyes of the nineteenth century.

Price bands

Singles only:
17th-century, £800–£1,500 + .
Queen Anne baluster, £750–£1,500.
Octafoil, faceted, £650–£1,000.
Pleated, shell base, £600–£850.
Figures, £800–£1,200 + .
Rococo, £800–£1,500.

Fused plate, £320–£480.

Above *Harlequin figure taperstick by specialist candlestick maker William Cafe. London 1757. 5½ in (14 cm) high. 166 g.*

Left *Full rococo style, cast and chased with flowers and scrolls. London c.1755. 4¾ in (12.5 cm) high. 178 g.*

Above *George II provincial taperstick with pleated base and shaped shoulder knop. Newcastle 1728. 4½ in (11 cm) high.*

Chambersticks

Signs of authenticity

1. Hallmarked with Britannia Standard 1697–1720 generally inside rim of pan.
2. Sconces, nozzles, extinguishers marked with maker's mark and sterling lion passant after *c.*1720.
3. From *c.*1710 to 1715 sconces threaded to screw into socket plate in centre of pan.
4. Openwork stems from *c.*1740 for snuffers.
5. Made in sets of six or more – pairs are two of a 'long set'.
6. From *c.*1770 in fused plate, following silver patterns.
7. Extinguisher caps with slots to hold them from *c.*1750 or later.
8. Chamberstick pan, sconce, nozzles and extinguisher cap all of sheet silver or Sheffield fused plate – none authentic if metals are mixed.

Likely restoration and repair
9. Small dark patches on underside indicates original feet which have broken off.
10. Signs of splitting and repair round socket, or where handle joins pan, with tell-tale dull patches.
11. Hallmarks on underside of base from *c.*1720 distorted, where denting has been beaten out.
12. Genuine signs of wear on underside not evident – dents, damage may have been hammered out and buffed up.
13. Absence of any seaming on sconce – either replaced or extensively repaired and electroplated.
14. Silver chamberstick with extinguisher caps in fused plate – replacement and not genuine.
15. Pan with minute cracking round sconce plate – could indicate some replacement of central boss.
16. From *c.*1765 should be fitted with detachable drip pan – absence decreases value.

Chambersticks or 'hand candlesticks' were used all over the house – upstairs, downstairs and in my lady's chamber – to light the way from room to room, particularly by servants scurrying about their duties after dark. Draughty passages and the fact that these useful little objects were almost always on the move required a large pan to catch the melting wax and prevent it falling on clothes and draperies.

The earliest type is affectionately known as the 'frying pan' from its shape. Mainly in sheet metal, rarely decorated with anything other than a simple pierced or shaped end to the handle, chambersticks did not get the benefit of any design until the end of the seventeenth century, when they were cast with well-shaped handles, lobed candle sconces and gadrooned rims. In the 1730s and 1740s the flat handle was replaced with a simple scroll or ring handle, with a socket for an extinguisher cap.

Between 1770 and the end of the century, chambersticks were made with a slot for snuffers – scissor-like implements with broad blades to trim the charred wick – but most of these have long since been lost or broken. Many chambersticks were made in fused plate and were in regular use until the end of the nineteenth century and even later. Rare in any other candleholder made in silver are the ejector-type sconces which pushed the candle-end out of the socket.

After the introduction of the self-consuming candle wick in 1799, many chambersticks reverted to older, more attractive patterns, often in earlier shapes, such as the pleated dish-shape or octafoil shapes derived from the eighteenth century, without slots for snuffers.

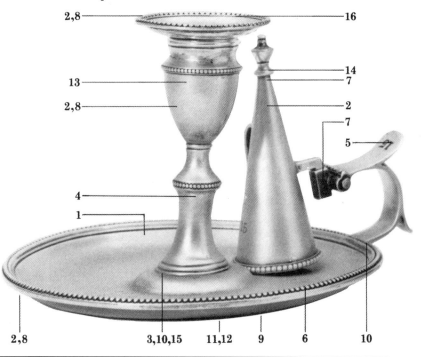

Construction and materials

The sconce was cast in two pieces and seamed together or, in the case of those made of sheet metal, should have one seam running vertically where the edges have been joined. Many of them were made with threaded sconces which could unscrew for cleaning out the candle stubs, and occasionally in the latter part of the eighteenth century and the nineteenth century were made with a push-up ejector.

Chambersticks were made in great quantities from the end of the eighteenth century in fused plate, and far less in sterling silver; in many large houses which had a large number of chambersticks – two dozen or more – original patterns were copied at far later dates to make replacements for those which were too damaged to be of use.

Decoration

Generally this consisted of a gadrooned, reeded or beaded rim to the pan, echoed round the drip pan and the sconce, and little else besides contemporary armorials or a crest. Simple scroll, ring or flying-scroll handles were often marked with a house inventory number, and sometimes the extinguisher caps were also engraved with a crest.

Fused plate chambersticks often lacked the extra decoration round the sconce, and the beading or gadrooning was made in a continuous edging ribbon and soldered on. There are enough examples with a pleated 'strawberry dish' pan to conclude that this was a genuine fashion current around c.1830–40 and not simply replacements made for earlier sets.

Reproductions

A distinction must be drawn between those genuine late copies made in households to replace badly damaged chambersticks, and those made in ones and twos as out-and-out copies. These may date from the 1900–20 period, either in fused plate or in sterling silver, but it is rare to find that the copyists have taken the trouble to have them made in Britannia Standard silver for the 'Queen Anne' period. Some genuine patterns based on earlier Queen Anne styles, such as the octafoil pan, were also made during the Victorian period. Since genuine chambersticks from the early eighteenth century rarely had any other decoration but a simple gadrooned or reeded border, the Victorian versions are obviously not intended to deceive.

Variations

Apart from those made in fused plate in almost identical patterns to sterling silver, the brief period of rococo in England c.1735–45 produced a number of heavy cast candlesticks with an ornate shell or leaf as pan, and a figure or leafy stem supporting a flower-bud sconce. Odd, charming fantasies which include snails and fishes or dolphins are also known, but they are rare indeed. If encountered, they are more likely to belong to the Victorian rococo revival period, c.1830–50.

Right *Late 19th-century copy of an early form with pleated base and sconce and nozzle made in one piece, screwing into the base.* 4½ in (12 cm) diameter.

Below left *One of a set in fused plate with gadrooned borders and rims, openwork stems for snuffers, vase-shaped sconces and detachable nozzles. Sheffield c.1810.* 6½ in (16.5 cm) diameter.

Below *Early 18th-century chamberstick with cast circular pans engraved with contemporary armorials and lobed decoration. London c.1715.* 4¼ in (11 cm) diameter. 387 g.

Price bands

Singles:
17th-century, £700–£1,500.
Queen Anne, £1,800–£2,500.

Pairs:
Georgian, £1,200–£2,000.
Rococo, £3,000 +.
Regency heavy quality, £1,800–£2,200.
Victorian heavy cast, £1,200–£1,800.

Fused plate, £380–£500.

Early pairs more than double.
Later singles less than half.

Salvers and waiters 1650–1730

Signs of authenticity

1. One full set of hallmarks generally on surface of salver to c.1720 – Britannia Standard and lion's head erased.
2. Sterling lion passant guardant after that date, generally marked on underside of tray.
3. From c.1720 salvers with three or four small cast feet – marked on underside but occasionally still on surface.
4. Cast feet – one or more – sometimes marked with sterling lion passant guardant and maker's mark.
5. No decoration on surface at this period except for armorials. Monograms rarer – exceptionally high prices for early engraved decoration.
6. Contemporary style, cartouche of armorials.
7. Uniform thickness of plate across whole surface area.
8. Four bracket feet common at this period, joined with fairly rough soldering to tray.
9. Some octafoil salvers made with central foot which should accord with shape of tray.

Likely restoration and repair
10. No provincial town marks on Britannia Standard until after c.1701.
11. Small holes, cracks, splits near rims due to wear reduce value.
12. Marked thinning of gauge in central area – armorials removed.
13. Later engraving of armorials reduces value.
14. Petal-shaped and octafoil salvers subject to splitting on edge of rims due to working up of decorative edge – may be repaired or concealed. Examine very closely for signs of parting of rims from trays.
15. Feet replaced – area directly above foot subject to splitting, cracking which reduces value.

Several surviving stands of fairly small size with a raised broad rim were definitely made as an accompaniment to grand porringers and caudle cups, as their almost identical decoration testifies. Larger versions of these 'presentoires' or presenters were certainly being made and used for a number of different functions during most of the seventeenth century, for a number of grand examples exist from that period. They stood on a central trumpet-shaped foot, and are often mistakenly called 'tazzas'. The actual derivation of the word 'salver' is obscure, but it may have meant 'to save', from the Latin root *salvare* – literally saving spilt wine or liquor. Smaller sizes measuring up to about 8 in in diameter are generally called 'waiters'.

Up to about 1700, broad decorative rims were often embossed or chased and salvers were none too sturdy. After that date, the gauge of metal was heavier, and the central trumpet-shaped foot was often cast and could be unscrewed. Simple cut card work may be applied underneath, surrounding the socket of the foot, to act as strengthening. Coinciding with the squared and faceted shapes of other silverware which had a brief and delightful popularity from about 1710, salvers were made in octagonal form. Petal-shaped octafoil salvers were made from about 1720, among the first to stand on four small cast feet.

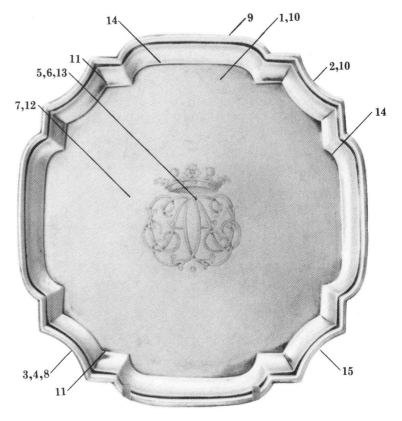

Construction and materials

In general, early salvers with rims decorated with chasing and embossing are lighter in weight than those with completely plain surfaces, because the chasing was in thin gauge metal. Plain, circular salvers dating from around 1700 often have applied moulded wires around the rim and at this period still have a central foot, but it is detachable and the socket on the underside is often strengthened with very decorative cut card work.

Engraved decoration of any sort except for armorials or monograms is extremely rare. Once the octagonal and octafoil form was adopted, between about 1710 and 1730, rims were moulded from the single piece and not added or applied – except on very rare examples, mainly by Huguenot silversmiths, whose borders were far more ornate, cast separately and either soldered or joined to the body with a lap-over join.

Decoration
Great attention should be paid to the quality, style and period of the central cartouche engraving. Some of the finest engravers worked on the difficult, plain surfaces of salvers and waiters, and it is essential that armorials should be correct and contemporary. Early salvers with chased and embossed broad rims should be in the Stuart style, either formal and stylised or with naturalistic fruit and flowers of the period. The 'piecrust' border is one of simple indentations, and should not be confused with what has come to be called 'piecrust' of the Chippendale period from c.1750.

Reproductions

The famous nineteenth-century silversmiths William Pitts and Edward Farrell made some remarkably fine 'Carolean' sideboard dishes, and it is possible that copies of seventeenth-century salvers were also made at the same period. Of the plain shapes dating from the first three decades of the eighteenth century there are very few reproductions, since the form was unsuitable for more modern techniques of manufacture. Circular salvers and waiters with applied reeded borders have been reproduced, but they stand on three rather than four feet, and certainly never on a single central foot.

Price bands

Singles:
17th-century, gadrooned on foot, £900–£1,300.
Octagonal, £1,500–£2,750.
Octafoil, petal, £2,200–£3,500.
Moulded borders, £1,800–£3,200.

Pairs more than double. Size, condition govern price.

Variations

Salvers of small size, generally known as 'waiters', can be as small as 5 in (12.5 cm) in diameter, but usually measure between 7 in (17.5 cm) and 9 in (23 cm). Larger salvers are rarer, and measure roughly 11 in (28 cm) to as much as 13 in (33 cm). Examples which are easiest to confuse come from Ireland, where fashions and styles lagged behind London by as much as 20 years – single-footed salvers and waiters were still being made with attractive but outdated gadrooned rims as late as the end of the 1730s. It is most unlikely that any of the more complicated shapes such as the octagonal and octafoil forms will bear provincial hallmarks, since they appear to have been made almost exclusively in London.

A Georgian shaped square salver with finely engraved armorials, probably those of the Company of Vintners. Francis Pages. London 1730. 8½ in (22 cm) diameter. 629 g.

Shaped square waiter with a moulded border, engraved with a scrolling contemporary cartouche. London 1731. 5½ in (14 cm) diameter. 209 g.

Two of four gadrooned waiters on a single trumpet foot, a pattern made in the late 17th century. These are from Dublin 1730. 6¾ in (17 cm) diameter.

Salvers and waiters 1730–1770

The Georgians had a passion for plain expanses of highly polished wood – mainly mahogany, which had replaced walnut – and delighted in the reflections of glass and silver in these rich surfaces. Table cloths were rarely used, and salvers became an essential part of life, protecting polished mahogany from glasses, teapots, coffee pots and chocolate pots. With regiments of footmen to attend on the wealthy, salvers were almost a part of their livery – when not in use, they were tucked under one arm, waiting for the moment when a drink or cup was empty.

Much larger salvers, measuring 19 in or more in diameter, were used for tea services – and at one time were known as silver tea tables. From the 1750s, with the all-embracing influence of Thomas Chippendale, small circular tripod tables and circular salvers both had 'piecrust' borders – a repeating border of forward and reverse curves – and sometimes stood on small hoofed feet. These complicated borders were not moulded, but cast, often in sections, and were of considerable weight, thus coming within the category of items which had to be assayed.

The rococo shell was ideally adapted in many of the borders of this period, sometimes combined with a bound and reeded edge. The plain surface decorated with a swirling rococo cartouche was further embellished with shell and foliage engraving, which was later much-copied on nineteenth-century versions, using flat chasing with great exuberance.

Signs of authenticity

1. Full set of hallmarks in roughly straight line generally on underside of salver.
2. Cast feet in volute or scrolling pattern, sometimes incorporating a shell motif.
3. Rarer, but desirable, ball and claw feet typical of early Chippendale influence.
4. Borders may be moulded and applied, or cast in far heavier silver.
5. Moulded borders usually soldered – cast borders crimped to the main body.
6. Cast borders should be struck with the sterling lion passant.
7. One foot at least should also bear sterling mark.
8. Signs of wear on undersides of feet through long years of use.
9. Engraving usually worn to deceptively blurred effect with wear, polishing. Should not be confused with later flat chasing.
10. Flat chasing occasionally contemporary from c.1740 but far more common after c.1840.

Likely restoration and repair
11. One or more feet damaged, replaced.
12. Slight dishing or thinning in centre – armorials, engraving removed with consequent loss of silver.
13. Armorials always engraved – not flat chased. Flat chased decoration round circumference may be of later date.
14. Noticeably sharp engraving usually denotes later-engraved.
15. Applied moulded borders, cast borders split and repaired.

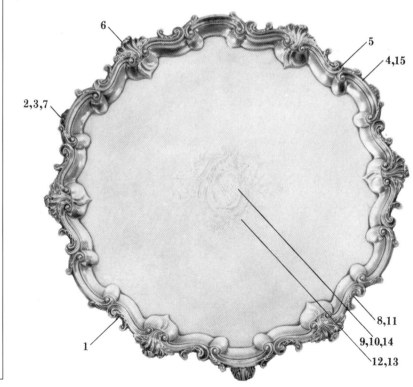

Construction and materials

This period is marked by a very high standard of workmanship and quality. It was before many of the mechanical methods of stamping and die-sinking were developed, and when the English engravers were coming into their own.

Comparing the work of this period with the engraving of earlier periods, it is interesting to note the increased amount of detail and additional 'colours' added to armorials, as well as the fine interpretations of cartouches. The forward and reverse curves, gradually becoming interspersed with a shell motif, are of excellent proportions, the cast feet are well finished in styles appropriate to the form of the salver or waiter, and if there are engraved decorative bands around the circumference, there is a natural feeling for spacing, so that the central armorial is not encroached upon.

Decoration
There is a remarkable simplicity in salvers and waiters of this period, but the starkness of the period immediately before it has been softened with curves of gentle proportions. The rather rigidly formal cartouches of previous amorials disappear during the 1740s as engravers became more fluid and confident, and there are some wonderful, free-flowing scrolling designs, within which the actual heraldic devices sometimes almost become a secondary consideration to the design.

Reproductions

The shell and scroll border was revived after the austerity of decoration during the latter part of the eighteenth century, in fused plate as well as in sterling silver. Close comparison by a critical eye will betray the over-indulgent use of additional grace-notes, such as vine leaves, gadrooning around the rim, and the fact that nineteenth-century salvers are almost always on three feet and not on four. Fused plate salvers almost always stood on four small ball feet until the end of the century, when technical advances enabled the platemakers to manufacture almost every variety of design, die-sunk and filled with lead to give them strength and rigidity.

Victorian salver in 18th-century style, but flat chased and not engraved, with an over-elaborate version of the shell and scroll border. London 1837. 20½in (52cm) diameter.

Variations

From about 1750 onwards, the cast border is often pierced with intricate patterns, which in some cases tends to overpower the simplicity of design, particularly when there is a band of engraved decoration as well. The small-sized waiter is less common than salvers, which increase in size until they are virtually the same dimensions as trays. At this period, both salvers and waiters were based on a circular shape – oval designs belong to the 'Adam period' immediately following the 'Chippendale period'. Nineteenth-century silversmiths, however, had no inhibitions about combining a rather more ornate version of the shell and scroll border with an oval shape.

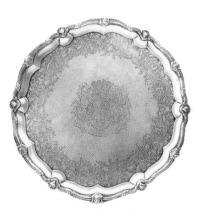

One of a graduated set of salvers with bound reeded rims decorated with leaves and shells and a band of engraved anthemion and foliage. George Wickes. London 1746. Numbered '5'. 15in (38cm) diameter.

One of a pair of George II waiters with shaped borders decorated with shells with finely engraved rococo cartouches, on three hoofed feet. London 1742. 6in (15cm) diameter.

Price bands

Singles:
'Chippendale' piecrust borders, £950–£1,800.
Shell and scroll, £700–£900.
Pierced borders, £1,800–£5,000.
Decorative engraving, £1,000–£5,000.

Pairs more than double. Size, condition govern price.

Salvers and waiters 1770–1840

Signs of authenticity

1. Hallmarks on underside correct for period and style.
2. Later marks from 1822 have leopard's head without a crown.
3. From 1836 sterling lion in profile walking to the left, no longer 'guardant'.
4. Three feet most common for period, in shell, scroll, ball and claw, on round sterling silver – plain ball or bun on fused plate.
5. Four feet on oblong and oval salvers.
6. Shape, style of cartouche extremely plain, formal, with highly detailed engraving.
7. From c.1780 bright cut engraving with drapes, swags, husks, medallions and urns.
8. Fused plate generally unmarked – may bear a crown as guarantee of quality from c.1815. Should not be confused with Sheffield Assay Office town mark.

Likely restoration and repair
9. Slight dishing, thinning in centre – armorials may have been removed.
10. Feet replaced in later style – outward scrolling panel feet may indicate Victorian replacement.
11. On flat chased salvers, examine style and design closely – may have been 'improved' at later date.
12. Slightly metallic, harsh colour – scratches, dents may have been removed and part or whole of piece electroplated.
13. Early salvers in fused plate frequently had tinned undersides – look for signs of single-faced plate which has been later electroplated.
14. Rims below borders split – poorer-quality ware made in one operation with drop-hammer, weakened with age and use.

England's fortunes expanded at an incredible rate during the second half of the eighteenth century. The building of the canal system coupled with the harnessing of steam engines to manufactories and workshops brought opportunities to the sons of labourers to prosper and grow rich in a manner which had never been possible before in the country's history. 'The middle class of people in this country', wrote Lord Chesterfield, 'are straining to imitate their betters,' and moreover, had the money to do so. Matthew Boulton's manufactory in Birmingham employed 500 workers, turning out silverware for this broad band of the market, in silver and in fused plate. Essential to first appearances in every household were salvers for receiving calling cards and letters, but they were still expensive to make, because of the sheer weight of metal required.

Bright cut engraving enjoyed a delightful period of fashion – the Adam influence brought oval-shaped salvers into the general design of things, and engraving was soft with drapes and ribbons looping round cartouches and delicately enhancing the plain surfaces. In 1773 Birmingham and Sheffield were granted their own Assay Offices and their output rose to overtake the London silversmiths.

Fused plate began to make inroads into the market and the high standards of design and attention to detail suffered in the hands of quick profit-makers who cut corners and used mechanical methods to produce an increasing range of 'silverware' at one-third of the cost of silver plate.

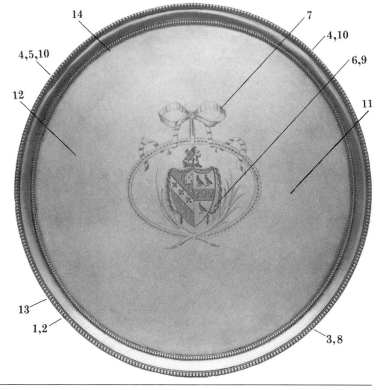

Construction and materials

There was little change in the way that salvers were made until the 1780s. Reeded and beaded borders were applied to rims, and the general rule was three rather than four feet except for oval and oblong salvers. The sizes changed, and it was quite common for sets of three to be made – one large salver measuring anything up to 15 in (38 cm) or more engraved with full armorials, and two smaller ones of about 6–8 in (15–20 cm) generally with a crest only. Bright cut engraving which was particularly in vogue from the 1780s, but flat chasing is more common on fused plate where the surface could not be cut into without exposing the copper core beneath. Borders shaped with forward and reverse curves were made of two plates of single-faced fused plate soldered together with the join hidden by silver solder. From the 1790s the central surface of fused plate salvers had insets of sterling silver so that coats of arms and crests could be engraved.

Decoration

This period covers a wide variety of delightful designs and techniques of decoration, from the plainest, simple salvers with beaded rims to virtuoso bright cut engraving. Decorative borders abandoned their stark reeding and beading in favour of a version of ribbon and reed or, more commonly, the 'Chippendale' piecrust design embellished with shells and, later, with fruiting vines or foliage. This became possible with the advances in mechanical techniques which could stamp out ever more elaborate borders in one operation.

Reproductions

The Victorian silversmiths reproduced many earlier patterns and designs, the most common being the forward and reverse curves of the eighteenth century, but the curves are too tight, and the extra embellishment of shells, fruiting vines and other extraneous motifs, as well as rather too much flat chasing over the surface of the salver, are quickly recognisable as belonging to a later date.

Variations

Silversmiths did not necessarily make salvers and waiters to precisely the same sizes – the Sheffield platers, however, because of their mass-production techniques, made sizes from 6 in (15 cm) to 10 in (25.5 cm) in diameter, each 1 in (2.5 cm) larger than the last. Salvers and waiters were made in one single operation with the use of a heavy drop-hammer and dies, with no additional applied border, since the whole piece was stamped, border included, at one blow.

Very few salvers and waiters were made in the eighteenth century 'Adam' style with pierced or fretted borders, but in the 1870s earlier neo-classical designs was revived. The flat chasing or engraving is often centred as opposed to following the outer rim. At this period, too, it is common to find monograms instead of armorials in the centre.

Above *Two plain circular salvers with beaded borders on three scroll feet in a standard pattern. One by Hester Bateman 1789, the other by Peter, Anne and William Bateman 1794. 7¼ in (19 cm) diameter.*

Above *Oval salver with applied gadrooned border engraved with a rococo revival cartouche by one of the most prolific silversmiths of the period, John Schofield. London 1795. 18¼ in (46 cm) diameter.*

Left *Plain salver with an applied wavy beaded border, engraved with armorials surrounded by bright cut engraving. London 1783. 15½ in (39 cm) diameter.*

Tankards 1660–1700

1. Full set of hallmarks on body near rim and to one side of handle.
2. Full set of marks on lid, usually towards the thumbpiece.
3. Up to c.1714 maker's mark on handle also.
4. Correct style of engraving for armorials for period.
5. Single step to lid with single peak or waved peak.
6. Thumbpiece in double cusp, openwork lattice, scrolled and from c.1680 twin dolphin.
7. Handles with seam where curved undersection joins flat outer section.
8. Height 7–8 in (18–20.5 cm).
9. Outward curve of handle should be set so low that it is almost level with foot rim.
10. Small hole in lower section of handle where inner curve ends.
11. Heavy solid hinge and hinge plates.

Likely restoration and repair
12. Lids with slight discrepancy in hallmark dates – replaced or 'married' from tankard of similar date.
13. Signs of tampering around thumbpiece, hinge – broken, torn and replaced.
14. Narrow foot rim – if too high may have been repaired with new foot rim added which will raise height of body.
15. Base of handle too high – either foot rim added or handle 'married' from tankard of similar date.
16. Armorials of considerably later date – drastically reduces value.
17. Different maker's mark on handle from rest of tankard – may be contemporary, made by specialist handle-makers, but may also be a replacement of similar style, later date.

The capacity of early English tankards, and the capacity of seventeenth- and eighteenth-century English gentlemen, is by today's standards awesome. English ale 'good and stale' was sold – and drunk – by the quart, the pottle and the gallon, a pottle being two quarts. Made from barley malt, it was sweet and strong. Hops came from Holland in the fifteenth century with the Flemish, who planted the first English hop fields in Kent. By the Restoration even ale was hopped – it kept better, but was bitter to the taste, and in the North, sweet ale was preferred to hopped beer or ale. Even sack or 'sec', a dry white wine, was drunk by the pint.

Conservative as their bibulous owners, the shape of tankards changed very little over a period of a hundred years or more. The only changes are gradual and can be seen in the applied rim round the base, a slight fretting of the lid where the peak overhangs the body, and the thumbpiece. Like the grand silver gilt sideboard dishes of the same period, tankards made in the first flush of riches after the Restoration were often silver gilt, extremely finely decorated with chased stiff acanthus leaves – occasionally with a leaf-wrapped bud as a finial on the leaf-chased lid – and engraved with characteristic Stuart crossed plumes and bold armorials with very little detail of heraldic 'colours' or cross-hatching.

Construction and materials

The stoutest tankards, and therefore the ones most likely to have survived, were hammered up on the sinking block and the raising stake, and have a slightly bellied base, round which the foot rim is soldered. Such is the nature of the metal that when made this way, the molecular structure changes so that the body is resilient and springy, and there is little likelihood of denting. Lids, foot rims and hinges were quite liable to damage, however, even though they were strongly made and well soldered to the body.

Handles were not cast in solid metal but in two pieces, with the underside curved into a half-round to meet the flat 'ribbon' of the outer side. Thumbpieces were cast, and hinges were proportionately large and perhaps a little clumsy, but they had do withstand a great deal of wear and tear.

Decoration

Many tankards were made without any decoration except for a shallow, reeded foot rim and a few lines of turning round the lid, which was slightly shaped, either in a single peak or in a slightly more decorative wavy edge. Thumbpieces were limited in pattern, the most common being the wing-shaped double cusp, a slightly more ornate openwork lattice or a volute or scroll. Grand tankards with chased decoration were frequently made in silver gilt, although through long usage the gilding may have worn off. Traces may occasionally be found in the indentations of chasing. Armorials should have crossed plumes or scrolling and foliage, with very little detailed engraving of 'colours' or heraldic cross-hatching.

Variations

The finest and most desirable are tankards with chinoiserie decoration which had a brief fashion from c.1675 to 1685. These tankards should have a slightly more pronounced single or double step, and the thumbpiece is of a pattern often known as a 'corkscrew' – a tight scroll twisting outwards at either side. The decoration may be engraved and very worn, or flat chased. Handles should still conform to the general pattern, although sometimes the curve at the bottom is a little more flourished. On tankards of this type the lid is often simply overlapping and without a peak.

Reproductions

There are two periods when lavish copies of the grand versions of these tankards were made – during the Victorian era, and at the turn of the century around 1900. But they were generally made as trophies or presentation pieces, and as such their size exceeded even the ample proportions of the originals, sometimes measuring 12 in (30.5 cm) or more in height. There were also some versions made of tankards with swirled lobes or heavy gadrooning, but often this decoration has been added later to early, very plain patterns.

Price bands

Charles II plain, £2,500–£5,000.
Embossed, £3,500–£6,000 + .
James II, £2,500–£4,000 + .
Chinoiserie decoration,
£4,000–£8,000 + .
Plain, late 17th-century,
£1,600–£2,400.

Charles II tankard of quart capacity with a single peak to the lid and a double cusp thumbpiece. London 1667. 7½ in (19 cm) high.

Charles II tankard, flat chased with chinoiserie figures and foliage on body and cover, with volute thumbpiece. London 1677. 6¼ in (16 cm) high.

The engraved armorials are typically Stuart, with stiff plumes and simple heraldic devices. Entwined dolphin thumbpiece. London 1682. 6½ in (16.5 cm) high.

Tankards 1700–1750

One reason for the enormous consumption of beer and ale was the fact that, certainly in the larger towns and in London, drinking water was so polluted that it was unsafe to drink – even for children. Brewers in London were supposed to use water from the lower reaches of the Thames when the tide was out and there was very little sea water in the estuary. In 1690 an Act of Parliament encouraged the populace to drink cider and perry – made from pears – as well as beer and ale. Tankards remained of large capacity nonetheless.

Beer-drinking, although common in Germany and Holland, was virtually unknown in France, and not many tankards were made by the Huguenots before the early eighteenth century, when they were well settled and admitted to the Goldsmiths Company. They changed the form of the English tankard with a curve in the base, so that it tucked in just above the foot, and added a dome to the cover. At about this time tankards were usually ringed with an applied or moulded girdle, plain or reeded, occasionally corded, running round the body on a level with the lower sweep of the handle. English silversmiths made few changes – the foot rim is deeper, the stepped lid is more pronounced, and the thumbpiece is generally simpler and better-proportioned. Armorials are excellently engraved within scrolling foliate cartouches, departing from the rigid heraldic formula to a certain extent, with additional elements of purely decorative motifs in more grand examples.

Signs of authenticity

1. Britannia Standard marks to c.1720.
2. Marked in straight line to one side of handle near rim.
3. Marked on inner side of lid from c.1735.
4. Foot rim applied, deeper and spreading slightly outwards.
5. Peaks of lids with generous overlap, sometimes plain, sometimes with wavy edge.
6. Thumbpieces cast in simpler, more elegant shapes, in scroll, corkscrew or foliate patterns to c.1735 – openwork chairback form after that date.
7. Handles with seam down outer edge where curved undersection joins outer section.
8. Cartouche of correct period, style, according with date mark.
9. Lower scroll of handle almost level with base.

Likely restoration and repair
10. Marks on lid do not accord with rest of tankard – may have been replaced or 'married' from tankard of similar period.
11. Foot rim too deep in proportion to handle and body – damage may have been repaired, foot rim replaced.
12. Armorials of later date – reduces value considerably.
13. Signs of tampering, heavy soldering, round hinge plates may indicate repairs or part replacement.
14. Height 7–8 in (18–20.5 cm) – if more, foot rim may be replaced.

Construction and materials

Britannia Standard silver with its accompanying hallmarks was used until 1720, and occasionally during the following 10 years, although seldom for everyday objects such as tankards. Bodies were hammered up on the sinking block and the raising stake, and there should be no mouth wire on tankards of this period. The foot rim and girdle were made separately and soldered on, and the handle was made in two parts, seamed and soldered to the body.

Hallmarks were struck on the outside of the lid until the advent of the pronounced dome, when they are often on the inner surface. Until c.1725 handles were often made by specialist handle-makers and may be struck with the maker's mark and not that on the rest of the tankard. Thumb-pieces were cast, and hinges were stout, though less clumsy than the previous period. Armorials were finely engraved in a more decorative form, always in the centre of the tankard opposite the handle.

Decoration
During this period, decoration on straight-sided tankards was almost entirely limited to the engraved cartouche, and sometimes the initials of the owner, or the triangle of a married couple, on the handle. The only addition was the applied girdle, in which case the armorials are set higher, between the girdle and the rim. The girdle ran round the body in line with the lower socket of the handle, and was sometimes reeded or corded, or with a very plain moulding. Thumbpieces, too, were less ornate.

Variations

Between about 1690 and 1720, a common variation on grander tankards was a lion thumbpiece – a seated heraldic lion forming the terminal to the hinge. Other variations of this period are tankards with tuck-in bases, at first rather squat and broad, often with some gadrooning round the foot rim and the rim of the lid. Sometimes there is stylised cut card work around the base, and a line of heavy beading down the outside of the handle. From c.1730, after the end of the Britannia Standard, the tuck-in base tankard became taller, often with a double C-scroll handle, and the lid was domed to come level with the top of the thumbpiece.

Reproductions

Many silver tankards have been made to this simple, elegant design, but they are seldom encountered in their original capacities, except occasionally when one with a lion thumbpiece, usually with considerably more detail and decoration, may have been made as a presentation or trophy piece. Later variations of this pattern are almost always pint-sized, and are of imperial measures, introduced in 1826, taking the place of the measures laid down during William III's reign and used for ale, wine and spirits right up to that date.

Price bands

Queen Anne, plain,
£1,500–£1,900.
Heavy quality, fine engraving,
£2,000–£4,000 + .

George I, £1,200–£2,750.

Below left *Plain large-capacity tankard with forward-scrolling thumbpiece and reeded borders. London 1699. 7¼ in (18.5 cm) high.*

Below centre *Queen Anne tankard with slightly domed cover and backward scrolling thumbpiece. London 1704. 6¾ in (17 cm) high.*

Below *Example of a 'marriage' between the body dated 1690 and the cover, with fretted peak which is dated 1686. Double scroll thumbpiece. London-made. 7 in (17.5 cm) high.*

Tankards 1750–1790

There had been a steady rise in the drinking of wines and spirits from the beginning of the eighteenth century onwards, and by mid-century the size and capacity of tankards began to decrease. The drinking habits of the upper classes changed, glass was freely available, and although beer filled the gut and quenched a mighty thirst, it was not a particularly decorous drink for the table. Generally consumed in the morning, at breakfast, along with a dish of pheasant, beer slipped a little down the social scale as tea and coffee drinking became more fashionable.

The shape of tankards gradually assumed the baluster form, a slightly more graceful evolution of the earlier tuck-in base with its rather dumpy lines. Handles became more elaborate, with a flourishing double C-scroll and a more pronounced heart-shaped terminal, and the girdle moved a little further up the body to balance the new shape. Lids were definitely domed, and the lower plate of the hinge was shaped like a leaf running down the top of the handle. The most common form of thumbpiece was the open chairback, sometimes simple, sometimes with a little open fretwork design.

Right at the end of this period, there was a revival of the plain cylindrical straight-sided tankard, in smaller sizes, and often decorated with reeded hoops, in imitation of barrels. This type had completely flat lids with no peak and an upstanding reeded thumbpiece.

Construction and materials

At this time cheaper methods of construction were used: instead of being made on the sinking block and raising stake, sheets of thick gauge silver were soldered into a cylinder and then shaped. This construction necessitated strengthening the rim with a mouth wire because the metal lacked the resilience of hammered silver.

Monograms became more common than armorials, since the average user of tankards was not titled. Handles tend to be more generously proportioned, rounder and less D-shaped, with the lower plate of the hinge longer, curving over the top of the handle.

The latter part of this period includes some tankards made in fused plate – generally of cylindrical form, sometimes reproducing the reeded, staved barrel-like design, but more often in convincing copies of the straight-sided, low-domed lid variety of the 1740s and 1750s.

Decoration

There is very little decoration on tankards of this last period, before they shrank to an unlidded pint-sized form, except for nicely engraved monograms and some turned decoration to the lid and foot. Thumbpieces are still of the openwork variety, slightly more elaborate in the latter decades than the plain openwork chairback pattern which characterised early baluster-shaped tankards. Handles may be of the conventional S-scroll variety, or a more elaborate double C-scroll with a more pronounced flourish.

Reproductions

With the return of tankards to favour at the end of the nineteenth century, almost every shape was copied, but they betray their late dates by their capacities. The Imperial measures introduced in 1825 give away even those made to identical patterns – although very few of them were made with lids.

Tankards in fused plate generally date from the 1790s and not earlier, because of problems connected with concealing the edges and the fact that the silver coating was thinner than early fused plate and wore down to the copper/ brass core with the amount of usage generally received by tankards. The most successful copies were made with a white metal alloy base known as 'Britannia Plate' but again, since they came into use from about 1830, their capacity is measured in Imperial measures and not in the older, slightly more generous sizes.

Variations

The most common variation on the baluster-shaped tankard of this period is the straight-sided, slightly tapering cylindrical pattern with either two or three horizontal bands of reeding, which were also made in fused plate. This shape was also quite genuinely made as a beer-jug from the 1780s and 1790s, but generally with slightly domed lids and handles of a completely different pattern.

Many beautiful early tankards were too large to be serviceable in the nineteenth century and were desecrated by being converted into jugs, or embossed and chased with quite unsuitable decorative designs, probably to be given as gifts or presentation pieces, in which case there are sometimes armorials dating from the nineteenth century also engraved.

Price bands

George II baluster,
£1,200–£1,800.
Heavy quality,
£1,500–£3,000+.

George III, £800–£1,500.

Far left *Late Georgian baluster tankard with raised spreading foot, scroll handle, reeded and domed lid, and pierced shell thumbpiece. London 1791. 7½ in (19 cm) high.*

Left *A slimmer baluster shape with spreading foot, double scroll handle and a pierced shell thumbpiece. London 1776. 7½ in (19 cm) high.*

Mugs

Mugs, as opposed to tankards, were lidless, and originally known as 'cannes' – a name which persisted in porcelain for coffee cans, as opposed to cups, which were more bowl-shaped. The earliest patterns seem to have developed from pottery shapes rather than any parallel metalware, and vary considerably in capacity, though it could be said that they held between a half-pint and a pint. They had the typical rounded bodies and broad, reeded collars of stoneware mugs dating from about 1680, with the added refinement of a beaded rat tail running down the handle. But it was only a short time before they began to follow first the fashion in decoration, and then the purer lines of other silverware, with gadrooning and lobing, and by the end of the seventeenth century were miniature lidless tankards in every respect. The only difference was that mugs generally had solid cast silver handles instead of wrought hollow ones.

Silver mugs may well have been used by ladies for their nips of strong ale, and by children for 'small beer', but probably were not used exclusively for alcoholic drinks, but for all manner of hot possets and spiced and herb concoctions. It must not be forgotten that for centuries the only alternative to silver was pottery – both brass and pewter were liable to release dangerous chemicals if they came into contact with acids in any form.

The custom of godparents giving christening mugs dates only from the nineteenth century, when there was such a demand for them that practically every style, period and decoration was ransacked in order to make original and memorable christening presents. Sadly, many early, plain half-pint mugs were seized and embossed or decorated for this purpose.

Signs of authenticity

1. Hallmarked in general on base until *c*.1770.
2. Britannia Standard marks 1697–*c*.1720.
3. Tankard-shaped mugs often marked near handle in similar place to tankards.
4. Shape and style correct for period.
5. Signs of wear on foot rim due to long wear and use.
6. Engraving, flat chasing, worn and rubbed due to age.
7. Seamed vertically along line of handle generally indicates end of eighteenth century.
8. Silver wire handles on early examples, similar to porringers.
9. Cast handles should be seamed down the centre – cast in two halves and then soldered.
10. Shaped outside curve to handle, spur or leaf-capped, generally rising slightly above level of rim from *c*.1720.

Likely restoration and repair
11. Bases badly dented, beaten out – may be hair splits around bottom.
12. Foot rims added, repaired may distort proportions of piece and lower value.
13. Later initials, crests, armorials engraved – lowers value.
14. Mouth wire repaired – minute signs of splitting round rim before restoration.
15. On mugs with pint capacities examine top curves of handles with great care – may originally have had lid which has been removed. Mugs by definition have no lids.

Construction and materials

Hallmarks on early mugs are often hard to find, due partly to wear and age, and partly to the fact that they were not always grouped together but sometimes separated, with the maker's mark on the base and the Assay marks on the body. The Britannia Standard 'lion's head erased' and Britannia mark should, of course, be struck on mugs made between 1697 and about 1720 – but these marks, which have remained valid for any silver made to a higher standard, may appear on christening mugs made in the nineteenth century.

Early mugs were hammered up and have no seams, but towards the end of the eighteenth century many were made in cylinders of sheet metal, seamed together down the line of the handle, in which case the mouth is reinforced with a wire. It is rare to find pairs of small-capacity mugs – although in the case of the late eighteenth and early nineteenth century christening mugs, several may have been made to the same pattern for successive children in one family.

Decoration

The fact that very few genuine seventeenth-century mugs with lobed bases survive should make a buyer extremely wary if offered one – it is more likely that the lobing has been carried out much later. It is safer to gauge the age of a mug by its outline and shape first, and then to determine whether the decoration accords with similar period silverware. Mugs were inevitable candidates for 'late embossing' in the nineteenth century.

Variations

Silver dram cups or tot cups which are shaped like a thistle were made well into the mid-eighteenth century, mainly by provincial makers in the north of England and Scotland; these have proved excellent candidates for later lobing around the base to give them the spurious appearance of having been made in the seventeenth century. More cup-shaped small mugs were made as individual hunt cups, often without foot rims and with the weight in the base in the same manner as tumblers but with loop handles, for a spirit-warming tot of cherry brandy or similar strong drink which was consumed in the saddle by huntsmen.

Above *Typical George II mug with a tuck-in base and spreading foot, with initials pricked on the capping of the scroll handle. London 1727. 3½in (9cm) high.*

Reproductions

It is notable that very few mugs seem to have been made in fused plate until this century, probably because during the height of production, solid sterling silver was the only material for christening mugs, and the use of mugs for general purposes had waned, only to be revived a century later, at the end of the nineteenth century. From that date onwards, however, both half-pint and pint mugs were made in all the early styles and patterns, in fused plate and in electroplate.

Heavily decorated mug embossed and chased with hops and hop leaves. London 1846. 4½in (11.5cm) high.

Left Classic tapered cylindrical shape with armorials easily distinguishable from early crossed plumes. Edward Fernell, London 1783. 5½in (14cm) high. 522g.

Monteiths and punch bowls

Punch bowls with scalloped rims were named after 'a fantasticall Scott called Monteigh who at that time or a little before wore the bottome of his cloake or coate so notched', and Anthony Wood's diary records that he first saw such a 'vessel or bason' in the summer of 1683. The purpose of these handsome bowls was to hang the glasses by the foot so that the bowls were suspended in water.

By about 1694 monteiths were made with detachable collars and heavy ring handles. Even in the profligate days of the late seventeenth century, a massive piece of silver which was used solely for carrying cool glasses seemed excessive, and the bowl itself, with the rim or collar removed, was used for mixing the punch, and was usually accompanied by a punch ladle and an orange or lemon strainer. Punch was a concoction brought back by the merchants of the East India Company in about 1672 and was concocted from 'one quart of claret wine, half a pint of brandy, grated nutmeg, sugar and the juice of a lemon'. Very Baroque in style, monteiths were fluted or lobed, mainly to increase the strength of the vessel. A few late examples were made with beautifully applied cut card work and strapwork, with heavy cast ornamental handles instead of simple drop rings. By about 1730 they had ceased to be made, and punch as a drink seems to have fallen from grace – although milk punch was greatly fashionable in the eighteenth century, made with milk instead of claret, liberal quantities of brandy, spices and citrus juice. There was a tremendous revival of both punch bowls and monteiths in the nineteenth century, when almost identical patterns were made.

Signs of authenticity

1. Monteiths without detachable collars of early date generally hallmarked on base.
2. Monteiths with detachable collars marked in full in roughly straight line near rim.
3. Detachable collars should have full set of hallmarks.
4. No handles on monteiths c.1683–93.
5. Detachable collars rarely found on monteiths c.1683–93.
6. At this period, notches pronounced in otherwise plain rim.
7. Detachable collars generally scalloped, often with masks, shells and scrolling.
8. Cartouches, armorials, correct in style for period.
9. Britannia standard marks 1697–c.1720.

Likely restoration and repair
10. No handles but signs of heavy repair on both sides where handles originally were – split, cracked, torn away from body and removed with subsequent patching and repair.
11. Plain silver bowl of later date fluted, gadrooned to resemble early monteiths – marks will be of far too late a date.
12. Plain early-eighteenth-century punch bowl with detachable collar made at considerably later date – check hallmarks on both body and collar.
13. Monteiths in one piece with scalloped rims, collars integral with body – nineteenth century. Occasionally these may have early marks 'let in' to the side and lion's mask ring handles added in deliberate attempt to deceive.

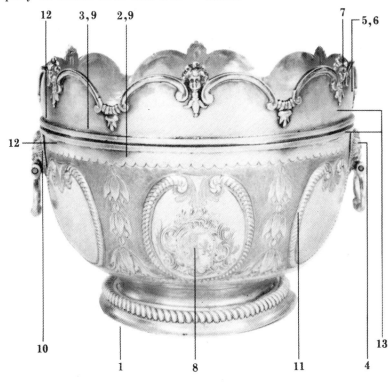

Construction and materials

Monteiths have applied foot rims, either plain and slightly spreading, or rounded, sometimes with gadrooning which generally slants from left to right in a continuous repetitive pattern, unlike later, eighteenth-century gadrooning which was often broken and slanted right to left and left to right to give symmetry. On rare and remarkable examples there was some applied cast decoration round the integral notched rims. Once monteiths were made with detachable collars, the rim of the bowl and the base of the collar were made with very simple moulding so that the join would be concealed when fitted together.

Cast lion's-mask and ring drop handles were added at about the same time that collars became detachable, but there was naturally a tremendous strain on them because of the weight of the contents they held.

Decoration
Rarest to find are monteiths with flat chased or engraved chinoiserie decoration on the bodies. This fashion had a brief spell of popularity between about 1675 and 1690, and is contemporary with the arrival of monteiths as an additional grand vessel for the service of punch. The few examples which have survived are those with some gadrooned decoration to the feet and in panels on the body, made in the first decade of the eighteenth century. The shape and pattern of the detachable collar with its cherubs' heads, shells, husks and scrolls was clearly the most popular, and one may deduce from the many nineteenth-century versions that at that time there were still some surviving for this particular design to have been so faithfully copied.

Variations

Plain silver punch bowls seem to have taken the place of monteiths between about 1725 and 1730, standing on a spreading foot, with an applied wire round the rim. After this date it seems possible that heavy cut-glass punch bowls took the place of silver – far more suitable for showing off the rich colours of wine punches, and more practical for milk and cream punches, when the alcoholic content settled quickly at the bottom and required frequent stirring.

Large silver punch bowls made during the Regency, were in the main presentation pieces for military or sporting organisations and establishments.

Reproductions

The return to fashion of punches and toddies in the nineteenth century brought with it such a plethora of monteith-type bowls that these are by far the most likely to be encountered rather than the rare surviving early examples. Variations on the theme include a large number of 'rose bowls' with a special wire grille for holding flowers, which were regularly given as wedding presents, presentations and gifts well into this century. There are also some very fine examples of nineteenth-century silversmiths' work in Adam-style silver bowls which, although based on themes from the eighteenth century, are purely original, since they do not seem to have been made during the 'Adam' period at all.

Elegant interpretation of a monteith with detachable collar, heavy cast handles and lion's masks by Mappin and Webb. London 1916. 12¾ in (33 cm) diameter.

Punch bowl with lobed body and foot below chased festoons of oak leaves and rams' heads by George Fox. London 1893. 10½ in (27 cm) diameter.

Plain heavy gauge silver punch bowl with reeded spreading foot and reeded rim. Thomas Newby. London 1818. 10½ in (26.5 cm) diameter.

Price bands

Monteiths:
Queen Anne, £8,000–£12,000 +.
Regency, £4,000–£6,000.
19th-century, £1,000–£2,500.

Punch bowls:
18th-century,
£5,000–£10,000 +.
19th-century, £400–£1,500.

Goblets

1. At least three, if not the full set of four hallmarks on rim near lip.

2. Early goblets sometimes marked with fourth mark – the lion passant guardant – on underside of base.

3. On slender-stemmed goblets, stems cast in two halves and seamed vertically.

4. Correct style and motif of decoration for date of goblet.

5. From c.1765 full set of marks on either bowl or foot.

6. Goblets from early period rarely engraved with armorials or crests – check dates, styles, for late engraving.

7. Beaded rims to feet on good quality late-18th-century goblets should be applied, not stamped.

8. Original gilding on insides of bowls with signs of wearing, due to constant use. Regilding in recent years can detract from value, conceal damage and repair.

Likely restoration and repair

9. Weakest part of goblets is the join between bowl and stem – check for signs of reinforcement, repair, inside and outside.

10. On baluster-stemmed goblets, foot may have been bent, dented sideways and repaired or replaced.

11. Check style, proportions of bowl and stem – may have been 'married' up.

12. Bright cut engraving most common decoration on late-18th-century goblets – other surface decoration apart from initials, monograms, armorials rare.

13. On early wine cup shapes, still used at later periods for Communion wine, ecclesiastical cypher of 'I.H.S.' may have been removed to distract attention from the fact that it is of much later date than secular versions.

A great quantity of wine was consumed in England when drinking glasses had to be imported from Venice at considerable expense. Horn beakers were elaborately mounted in silver, but there must also have been large numbers of silver cups and goblets in use from earliest times.

In shape, the goblet is descended from early English Communion chalices dating roughly from Elizabethan times, when almost every church had a silver wine cup of simple shape, with a straight-sided, slightly flaring body mounted on a trumpet shaped foot. Most of these wine cups originally had covers with capstan finials which were used as patens for the Communion wafers. Parallel with this shape is the baluster-stemmed glass-shaped goblet which goes back as far as the first decades of the seventeenth century, flat chased or punched with vine leaf and grapes, many of which were originally silver gilt.

Once glass became freely-available the use of goblets virtually died out, to be revived in the second half of the eighteenth century. From about 1765 onwards, silver goblets became part of the accepted display of silverware in wealthy households, generally engraved with a crest at least, if not full armorials. From the early 1800s they were more commonly engraved with monograms, or decorated with the fashionable designs of the day.

Construction and materials

It is uncommon to find goblets in the higher, Britannia Standard sterling silver, since by the time this came in, the English glasshouses were making quantities of extremely fine flint glass, and the goblet had in general been relegated to an occasional commission.

Prior to 1697, most goblets were made with solid cast stems and plain or slightly flared bowls. Feet were made separately, and the goblet was soldered together from three separate pieces. The wine cup shape was generally made in two parts: wide, almost trumpet-shaped stem and deep straight-sided cup, soldered at the base of the vessel.

When goblets came back into fashion and more or less followed the lines of glass, they too were made in two parts only, with stem and foot in one piece.

Decoration

Early wine cups were engraved with simple bands of arabesques in a very similar manner to beakers of the same period. The wine-glass-shaped goblet was often chased with fruiting vines and leaves in a broad band above flat, geometric lobe shapes, sometimes with a matted surface which contrasted most effectively with the plain parts of the design. Eighteenth-century wine goblets were generally plain, with a gadrooned or beaded rim to the foot, and sometimes a slender annulet of cording or beading on the stem and at the base of the bowl. Crests, armorials and heraldic devices were common until around the 1790s, when wreathed monograms or initials took their place. Only during the nineteenth century did surface decoration become effusive and prolific.

Reproductions

In the second half of the nineteenth century goblets were made in a wide range of pastiche designs, drawing elements from earlier periods and mixing them together into a rather over-decorated, overladen style which is not very appealing. Some of the purer forms are quite attractive, but most of them were made from mechanically spun silver which was of thin gauge. The joins between the rather spindly stems and bowls are none too sturdy, and many of them have been badly damaged – not through ill-use but as a result of their somewhat flimsy construction and materials.

Victorian goblet with 'medieval gothic' formalised decoration, with beaded collar and foot rim. London 1877. 6¼ in (16 cm) high.

Variations

The only important variation to the goblet was a more shallow, wider wine cup set on a flaring trumpet base which was made during the middle of the seventeenth century. It is not particularly attractive apart from its interest to collectors, and has a plain or matted surface in simple geometric patterns. The shape was, however, revived in the early decades of this century. Many of these wine cups were not very practical, since they were decorated with Gothic peaks and frills around the foot or on the stem, but they were among the few genuinely creative efforts of a small group of artist silversmiths of the day.

George III goblet with vase-shaped bowl and a plain foot, engraved with a crest and motto. York. 1784. 6¾ in (17 cm) high.

Bright cut decoration on rim and foot, with engraved armorials within crossed leafy sprays, surmounted by an earl's coronet. London 1794. 6¼ in (16 cm) high.

Price bands

Singles:
Early wine cups,
£850–£1,800 + .

Pairs:
Georgian goblets,
£1,000–£1,500.
19th-century, £280–£800.
Singles less than half.

Wine coolers and ice buckets

Winter ice was collected from frozen ponds and lakes and stored in specially built ice-houses. These brick vaults, where ice was laid on wooden slats between layers of straw sprinkled with salt to lower the temperature, were certainly constructed from the time of William and Mary onwards. If glasses were laid on salty ice in monteiths, as has been said, the taste cannot have improved the punch – soon ice pails or wine coolers became an essential part of the service of wine, to cool individual bottles now being made by the thousand in England.

In the 1690s, bucket-shaped containers held bottles on ice, with separate lift-out liners which were sluiced down to prevent the salt in the ice from corroding the silver. Ice pails and buckets were soon treated as decorative objects, and plain shapes were enriched with swirled lobes and gadrooning, lion's mask handles, and a few quite exotic and beautiful pairs of massive wine coolers were made for the great houses of the land, heavy with cast decoration.

Between 1730 and about 1790 these magnificent objects seem to have gone out of fashion, no doubt because of the renewed popularity for claret, drunk at room temperature, the enormous rise in the consumption of distilled spirits and, of course, port, which was decanted and not chilled.

In the 1800s there was a return to hock and white wine, and with them came a new style of ice bucket, with designs which ran the gamut of patterns from early gadrooned shapes through 'Adam' vase shapes to campana shapes with high relief stamped decoration.

Signs of authenticity

1. Hallmarked in full round rim of base in 18th century but occasionally near upper rim, as they were in the 17th century.
2. From 1784 hallmarks must include sovereign's head duty mark.
3. Detachable rims and liners intact – liners often showing good signs of wear.
4. Detachable rims and liners should bear full set of marks except for town mark – from c.1780 often in fused plate.
5. Heavy cast handles, in correct style for rest of piece.
6. Finest-quality fused plate made from late 1770s, gauge of silver slowly reduced to poor quality c.1820.

Likely restoration and repair
7. Handles weakest point – cracking, splitting, tearing repaired, often with addition of reinforcing plate.
8. No signs of seaming vertically down body – may have been electroplated at later date to conceal repairs and on fused plate to re-silver where original coating has worn.
9. Detachable rims with slightly different edge patterns to main body – not original, replaced or 'married' from others of similar date and style.
10. Different marks on one detachable rim on pairs – may be made up to make a pair thus considerably reducing value.
11. Plain campana-shaped wine coolers in poor-quality fused plate or electroplate with die-stamped rim and border decoration, not cast. Low in value and quality.

Construction and materials

Even though most wine coolers were made from sheet silver seamed vertically, and not beaten up without seams, their sheer size and the amount of cast and applied decoration makes them very heavy pieces, and therefore not cheap, either to make or to buy.

Inevitably, the fused plate makers saw a golden opportunity for copying almost every silver shape in less expensive materials, using die-stamping and mass-production methods, but this is not to decry their early work. The quality was fine; attention to detail, proportion and design was excellent; and, since wine coolers did not get an enormous amount of wear and tear, fused plate was eminently suitable for the rich industrial barons and wealthy middle classes. The almost simultaneous introduction of the railways, with their attendant hotels, with the technique of electro-

plating swamped the lower end of the market with all the trappings of the rich, made on the cheap.

Decoration

On sterling silver wine coolers, handles were cast in the most intricate and often impracticable forms, from great rams' heads to writhing serpents, entwined vines, and elaborately wrought leaves and grapes. Borders, rims and liners were embellished with cast and applied decorative edges, and the shapes themselves were so laden with classical and mythological themes that the underlying pattern became difficult to detect. Wine coolers from Sheffield, whether in sterling silver or fused plate, are made with mass-production techniques, and the ornament is not cast, but stamped, filled with a lead solder, and then applied.

Variations

Probably the true variations are those made in fused plate in the last decades of the eighteenth century, but since they were genuinely original products, it is hard to separate them from sterling silver examples, except naturally in terms of cost and difference of workmanship. There

may be some confusion over the fact that the Sheffield crown was occasionally used on fused plate as well as sterling silver, but the hallmarks on silver are so distinctive that only the fact that fused plate is so often called 'Sheffield' plate may muddle a first-time buyer. As for variations in style and shape, so many different designs were made that it is better to trust the eye first and investigate the details later.

Above *Based on an early 18th-century pattern, with lobed lower body, heavy cast lion's mask ring handles, detachable collars. London 1835. 9¼in (23.5cm) high.*

Reproductions

An arbitrary line can be drawn around about 1830, after which both the silversmiths and the plate makers began to repeat earlier shapes and styles from the eighteenth century. The great nostalgia of the Edwardian era produced another run of reproductions, mainly in fused plate, but also in sterling silver for the last days of dying splendour of great houses and institutions. Any found marked 'Sheffield Plated' should be avoided – this was a deliberate deception on the part of the electroplaters. Genuine fused plate or 'Sheffield Plate' was never marked thus.

Plain campana-shaped wine cooler in fused plate, with die-stamped rims and handles, detachable collars and original liners. c.1925. 9in (23cm) high.

Price bands

Pairs:
Queen Anne, £20,000+.
Georgian heavy quality, £15,000+.
Regency, £12,000+.
Paul Storr, £18,000+.

Fused plate, early patterns, £1,000–£2,500.

Singles considerably less than half.

Left *Vase-shaped rococo revival, with asymmetric cast shell bases and applied decoration. London 1840. 9in (23cm) high.*

Ewers and jugs

The elegant covered jugs which do not seem to have been made much before the end of the eighteenth century constitute something of a mystery. While it might be assumed that covered jugs of the first part of the century were for serving mulled ales and wines, these had largely died out by mid-century. Ewers and jugs for this purpose do not seem to have been made in pottery or porcelain either during this period, unlike tea and coffee wares.

These proud, haughty jugs, usually designated as 'hot water jugs', are sometimes made with silver handles, indicating the service of cold drinks of some kind, and sometimes with ebony or fruitwood handles, which generally indicates a hot liquid of some sort. A few of these enigmatic jugs are made in sets with sugar bowls and smaller, uncovered jugs, as well as with pairs of matching goblets. It was customary at that time to serve almost every wine 'with or without sugar'. From the 1770s onwards, a wide variety of 'physical ales' and health drinks were also fashionable. These ranged from purgatives of a nauseous kind to scurvy grass ale, and countless cordials made from elderflower, elderberry, cress and a wide selection of herbs and roots as well as herbal ales flavoured with anything from wormwood to sage and rosemary.

In the nineteenth century the form of these jugs changed when many fortified wines such as madeira, as well as wine, were frequently diluted with pure water or spa water.

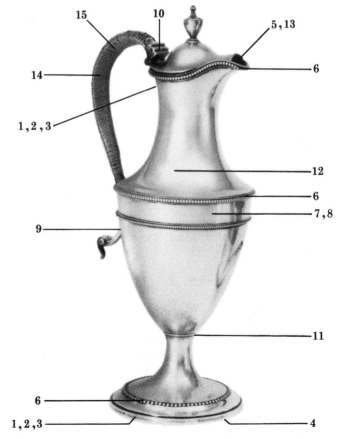

Construction and materials

The most sought-after ewers and jugs are made in very heavy gauge silver, and date from about 1775 to 1790. Standing on plinth feet, with luxurious classical decoration in the form of acanthus leaf, swags, husks and urn-shaped finials, every detail including the handle sockets forms part of the overall design.

By the 1780s the ever-widening demand for silverware meant that on more pedestrian designs the gauge was often quite thin, and detail was skimpy. Some of the best examples were made at the Birmingham works of Boulton and Fothergill, in both silver plate and early fused plate. Once the plate makers of Sheffield began to make large quantities of domestic ware, the quality of both materials and workmanship gradually deteriorated, until the silver coating was reduced to a paper-thin layer in the 1820s.

Decoration
The most typical decoration for these ewers of the latter part of the eighteenth century is bright cut engraving, in bands around the body, or round the neck and foot, sometimes with a crest or decorative motif encircled by a wreath rather than a full set of armorials. Simple beading round the neck, body and foot characterise the thinner gauge, more mass-produced versions, which are often a little too tall and slender to be the genuine Adam-style urn shape, but are very attractive nevertheless.

Care should be taken if pairs of goblets, apparently matching, are offered together with ewers – many, many such objects were made during the period by different makers, and although the decoration seems identical, they may not actually belong together.

Variations

The best-known variations, fashionable from the 1850s onwards, are silver-mounted glass claret jugs. These often handsome examples of nineteenth-century design have become very much in demand, although there are many which are either not very attractive or not very practical, made towards the end of the century. The best pieces are those decorated with vine leaves and grapes on both the glass body and the silver mounts, some of which are of remarkably high quality. There should be a full set of marks on the silver collar, and condition is of prime importance.

Reproductions

Once its relatively brief period of fashion was over, this particular form declined in popularity as the silver-mounted claret jug took its place. It could not truthfully be said that fused plate ewers and jugs were reproductions, since they were made at the same time as silver plate versions, although their manufacture continued long after the silversmiths had ceased making this particular pattern. The plate makers continued to make the 'Adam' urn-shaped covered jug until the 1820s and 1830s, and this latter period, of poor-quality fused plate with mass-produced techniques of die-stamping, has little merit.

Price bands

Adam-style, cast decoration, £3,000–£5,000.
Plain, good quality, £800–£1,500.

Baluster beer jugs, £800–£2,000 +.

Silver-mounted claret jugs, £500–£1,800 +.

Far left *Baluster-shaped beer jug with cast shell handle mounts and simple button finial. 18th-century beer jugs were usually made without lids. London 1801. $9\frac{1}{2}$ in (24 cm) high.*

Centre *Covered jug with vase-shaped body decorated with a band of bright cut engraving and a crest engraved on an inset panel, in fused plate. c.1790. $12\frac{1}{4}$ in (31 cm) high.*

Left *Silver-mounted glass claret jug with neck and handle in similar form to the 'Armada' jugs of the period. London 1870. 10 in (25.5 cm) high.*

Wine coasters and decanter stands

Although there are some rare examples dating from before the mid-eighteenth century, decanter stands or wine coasters seem to have become a regular part of wine equipage from about 1760. It is interesting that at about this time there was a change in the manner of storage and bottling of wines, particularly port, as a result of a prohibitive tax on glass. The thoroughly English custom of leaving the gentlemen to drink alone after dinner while the ladies withdrew appears to have begun at about the same date. Wine was generally served by footmen and servants – port was the only drink which the gentlemen served themselves. By custom and ritual the port passed round the table in a clockwise direction, and anyone impeding its progress was severely called to order.

Most wine, including port, was decanted, and poured through a wine funnel to make sure none of the sediment disturbed by the pouring was allowed to pass through to the decanter. From the shape and size of most Georgian wine coasters, it seems they were intended for decanters and not bottles. Those intended for the latter are less common, and usually have a higher gallery and straight sides.

Signs of authenticity

1. Full set of hallmarks on plain rim of base.
2. From 1784 must include sovereign's head duty mark.
3. Signs of wear on undersides and inside wooden turned bases from bottles, decanters, use and age.
4. Medallions, cartouches with contemporary crests.
5. Those with central silver boss engraved with crest, also contemporary, not later addition.
6. Pairs more than double the value of a single.
7. Pairs must have identical hallmarks, dates, as well as design and pattern.
8. All-silver stands, coasters generally silver gilt.
9. Signs of wear on gilding where gadrooning, rim decoration have been rubbed.
10. Signs of single seam where sheet silver has been joined.

Likely restoration and repair
11. Wooden bases replaced – may not detract too much from value if correctly done.
12. Signs of splitting, cracking in pierced examples.
13. Central silver bosses added at later date with later crests, armorials – reduces value.
14. Recent gilding on early coasters may conceal repairs to pierced and fretted galleries.
15. Anachronistic chased, embossed decorative motifs – later embossed plain coasters from earlier period.
16. Absence of sterling lion passant on central silver boss may indicate later addition.

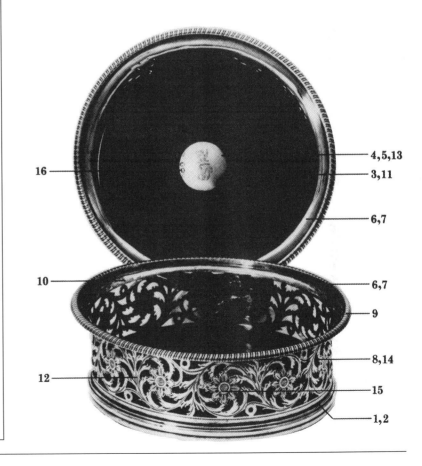

Construction and materials

Early wine coasters were pierced with delicate designs of leaves, flowers and abstract arabesque patterns, generally with a small medallion for a coat of arms or cartouche incorporated in the design. From the 1780s an alternative design of upright pales was common, interspersed with medallions, sometimes enriched with bands of bright cut engraving. Decanter stands were not made in fused plate until double-faced plate evolved in the 1780s. From the 1790s fused plate coasters and stands were often fluted or reeded, which increased the strength of the metal. From about 1800, die-stamped rims on both fused plate and silver plate became more elaborate and extended in a flat decorative edge from the top of the gallery.

Decoration
The earliest form of coaster had an undulating rim with an applied decorative edge, adding strength to the rather delicate galleries of pierced work. By the 1790s the sides were of sheet metal, and had applied or chased decoration in the Adam manner, with swags, rams' heads, medallions or paterae, and bright cut engraving. Taller bottle stands were made from c.1780 with a gallery of about 3–3½ in (7.5–9 cm) and almost the same diameter. These allowed greater freedom for decoration, and scenes of bacchic delight, vine leaves, grapes and putti were typical – pierced, with reeded rims. Decanter stands from about 1810 were often lobed with gadrooned edges standing out from the rim, interspersed with shells or vine leaves.

Variations

Double decanter stands were made from about 1790 onwards, with two galleries on a single hardwood base, often with a handle to push them across the table. A particularly delightful version of these was the 'jolly boat' double decanter stand, shaped like a rowing boat with little rowlocks down either side, a coiled rope ring to pull it along on four small castors, two depressions for the decanters, and sockets for the stoppers. Far more elaborate 'wine waggons' or decanter carriages followed in the 1830s, with proper wheels on axles and a central shaft with a bar and handle. These variations were made in silver and in fused plate, generally a few years after the first silver model had appeared.

Reproductions

Ever since their first appearance, wine coasters – as they are known today – have been made in patterns from earlier periods, in both silver plate and fused plate, with widely varying finish and quality. From about 1850 many dozens of the plainer patterns were made in electroplate, and possibly the early production of these could today have achieved a patina which is very similar to early fused plate. By the 1830s, however, much of the pierced work done by the plate makers was with a white metal core to the fused plate, known as British plate. This nickel alloy withstood piercing far better than the softer copper alloy, and the designs were crisper, without the pinkish tinge that fly-punching produced by stretching the silver coating.

Remarkably fine copy of 18th-century work, with pierced and engraved pales, perching birds and leafy branches, medallions engraved with armorials and gadrooned wavy edges. George Fox. c.1890. 5½ in (14 cm) diameter.

Silver gilt wine coaster with gadrooned rim and sheet silver loaded base. Robert and Samuel Hennell. London 1806. 5½ in (14 cm) diameter.

Standard pattern made in silver and in fused plate over a long period, with stamped and applied borders and turned hardwood bases. 1830 onwards.

Price bands

Pairs:
Georgian pierced, £1,200–£2,400.
Silver-based, £1,900–£3,500.
Regency cast, heavy, £1,200–£3,000 +.

19th-century, £350–£1,200.

Fused plate, £120–£350.

Singles less than half.

Wine labels and bottle tickets

Signs of authenticity

1. Sterling lion passant guardant and maker's mark as minimum hallmarking to c.1784.
2. From c.1784 date letter should also be included, although not necessarily town mark.
3. From 1784 sovereign's head duty mark must be included.
4. Provincial town marks more valuable than London.
5. Rings intact, no damage round ring-holes.
6. Complete with original chain adds to value.
7. In fused plate, earliest examples from c.1760 single-faced plate with close-plating on reverse side, sometimes just tinned.
8. Rings, chains on fused plate are sterling silver if genuine, not fused plate wire with copper core.
9. Slight convex curve to match curve of bottle or decanter.

Likely restoration and repair
10. New rings, chains – lessens value.
11. Ring-holes close to edge worn through, repaired.
12. On early fused plate, single-faced only. Uniform silver surface on both sides may suggest replating or electroplating.
13. From c.1790 fused plate stamped out and backed with plain strip of metal – very thin examples with stamping visible on back denotes loss of lead filling and backing plate.
14. Badly worn, rubbed – considerably less in value.
15. Rare wines, names highly sought after – must be correct for period.
16. Specialist field – further study of subject advisable if contemplating purchase of any value.

'Label decanters' in blue glass for cordials and spirits were embellished with gilded vines and the names of their contents from about 1745 onwards. By the 1750s small, plain silver bottle tickets hung round the necks of dark green quart bottles of wine, for the Georgians were prodigious topers. Some early clear glass decanters were engraved with the name of the wine, but soon more elaborate decanter labels indicated 'Port', 'Madeira' and 'Mountain', a Spanish wine from Malaga. Other Spanish wines such as 'Alicant' and 'Tent' or vino tinto joined 'Sherry' from Jerez, 'Marsala' and a white wine from Frontignan known as 'Frontiniac', as well as burnt wine or 'brandewijn' and 'Hollands' gin.

The names of many wines, such as 'Vidonia' – a Canary wine from Vidogne, which was wiped out by disease in 1820 and never replanted – help to date these highly collectable items. Dozens of home-brewed concoctions were made from clary, a sweet wine, distilled and added to Malaga raisins, old claret wine-lees and the juice of mulberries, known as 'Raisin' wine. The same basic concoction could be made into 'Canary' by adding some sharp pippin cider and a little good white wine.

These small but highly visible items seem to have encouraged the silversmith to use his ingenuity, and some of the solid cast silver wine labels are remarkable examples of skilled craftsmanship and invention in miniature.

Construction and materials

Early bottle tickets and decanter labels were purely functional, made in small plain shapes, such as an escutcheon or shield, a crescent, or a rectangular shape with cut corners, with a slightly convex curve to fit snugly against the glass bottle or decanter. Bottle tickets were among the earliest objects to be made in fused plate, starkly simple, and stamped out with the name of the wine in plain shapes. Silver versions were engraved and the letters rubbed with black wax to make them stand out. With the improvement in die-stamping and the development of cold steel dies, both silver and fused plate labels were stamped out and finished by hand, and by the 1790s fused plate labels were being made in very thin gauge metal, backed with lead filling and covered with a plain strip of metal on the reverse.

Decoration
Edges of bottle tickets and decanter labels were often finished with two lines of reeding in the mid-eighteenth century. Later, feathering or tiny gadroons were also used on escutcheon-shaped or rectangular labels. Shapes remained fairly simple until the 1790s, when an Adam-style urn or festoons or drapes were added to the crescent shape, which became more of an escutcheon, deeper and more elaborate. Grapes and vine leaves with a scroll supported by two putti was a popular design at the end of the eighteenth century, much copied in a stamped version in the nineteenth century. Single shapes of vine leaves or shells date from about 1815 onwards.

Variations

The single letter label dates from about 1790 onwards, and pierced examples were originally intended to mark the ownership of a bottle in a gentlemen's club rather than the initial letter of the contents. However from the mid-nineteenth century onwards single letters for wines and spirits became fashionable, for decanters rather than bottles. A large number of silver labels were also made for sauce bottles and toilet waters – anyone coming across a label marked 'Harvey' should not be carried away with the idea that this was for sherry: it was for one of the first bottled sauces, made in the late eighteenth century.

Reproductions

From the 1860s onwards wine merchants labelled their own bottles, and the demand for bottle tickets more or less died out. Cheap copies of decanter labels continued to be made in electroplate until the end of the century, however, to add class to the blurred pressed glass and moulded glass copies of early grand cut and faceted decanters used by the rich and privileged Georgian households.

Price bands

Singles:
Georgian cast, £280–£400.
Escutcheon, crescent,
£150–£300.
Decorative, bacchic,
£210–£600.
Plain, £90–£180.
Pierced, £150–£400.

19th-century cast, decorative,
£200–£500.

Stamped, pierced, £40–£160.

Fused plate, £20–£80.

Reproductions, £20–£50.

Collector's market. Prices vary greatly for rare names, patterns, and exceptional examples may be £800 + .

Cast silver crescent-shaped wine label for Orange cordial with plain reeded border, slightly curved to fit the neck of the decanter. c.1797.

From c.1815 and right through the 19th century, variations on a vine leaf became very popular, often mass-produced with the new die-stamping techniques, in silver and in fused plate, of varying quality.

During the Regency, more ornate, elaborate designs were fashionable, at first in heavy cast silver or silver gilt, and then in stamped sterling silver and fused plate. This design is often known as the 'Bacchus and Banner'.

Salts

Even before the days of the great standing salt of medieval England had passed, small individual salts called trencher salts had been added to the very basic tableware of dining halls. Wooden trenchers were hollowed out to hold the sloppy 'spoon meats' of the time, with small depressions in one corner to hold the salt. The earliest trencher salts were made in exactly the same shape, like a corner of the platter, triangular with a central well.

From the Restoration period onwards, traingular trencher salts were replaced with capstan salts, often with gadrooned rims, made from sheet silver and fairly insubstantial. With the arrival of the Huguenot silversmiths towards the end of the century the shape and weight became heavier and rounder, and sets of four, six or more were made for a grand household, engraved with the crest of the owner. Salts were made in a variety of bowl and cup shapes until about 1730–35 when they were raised, on cast feet, often headed with a heavy lion's mask and terminating in paw feet. By the 1740s the extravagant influence of rococo design was given free rein in the design of salt cellars, with applied festoons, conches, shells and flared rims. The interiors were often gilded to help prevent the corrosive action of the salt from damaging the silver.

Coloured glass liners date from about 1760, and with them came a wide range of pierced decoration in the Adam manner. At the same time, far heavier, more elegant salts were made, generally in pairs, fours or sixes, in the typical compressed oval shape of the period, standing on oval feet and often embellished with rams' heads and festoons.

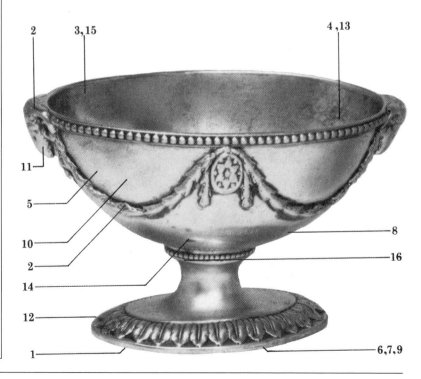

Construction and materials

Salts made in bowl or cup shapes were beaten up from sheet in a single piece and should have no sign of seaming. Feet and headings were cast and applied, as were any other swags or floral decoration. From the 1780s new techniques of die-stamping and sinking enabled feet to be stamped out in many traditional patterns such as ball and claw or hoof, but they are hollow on the inner side and none too strong.

This type of foot is generally associated with the pierced oval salts made by such experienced makers as Hester Bateman, with an eye to the broad middle-class market which could not afford as much for such ordinary domestic items as its grander counterpart. Fused plate salts, mustards and pepperettes date from the mid-1770s, when pierced work became fashionable. But the plate makers also made a wide variety of far earlier designs, dating back to the cup-shaped salt with a calyx of stiff leaves made at the beginning of the eighteenth century, as well as copies of the Adam-style boat-shaped salts standing on low pedestal feet.

Decoration

Common to almost all salts of the first half of the eighteenth century is a flaring gadrooned rim, sometimes interspersed with a small shell or leaf motif. Feet were lion's paw, hoof or shell until the 1760s, when a simple scroll or even a plain ball foot was used. On openwork salt cellars, a band of bright cut engraving often encircled the body or added sparkle to the pierced pales, festoons and medallions. Lobed bodies were popular from about 1800, with gadrooned rims and bases in oval or oblong shapes, and there was also a return to the early four-footed plain circular salt at about the same time.

Variations

Although strictly speaking the Victorian fantasies should be called rococo revival, the tradition for exuberant interpretations of shells, tritons and sea creatures runs as a continuous thread from its first introduction in the 1730s right through to the end of the nineteenth century and even later. Generally of great weight and ostentation, often silver gilt, and always cast and not made in thin sheet, these run the gamut from relatively modest scallop shells on snail feet to full-blown mermaids, tritons and water-babies twined or perched on shells, supported by waves or dolphins, and are certainly among the most decorative if not the most practical of all types of salts.

Reproductions

While the plate makers of Sheffield and Birmingham produced a profitable line of early reproductions called 'Queen Anne', in the nineteenth century the silversmiths too returned to earlier designs for salts, or salt cellars as they were known after about 1820. The gadrooned bodies most often deceive, as they have a strong Georgian air about them, but in fact were made from about 1800 onwards. Pierced and openwork salt cellars, mustards and pepperettes have also been made continuously from the 1780s onwards, in silver plate, rolled silver, fused plate and electroplate.

19th-century version of an 18th-century design, with lion's paw feet, scrolled headings, with gadroon and shell rims and gilt interiors. London 1824. 2½ in (6.5 cm) wide.

One of a set of six shell-shaped salts on snail-shaped feet, engraved underneath with a crest and coronet. London 1825. 4 in (10 cm) wide.

One of a pair of heavy cast silver salts supported by dolphins and figures of water babies at the tiller. R. & S. Garrard. London 1857. 5¾ in (14.5 cm) wide. 1772 g pair.

Casters and dredgers 1680–1710

Before the founding of the East India Company in 1600, spices had been reserved for the rich and privileged, and in the latter part of the sixteenth century spice compartments

had been incorporated into separate divisions of tall bell salts.

Little thought is generally spared for these lowly objects today, yet when they first made their appearance on the tables of England they signified wealth and sophistication, and their importance can be judged by the well-engraved armorials accorded to them. From the Restoration onwards, pairs of casters were made for black and cayenne pepper, of plain cylindrical form with simple piercing and a slip-lock or bayonet fitting to secure the lid, and rope-twist borders round the base of the two halves.

Extremely grand and showy sets of casters were made by such Huguenot silversmiths as Philip Rollos, with ornate cut card work and applied

decoration, and their shakers pierced in such small designs that it is a wonder they were serviceable – black pepper was coarse and grainy, and sugar – contained in a third, larger caster, was lumpy. From the 1700s onwards the finest double-refined sugar was known as 'castor sugar' this being the old spelling of the word 'caster'.

From this time onwards, one of the smaller casters was evidently intended for use with a long spoon rather than as a sprinkler, since the top was 'blind' or unpierced. It is doubtful if mustard was ever served this way, as it is often referred to as being served in earthenware pots, ready-made, and the secret of milling it to a fine powder was not discovered until the mid-eighteenth century.

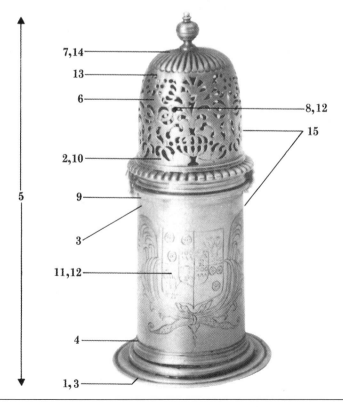

Construction and materials

Up to about 1700, casters and dredgers were made in plain cylindrical form, from sheet silver seamed vertically down the body, with applied foot rims, regardless of whether they were in old sterling standard or Britannia Standard. The bayonet fitting is the most common between base and cover.

For a brief period ending in about 1710, some casters were made with a 'long sleeve' fastening – the pierced cover extended in a plain cylinder fitting tightly inside the body. It was expensive, as it needed an extra length of silver, and probably none too efficient, and was soon discarded with the arrival of the baluster body and a new type of fitting between body and cover.

Decoration

Lobed or gadrooned foot rims and rims to covers, or rope-twist rims and a simple baluster or button finial were all the decoration on casters except for the piercing and an engraved armorial or a set of initials of a married couple set in a triangle. Casters of this early period have almost flattened covers, barely rounded where the finial and its plate are soldered to the cover. In the last years of the seventeenth century an applied girdle was set low on body, and the flat spreading foot changed to a rounded, stepped base.

Variations

A caster or dredger of simpler form was made throughout the eighteenth century and probably earlier, although few have survived from the seventeenth century. This is known inaccurately as a 'kitchen pepper' or, more generally, as a 'muffineer'. Straight-sided with a flat or bun-shaped perforated cover, it was made with a simple ring handle until about 1730, when some slightly more sophisticated versions were made in baluster form. This form of caster is very common in brass, and may have been used either for sugar or pepper, or in pairs for both, for seasoning oat cakes and wheat cakes which were buttered and toasted.

Below left *Queen Anne caster with long sleeve covers, baluster finial and less ornate piercing. London 1706. One of three, 7½in (19cm) and 6in (15cm) high.*

Below centre *Plain 'kitchen pepper' of baluster form with a bun top and a simple applied girdle. 1755. 5½in (14cm) high.*

Reproductions

Late seventeenth and early eighteenth century examples are very large by today's standards. During the 1900s and 1920s, when reproductions of 'Queen Anne' silver were made, casters were frequently made to a smaller size, and seldom from Britannia Standard silver. There is nearly always some detail that is not quite correct, such as the placing of the girdle or the addition of a cut card plate beneath the finial.

Queen Anne pattern lighthouse caster with a small amount of additional cut card work below the finial. Chrichton Brothers. London 1936. 5½in (14cm) high.

Price bands

Singles:
17th-century lighthouse, £890–£2,000.
Queen Anne baluster, £780–£1,800.
Octagonal, faceted, £850–£2,100.

Reproductions, £120–£400.

Pairs more than double, threes more than treble.

Left Octagonal faceted caster with decoratively pierced cover. The body is engraved with a crest within formal shell, scroll and foliate cartouche. London 1716. 6½in (16.5cm) high.

Casters and dredgers 1710–1750

1. Hallmarks for Britannia Standard to c.1720.
2. Full set of hallmarks near top rim of body.
3. Maker's mark and lion's head erased on cover to c.1720.
4. With sterling lion passant guardant after that date.
5. On baluster, pear and vase shapes, vertical seams on upper part of body – lower part raised from single sheet.
6. Covers with vertical, circular girdles, ribs, separating pierced panels.
7. Pierced part of cover raised in seamless piece strengthened with ribs applied over unpierced strips between panels, or in separate panels soldered to ribs, girdles.
8. Covers of octagonal, hexagonal casters, marked on bezel where it fits into the body.
9. Bases of octagonal, hexagonal casters marked on underside.

Likely restoration and repair
10. Covers of casters originally 'blind' i.e. unpierced, pierced at later date. Does not necessarily detract from value unless the work has been clumsily done.
11. Piercing on covers with lattice patterns not lining up – either made with mass-production techniques from c.1780, or pierced later.
12. Part of pierced cover blocked with thin sheet silver – often found on early casters when piercing was too coarse for practical use at later date.
13. Crests, initials removed or engraved at later date – detracts from value.
14. Maker's mark absent or different on cover – replacement or 'marriage'.
15. On casters marked on rim, foot too high – restored, replaced at later date.

Baluster-shaped casters and dredgers began to appear around 1705, still with a bayonet fitting between cover and body, and still with a low-set girdle. Finials were plain and ball-shaped – towards the middle of the century crests were more common than full armorials.

Around 1710 the standard bayonet fitting was abandoned in favour of a tightly fitting slip-on cover, known as a friction join, with a sleeve of springy silver lining the inside of the body which held the cover firmly when it was slid into place. Octagonal baluster casters were made from about 1720 onwards, making full use of faceted and reflecting surfaces on plain undecorated silver.

Sets of three casters in frames seem to have been a French innovation, and in general English silversmiths continued to make free-standing sets which gradually became more pear-shaped, sleeker and slightly smaller until, with the advent of glass liners towards the end of the eighteenth century, sets of salts, peppers and mustards were made. It is a little surprising that the Adam vase shape is uncommon – perhaps it is because of the difficulty of construction, which had become quite complicated, or perhaps because the new-fangled blue glass liners which date from about 1765 lent themselves better to the neo-classical style, with pierced and fretted silver, decorated with swags, festoons and rams' heads.

Construction and materials

Baluster-shaped casters were made in several parts – the lower part of the body was raised from a seamless piece, the upper part made from sheet silver soldered into a cylinder. The two halves were then soldered together and the join concealed by an applied girdle.

Octagonal and hexagonal casters were sometimes made with hinged covers and over-riding lugs that clipped over a moulded lip, which were intricate pieces of work and none too strong. The bodies were made from sheet silver, seamed vertically.

The third, taller sugar caster seems to have been dropped from condiment sets around 1765–70, when salts, pepperettes and mus-tard pots were made *en suite* with blue glass liners and fretted and pierced bodies.

Decoration
Decoration continued to be mini-mal on casters and dredgers, with little more than a corded or rope-twist girdle and a change in the shape of finials from plain balus-ter to a flame finial or an acorn shape. The shape of covers became a little more pointed, par-ticularly on those with vertical ribbing and alternate panels of piercing, but generally the only extra decoration was a crest – full armorials are rare after about 1725–30 except on very heavy quality casters made by the best London silversmiths.

Reproductions

Sets of three casters were made in the nineteenth century to the same design as those of the early Georgian period, but they are quite easily distinguishable from the originals by their shape, which is a little more bulgy, and above all by the mechanically pierced covers, which have little more than plain holes, occa-sionally enlivened by two decora-tive panels. The vertical ribs are not applied but simply form part of the cover, and the bases are not generally seamed horizontally but made in a single piece with one vertical seam. This type of caster was not, it seems, ever made in fused plate.

Variations

During the mid-eighteenth cen-tury sets of casters and dredgers were made in full rococo style, with swirling, spiralling flutes, chased with scrolls and rococo cartouches. It would appear that they were originally part of 'French-style' cruet sets in heavily decorated frames, and were accompanied by silver-mounted bottles in cut glass. Simpler versions of these cruet frames were made from the 1730s onwards, and the plain-surfaced casters have often been later embossed with Victorian rococo revival decoration which drama-tically reduces their value.

George II vase-shaped caster, decorated with chased and flat chased rococo scrolls and festoons of a type often added later. London 1733. 7¼ in (19 cm) high.

Pear-shaped baluster casters with spreading bases, with covers pierced with saltires and stylised foliage. London 1737/8. 7¼ in (18.5 cm) and 6 in (15 cm) high.

Cruets

English eating habits before the eighteenth century did not generally include 'French dressing'. Most of the early surviving condiment sets in a frame appear to have been made by Huguenot silversmiths and it seems possible that this design originated in France. Quite a number of two-bottle frames exist from early dates – the silver-mounted bottles for these usually have silver handles as well and the mounts have pouring lips. These would have been more common, not for the table, but as part of the ecclesiastical equipment for Communion, the bottles containing wine and water respectively.

Early cruet frames were hardly an easy object to design with any great felicity. They generally held five containers or more – three casters and at least two silver-mounted bottles, either for oil and vinegar or for more fiery concoctions such as tabasco, cayenne or mustard sauce. By the middle of the eighteenth century 'soy frames' were quite common, holding two or more bottles and receptacles for peppers and mustards, with a far better-proportioned frame. Pairs of siver-mounted bottles shaped like miniature ewers on boat-shaped stands were made during the Adam period as well as 'sauce bottle stands' holding five or six bottles for assorted condiments and spicy sauces, ready-made by Lazenby's or Harvey's from the 1780s onwards.

Signs of authenticity

1. Sets of casters with same hallmarks, maker's mark.
2. Casters frequently made by specialists – cruet frame, handle, silver mounts to bottles may bear different maker's mark.
3. Full set of marks on frame – maker's mark and sterling lion on detachable handle.
4. Glass bottles all same height with matching stoppers, mounts.
5. Cartouches, crests on casters and frame must match.
6. Contemporary engraving of arms, crests, etc.
7. Rococo chasing, piercing to covers, contemporary with period, date marks.
8. Feet original, in good condition, worn on undersides through age and use.

Likely restoration and repair
9. Symmetrical floral chasing with blind rococo cartouche – probably later embossed.
10. Feet bent, cracked or broken off and replaced.
11. Silver mounts to bottles of later date – colour of silver plate will differ from rest of set.
12. Bottles of different heights – chipped, ground down, mounts replaced.
13. Bases of hardwood covered with thin sheet, either silver or fused plate – made from 1770s mainly in Sheffield, and of considerably less value than silver frames.
14. Many versions of silver patterns made in fused plate – check that no item has been replaced with identical pattern in fused plate.

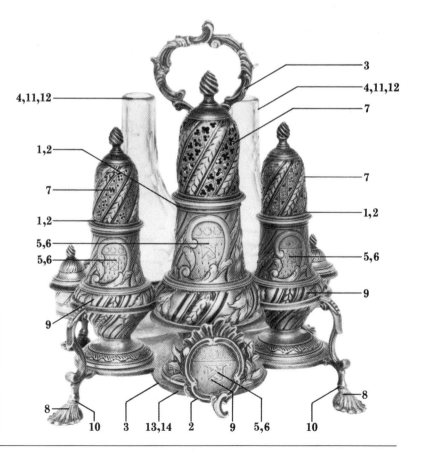

Construction and materials

Cruet frames and soy frames were made as fashionable additions to the table for well over a hundred years, from the 1720s until the 1850s, when the French chef Alexis Soyer decreed that they should no longer be placed on the table but stand on the sideboard. They ranged from heavy cast silver to the lightest of rolled silver, and were made in dozens of patterns in fused plate from the 1770s onwards. In many ways, the cutting and faceting of the glass containers is almost more important than the silver mounts and frames, for, to be genuine, all the original fittings should still be there. Early flint glass condiment bottles lacked the sparkle and fire of glass made from the 1780s – bottles made from the 1770s to the 1830s frequently had a star-cut base to compensate for the grinding down of the pontil mark on the base. Cheap soda glass, thin and sparsely cut, was used from the end of the eighteenth century, chiefly by the fused plate makers.

Decoration

Some of the most pleasing designs were made in the neo-classical style of the Adam period from the 1780s, by such makers as Hester Bateman and other well-known silversmiths making exclusively domestic silver articles. They have plain oval galleries with pierced decoration and beaded edges, and are decorated with bright cut engraving with swags and festoons. Among the least clumsy and most decorative are the two-bottle soy frames with boat-shaped stands, small ball and claw or hoof feet, decorated with garlands and rams' heads, with well-shaped bottles and elegant silver mounts and handles.

Reproductions

Cruet frames made from the 1770s onwards were at the same time contemporary and reproduction, since they imitated silver patterns as closely as they could within the limitations of materials. Often the frames have hardwood bases, covered with a sheet of fused plate, but Sheffield silversmiths also made identical cruets using thin rolled silver over the wooden bases. Mounts and mouldings were stamped out in thin sheet and filled with lead, then soldered together – fused plate handles were made the same way.

Price bands

Georgian heavy quality, £1,200–£2,500.
Rococo, £890–£2,200.
Pierced, £850–£1,700.
Adam-style, £700–£1,200.
Regency, £450–£1,750.

Victorian, £180–£1,000.

Fused plate, pierced, £75–£320.

Variations

The range of patterns, functions and designs of cruet frames varies enormously over the years, but probably the best-known later sauce bottle frames depart from the earlier versions in their square base on ball feet, with typical nineteenth-century interpretations of shell and gadroon borders. An even plainer version, with a squared-off gallery not individually shaped to the bottles, was made in great quantities in Sheffield for the burgeoning hotel and catering trade from the 1840s onwards, using a core of white alloy known as British plate as well as a copper core.

Below *Adam-style two-bottle cruet on a boat-shaped base with applied and chased rams' heads, paterae and husk swags. London 1780. 13¾ in (35 cm) diameter.*

Above *Typical pattern with gadroon and shell decoration, made cheaply with die-stamped borders in silver and fused plate. London 1813. 9 in (23 cm) diameter.*

Left *Lighter, pierced frames typical of the beginning of the 19th century. John Emes. London 1802. 13 in (33 cm) diameter.*

Sauce boats

Many an Englishman still chooses to call a sauce boat a 'gravy boat' but England seems to be alone in this particular accompaniment to roast meat. English gravy was simply the juices from roasted meat – often a separate chunk was half-roasted and pressed purely to provide the gravy. It has medieval origins, but the derivation of the word itself is unsure. With the arrival of George I, the first of the Hanoverian kings, there was a kitchen revolution and many Continental dishes took their place on English tables, expanding the only garnishes of melted butter and gravy with a host of rich and delicious sauces.

The first sauce boats were double-lipped, with a handle on either side. Restrained and elegant, they are most delightful pieces in every way, and when English porcelain makers at last succeeded in manufacturing soft paste porcelain, among the first objects recorded were double-lipped sauce boats, although the design was 20 years or more out of date in silver.

By the 1740s sauce boats had become a vehicle for frustrated feelings of silversmiths who longed to swirl rococo shapes and follow French fashions. Some of the grandest, in the shape of shells, with dolphin handles, eagles or caryatids, heavy with applied rococo scrolls and cartouches, were made by second-generation Huguenots in the 1740s.

Full matching silver services date from about 1745 onwards when, considerably toned down, sauce boats in pairs, four or sixes were made in the shape which has remained more or less constant ever since, although it has grown less and less imaginative over the years.

Construction and materials

It is very unlikely that any sauce boats will be found in Britannia Standard, although some silversmiths did continue to use the higher standard until the 1730s. Hallmarks should be examined very closely since there were many changes in the design of the sterling lion passant guardant and the leopard's head between 1719 and 1729 which may look unfamiliar. The bodies were raised from a single piece of silver plate without seams, and up to about 1745 handles were cast in fantastic shapes or in a double scroll, and applied. After that date the flying scroll handle became more fashionable until it was superseded by a tall loop handle, generally on sauce boats on a pedestal or collet foot. The three-footed pattern, usually with shell or hoof feet, appears in about 1735 – feet and headings were cast and applied, as were the gadrooned rim wires.

Decoration

On more prosaic sauce boats, the common factors were the feet, usually with shell terminals but occasionally with a heavier lion's mask on paw feet, and the leaf-capped double scroll handle, followed by a leaf-capped flying scroll. On more exotic versions, all manner of decorative handles were made, from twining sea-snakes to formalised dolphins, herons, cranes and even mermaids or caryatids. Bodies were sometimes embellished with cast applied rococo decoration, but more often fashioned in the shape of shells. Full armorials were usually engraved under the lip, crests on either side.

Variations

Rare to find in the original are the deep-bodied, almost helmet-shaped single-lipped sauce boats which had a brief span of popularity from about 1725 to 1735. They stand on a circular collet foot, and have relatively thin cast handles and shaped wavy-edged rims. This pattern was, however, copied in some quantity during the first decade of the twentieth century.

Reproductions

Among the rather surprising designs chosen by the fused plate makers in the 1820s and 1830s was the original double-lipped sauce boat, except that it has high inward curving scrolled handles, and is a poor interpretation of the original. In silver, almost every pattern except the extremely expensive early designs has been copied and reproduced at one time or another. And simplified versions of sauce and gravy boats in fused plate and electroplate were made in great quantities for the hotel and catering trades from the 1840s onwards.

Reproduction of a mid-18th-century rococo-style pattern on collet foot with shell-shaped body. C. S. Harris & Sons Ltd. London 1901. 7½ in (19 cm) long.

Fine-quality sauce boat with flying scroll leaf-capped handle, on rocaille shell feet. Walter Brind. London 1753. 8½ in (21.5 cm) long.

George III sauce boat with oval body engraved with a monogram beneath the lip and crests on either side, with punch-beaded rim, on three hoof feet. London 1767. 8¼ in (21 cm) long.

Price bands

Pairs:
Georgian collet foot, £1,100–£2,500.
Rococo, £3,800–£5,000 +.
Flying scroll handle, £1,000–£3,500.
Victorian heavy quality, £1,200–£3,000.
Pedestal foot, £800–£2,300.
Plain 3-footed, £600–£1,500.

Reproductions, £90–£1,000.

Singles much less than half, fours more than double.

Sauce tureens

Signs of authenticity

1. Full set of hallmarks on underside of base – occasionally on body or foot rim.
2. Covers marked with minimum of maker's mark and lion passant guardant – from 1784 including sovereign's head duty mark.
3. Finials soldered to covers.
4. Originally made with matching ladles, with square-cut slots in covers.
5. Boat-shaped, compressed oval shape basic design with typical upswept handles, urn-shaped finials.
6. Reeded rims, feet to c.1775, gadrooned, beaded from c.1780.
7. Pedestal feet cast, soldered on to body with small collar, sometimes decorated with similar motifs as foot and rim.
8. Reeded or plain ring handles to covers from c.1790.
9. Square bases to pedestals from c.1800 onwards.

Likely restoration and repair
10. Weak points to examine: joins between body and foot, handle, and area round finial.
11. Signs of dullness, obvious seam where body and foot join repaired, restored, replaced upper part of foot.
12. Reinforcing plate directly below finial – cover cracked, split, finial damaged with consequent tearing which has been restored, repaired.
13. Armorials on either body or cover, not both. Suspicious, since crests at least normally on both – or crest on cover and armorials on body.
14. Rounded ladle slot may indicate cover of later date, or slot cut at later period.
15. Hallmarks in compressed straight line round outer rim of foot – examine closely. Marks from earlier pieces have sometimes been 'let in' on later copies.

Although a great deal of French cuisine had been accepted by the English, mid-eighteenth-century kitchens and cooks still continued to resist the extravagant use of expensive ingredients for making *coulis* and ragouts – extra, rich, thick sauces to accompany many dishes, while the Englishman still preferred plain 'boyled' or good roast meat seasoned with nothing more than a plain gravy.

These French sauces were made with oysters, lobsters' tails, crayfish and other seafood delicacies, and for meat, with veal stock, ham, bacon, truffles, herbs and spices. They were served as piping hot as the main dish they accompanied, unlike most English sauces – mustard, herb, plum, redcurrant – which came cold or tepid to the table. It was not until the 1760s that covered sauce tureens as well as sauce and butter boats were added to a full table service, and Frenchified garnishes of unbelievable richness were ladled over entrées, *relevés* and main courses.

After 1789, when the French Revolution sent the kings of cuisine – Carême, Escoffier, Brillat Savarin – fleeing to England, pairs of covered silver sauce boats were regularly seen on the tables of lesser households who learned their recipes from good, sound cookery books written by Englishwomen. 'A New System of Domestic Cookery, founded upon principles of economy, and adapted to the use of Private Families' sums up the attitude of Englishwomen at the turn of the century. Published in 1808 and a runaway bestseller, it was compiled and written by Mrs Rundell, close relative of the founder of that most famous nineteenth-century firm of silversmiths, Rundell, Bridge and Rundell.

Construction and materials

Sauce tureens were generally raised from a single sheet without seams, with the pedestal foot made separately and soldered on to the base of the body. Handles and finials were also cast in heavier examples, although from *c.*1780 thinner reeded handles were often made from thick silver wire. Covers were quite steeply domed, so that the finial came to the same height as the upper curve of the handles, if not higher.

It is more common to find a single crest or the crests of husband and wife on both bodies and lids rather than a full set of armorials, although very heavy-quality sauce tureens may have a full coat of arms. Crests were usually displayed on either side of the body. The lower curve of upswept handles was sometimes reinforced with an extra thickness of silver.

Sauce tureens were made in fused plate, double-faced, from about 1780, and the plate makers made good use of the exemptions for duty on silver by using sterling silver for part or all of the handles.

Decoration

The majority of boat-shaped sauce tureens had very little decoration, since their design depended on simplicity and proportion. Occasionally, for rich commissions, silversmiths added applied swags, with leaf motifs on the handles, as well as making more decorative fruit or bud-shaped finials, but these examples are rare compared to the many plain versions with nothing but simple reeding, gadrooning or beading round rims, covers and feet. Sometimes, after the fashion of the day, armorials might be enclosed within a wreath, or engraved with a ribbon cartouche.

Variations

From about 1810 to 1850, rich, heavy and ornate designs standing on four feet became popular, in styles and forms of early-eighteenth-century soup tureens in miniature. These, as well as boat-shaped patterns, were made with great success in fused plate, using thin rolled silver to stamp out handles which were then filled and soldered together, giving an illusion of expense. On heavier sauce tureens, it was customary to display an engraved coat of arms on one side of the body and a crest on the cover. In fused plate the thin layer of silver soldered or sweated on can often be seen quite clearly.

One of a set of four George III sauce tureens with heavy cast lion's mask terminals, coiled serpent handles, with bound and reeded rims overlaid with vines. Benjamin Smith II. London 1807. 7 in (17.5 cm) wide. 3934 g four.

One of a pair in fused plate with urn-shaped finials a little too large, and covers which curve up at the sides. Sheffield, early 19th century.

Reproductions

The most popular form to be reproduced in the last hundred years has been the heavy, lobed and gadrooned design which dates from the late Regency period, from patterns made by such eminent silversmiths as Rundell, Bridge and Rundell in remarkably heavy quality, with generous cast handles, decorative finials and applied decorative borders. Although extravagant, they do not equal the massive 1000–1500 g weight of those made during the Regency period.

Based on an 18th-century pattern, with cast paw feet and deep leaf headings, plain reeded handles and reeded bands around the covers. Scottish. 1813. 8¼ in (21 cm) wide.

Tureens and dishes

Signs of authenticity

1. Full set of hallmarks on underside of base.
2. Full set of hallmarks on covers until 1784.
3. From 1784 covers may be marked with sterling lion passant guardant, maker's mark and duty mark only.
4. Cast, detachable handles to covers should also bear this set of marks from 1784.
5. Heavy, cast handles on covers detachable, fixed with threaded screw and small nut inside – on Adam-style tureens neatly soldered.
6. Handles, feet cast in solid metal – no sign of seaming.
7. Decorative rims, mounts cast and applied.
8. On massive, important pieces, full set of armorials on body, crest on cover.
9. On lesser pieces, crest on both sides of body and cover.
10. No sign of seaming on body or cover – raised from single heavy gauge sheet.

Likely restoration and repair
11. Reinforcing plate on inside of cover where screws of handle have worn, torn.
12. Screw threads on cover handles recut, replaced with new securing nuts. Possibly entire handle is a replacement – check hallmarks.
13. Interior remarkably mint-new in appearance for age – original inner liner missing. Possibly also electroplated to conceal repairs, damage, marking on interior.
14. Armorials, crests, initials removed – panels on either side of cover and body will be thinner between thumb and forefinger than rest of piece.
15. Applied cartouches in rococo style, florid design, on relatively plain tureens – may have been added at later date.

There is a clash of language and custom over the simple word 'soup' in English cookery. Old English 'pottages' were white meat stews, full of vegetables, wheat or barley and herbs. The actual 'soup' was the liquid, as today a French *soupe* generally describes a bouillon or clear broth. A French *potage*, however, is a peasant soup, far more akin to the dishes served in England right up to the middle of the eighteenth century and beyond. Depending on how solid the dish was, the serving dish varied from a deep bowl to a far more shallow one – and as late as the 1770s, middle-class ladies referred to 'tureens' as 'terrines' or dishes in which meat was cooked and served.

It was not until the 1740s that 'soup' was served at the beginning of a meal, and it was still a fairly substantial dish. In the 1760s the rich households and institutions first tasted turtle soup, brought into the country by the East India Company and still, by tradition, the first course for the Lord Mayor's banquet. Clear soups assumed an individual identity from that time on, although towards the end of the century two soups were served, thick and clear, at the opening of a grand dinner. Serving dishes for these widely different broths and stews were originally modelled on the massive designs of wine coolers of a century earlier, deep and capacious, standing on four solid feet, and covered with a lid of such pretensions that it often featured a solid cast silver crest as a finial.

Once clear broths became an accepted dish, urn-shaped tureens were ideally suited for placing on the table, often in pairs for a choice of clear or thick soup. This form was first introduced around 1765 and continued to be practical and popular until the early 1800s, when the fashion returned for massive tureens, often gadrooned, on four heavy cast feet, frequently made with a stand of fused plate which matched the overall design.

Construction and materials

Tureens were generally placed on the table for the host or hostess to serve from, and as such were conceived as massive, showy pieces of tableware, rich in applied ornament with solid cast handles and massive paw feet with lion's-mask headings, or shell and scroll feet. Both the bodies and the covers were raised from thick gauge silver, and tureens without their contents could weigh as much as 5000 g or more. They were seldom embellished with anything but cast and applied decoration, with applied gadrooned rims, usually fairly wide and overhanging the rim of the body.

Up to about 1770, many tureens were fitted with detachable liners in thinner sheet silver, but after that date it is not uncommon to find liners made of fused plate. Later tureens often have pleated shapes to bodies and covers, and the weight of metal and thickness of gauge is considerably less than those made before the late 1770s. Tureens were also made in fused plate from about that time, with feet and handles made from thin rolled silver, stamped into relief, filled and then soldered together. Edges were die-stamped, filled and applied, and many were engraved with armorials – the silver panel can often be very easily seen.

Decoration

Massive high-relief lion's masks heading heavy paw or ball and claw feet, gadrooned rims and foliate handles characterise early tureens. During the period 1755–65 just before the urn shape took over, beautifully cast finials in the shape of vegetables and fruit, fish and shellfish were typical of heavy, quality pieces, but after the urn shape was discarded and tureens resumed a more oval, squat shape, the ring handle returned, with the occasional exception of solid cast crests and heraldic devices. Shell and scroll or foliate scrolled feet were more common than earlier types, even on copies of tureens which originally had paw feet.

Variations

Dishes served after the soup were generally known as 'removes' or 'relevés' and came before the 'entrées'. These included a great variety of fricassees, ragouts, blanquettes, poached fish and sauced meats, served from deep dishes quite similar to tureens, but usually longer and lower, often oblong or oval, with deep covers and frequently fitted with detachable liners. Neither tureens nor large serving dishes were necessarily made *en suite* until the 1750s, when it was at last *de rigueur* to have huge silver table services.

Below *One of a pair of heavy serving dishes with lobed bases on scrolling leaf-capped feet, with heavy cast lion's mask and foliate handle to the lid, by Rundell, Bridge & Rundell. London 1816. 15¾ in (40 cm) wide. 4292 g pair.*

Reproductions

From the 1780s onwards, many earlier patterns of tureen and serving dish were made in fused plate – already it had become customary for dishes to stand on plated stands, often heated with an iron block in the centre or with hot water and a spirit lamp, and Sheffield took to making the dishes themselves, in slightly simplified form, from the end of the eighteenth century. Sheffield silversmiths also made excellent copies of earlier styles in thinner gauge silver plate, often distinguishable on sight by the addition of a band of lobing round the cover and gadrooned rims with added shell or leaf decoration.

Based on an 18th-century form, a fused plate tureen and cover with armorials engraved on a panel of silver. c.1840. 16 in (41 cm) wide.

Price bands

Georgian, £3,000–£5,000 + .
Regency, £8,000–£11,000.
Paul Storr, £12,000 + .
William IV, £3,500–£4,800.

Victorian heavy quality,
£2,800–£3,600.

Fused plate, good quality,
£750–£1,800.

Left *The Moor's head was used as an impressive finial on this large pleated serving dish, with scalloped borders, reeded handles and shell and leaf feet. 14½ in (37 cm) wide.*

Entrée dishes and vegetable dishes

Signs of authenticity

1. Full set of hallmarks on both base and cover – usually in straight line close to rims.
2. Hallmarks must include sovereign's head duty mark from 1784 onwards.
3. Detachable finials and handles should bear maker's mark and lion passant guardant – after 1784 also the sovereign's head duty mark.
4. Unlike tureens, full armorials more common on covers with crests on bases.
5. Covers with detachable handles, finials, with gadrooned rims on inside, so that they match bases when used as separate dishes.
6. Good signs of wear on base through age and use.
7. Matching bases and covers marked with numerals to distinguish correct pairs.
8. Locking plates for handles showing circular rubbing where they have been turned frequently while in use.

Likely restoration and repair
9. Fused plate covers on dishes of early date – genuine additions in many cases, but could be deliberate enhancement of value in more recent times.
10. Rims, edges split, damaged, cracked and soldered – repair can be seen on underside of rims.
11. On later double entrée dishes, signs of splitting in lobes, 'pleats' if gauge of metal is relatively thin.
12. Locking plates out of true, buckled, damaged – handles soldered, no longer detachable reduces value considerably.
13. On early fused plate examples, colour of metal too sharp, cold – may have been electroplated to cover patches of wear where copper core was exposed.

After the 'remove' came the 'entrées'. These were of such enormous variety that it is not surprising that there are many covered dishes of various shapes and sizes which today are lumped together and classified as 'entrée dishes'. Shallow covered dishes were known almost throughout the eighteenth century as 'hash dishes' or, from about 1760, 'curry dishes', as the expanding East India Company and its new stations in India meant that very hot, spicy curries became highly fashionable. In many households footmen stood ready to administer a glass of vinegar and water to those guests who choked on the extremes of hot chillis and fiery curries.

Entrées included all small game, hare, partridge, pheasant, and all meat except for the main roast joint. There were also entrées 'volants', vol-au-vents, bouchées, brochettes and croquettes, all to be kept warm, if not hot, while the dinner wound its way through anything from five to seven hours. Among the many receptacles used for the service of all these, cushion-shaped uncovered dishes seem to be early forerunners of the rectangular covered dishes made from the 1760s onwards. From the 1770s sets of covered dishes were part of large silver table services. The covers had removable handles so that they could perform the same function as the bases, making a pair of almost identical shallow serving dishes.

It is difficult to lay down a hard-and-fast demarcation line between entrée dishes and vegetable dishes, since they were almost certainly interchangeable, but pairs of round dishes with ivory or ebony handles were often definitely described as vegetable dishes – and there are many other dishes which originally had compartmented liners so that several vegetables could be handed round by one servant.

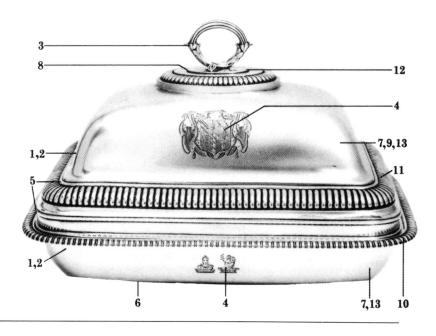

Construction and materials

In the 1760s entrée dishes were made in thick gauge silver, hammered up from a single sheet, with applied rims which were invariably gadrooned, with equally heavy covers, generally engraved with armorials. Handles or finials were detachable, and cast in solid silver.

By the 1790s, when table services in silver were being used by less wealthy, more middle-class households, the gauge became considerably thinner, and quantities of entrée dishes were made in both silver plate and fused plate. The ring handles so typical from this period onwards were secured by a locking plate which twisted into place, and 'double dishes' were made with the rims of base and cover decorated identically, generally with gadrooning, so that when the cover was used as a separate dish it matched its base.

Decoration

Very grand entrée dishes could have heavy cast finials in the shape and form of a family crest, but in the main fairly simple loop handles with leaf-wrapped bases and reeded rings were more common. Gadrooned rims remained popular until the 1830s, when die-stamped borders of more elaborate designs were applied to both silver plate and fused plate, and for a time the handles became ornate and laden with leafy ornament, or shaped like globe artichokes or similarly attractive-looking vegetables. Bound and reeded rims interspersed with leaves or shells also enjoyed a considerable span of popularity.

Variations

Entrée dishes were made in fused plate from the mid-1780s onwards, in a particularly ingenious design which included two extra pieces as well as the two parts of the entrée dish itself – a base dish which held a block of heated iron resting on a stand and a perforated plate which fitted into the heating dish. The two parts of the entrée dish were in double-faced fused plate, the heating dish and perforated plate were tinned inside. This form of heating stand was frequently used in conjunction with silver plate entrée dishes. Occasionally grander pairs of oblong dishes of very heavy gauge, made originally for rich commissions, were known as 'flank dishes', since they flanked the main dish on the table or sideboard.

Reproductions

The shape and design of entrée dishes has always been so practical and functional that it has been made almost continuously ever since it first developed – for private households in silver or fused plate of good quality, and for hotels and catering establishments in poorer-quality fused plate and in electroplate. They have become so commonplace that at first sight even the finest-quality thickest gauge silver plate seems remarkably ordinary and dull, but some examples are quite remarkable for their craftsmanship and simplicity.

Price bands

Pairs:
Georgian plain, £1,200–£2,800.
Regency heavy quality, £4,000–£6,000.
Paul Storr, £8,000 + .
Cushion shaped, £1,200–£2,500.
Round shapes, £1,500–£2,200.
19th-century plain, £850–£1,200.

Fused plate fine quality, £280–£350.

Reproductions, £250–£1,000.

Singles less than half.

Cushion-shaped entree dish with detachable snake handles. Paul Storr. 1806, 10¾ in (27 cm) wide. 3842 g pair.

Circular vegetable dish with fused plate heater base which has ivory handles and lobed bun feet. Paul Storr. 1807/8. 9¾ in (25 cm) diameter. 3160 g pair.

Heavy-quality circular dish with covers engraved on either side with armorials, the bases with crests. Richard Cooke. London 1807. 11 in (28 cm) diameter. 4167 g pair.

Plates and dishes

Records existing from the fourteenth century mention 'spice plates' in silver, as well as small plates in sets of 12, parcel gilt and with elaborate engraved or decorated borders and centres. By the mid-sixteenth century a dozen silver plates were known as a 'garnish' and six 'half a garnish', but these were not plates as we know them today. They weighed about 187 g each and were made as liner plates for wooden trenchers – an eighteenth-century dinner plate was seldom less than 466 g at least.

Although it is most likely that sets of silver and silver gilt plates would have been among the first items to be melted down for levies during the Civil War, in 1689 Celia Fiennes mentions her visit to Lowther Hall in Westmorland, where 'the Lady Landsdown sent and treated me with a breakfast, cold things and sweetmeates all serv'd in plaite'. By 1700 plates with wide rims and plain or reeded borders were made in con-siderable quantities as well as with gadrooned borders.

These proved to be the most enduring when they were re-vived in the 1760s and became the most common pattern of all. It is interesting to note that a lady ordered a silver soup tureen from Matthew Boulton in the 1780s, adding that she used only china plates for soup. She had considered ordering a dessert service in silver plate from him too, but had learned that the French used only glass or china and never metal for fruit or dessert.

Huge silver services made from about 1745 onwards could consist of as many as 150 to 200 pieces, including plates of two sizes, and by the 1820s a full service would have in-cluded as many as six dozen plates of varying sizes – a size-able outlay at an average of 560 g a plate.

Signs of authenticity

1. Britannia Standard marks 1697–c.1720.
2. Up to c.1730 hallmarks struck on surface of border.
3. Correct style, form of cartouche, armorials for period.
4. Applied border wire from c.1740 onwards on heavyweight plates.
5. Size 9–10 in (23–25.5 cm) diameter for large plates, 8 in (20 cm) for first course plates.
6. Sets of 12 marked with same maker's mark although date letters may span more than one year.
7. Shaped circular made in quantity c.1780–c.1830.
8. Sovereign's head duty mark from 1784.

Likely restoration and repair
9. Armorials engraved at later period – lowers value.
10. Armorials, initials, crest removed, decreasing value.
11. Rims bent, dented, part of rim wire removed, restored.
12. Centres shiny, bright, new-looking – knife-marks and signs of wear buffed out.
13. Soup plates with 18th-century date marks – possibly converted from plates during 19th century – soup plates seldom made in silver before that date.
14. Genuine replacements in identical matching patterns, mixed makers and dates considerably lowers value.
15. Late period soup plates converted to more desirable plates – check for date marks, hallmarks. Quickest giveaway – five marks means a date after 1784.

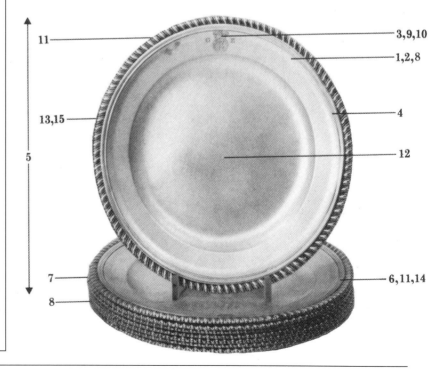

Construction and materials

It is unlikely that many ordinary plates of the higher Britannia Standard will be found today. Far more common are those dating from the 1750s onwards, in sterling silver, most likely with gadrooned rims or reeded rims. Dinner plates measure on average just under or over 10 in (25.5 cm) in diameter and can weigh from 498 g to 622 g each. They were beaten up from a single sheet, and a rim wire was then applied, partly to prevent warping, partly for decoration.

On some plates of early date, there is no border wire and the rim has simply been hammered in to add strength and then chased with a reeded border. This method of construction was revived at the end of the eighteenth century and in the nineteenth century – the plates are lighter in weight and therefore less costly to make.

Decoration
Up to about 1720 borders were generally reeded, and the only decoration was an engraved coat of arms on the broad flat rim. From the 1730s onwards gadrooned borders became popular and the shape of the plate changed slightly. Cast and applied shell and gadroon borders, or shaped gadrooned rims were most common from the 1740s onwards, with the armorials engraved on the rims. The bound and reeded border had a brief popularity in the 1760s, and was revived in the 1820s as a standard rim decoration.

Variations

There was a fashion in nineteenth-century provincial households of some financial status to use either silver or fused plate services almost as table mats are used today – underneath a soup or main-course plate of fine bone china or stoneware, purely for display. Silver plate and fused plate for this purpose was of thin gauge, either spun or rolled, and often with mechanically stamped borders which were first turned back on themselves to provide a double thickness. The underside of rims will show unsightly puckering where the extra metal has been turned over before stamping. Other variations include far too ornate stamped and applied borders with too much overhang round the outer rim.

Reproductions

The most common pattern of all, the shaped circular plate with gadrooned borders has been made almost continuously since it first appeared – for institutions, clubs, restaurants and private households, either in silver plate or in fused plate or even electroplate. Most of the latter were made in the second half of the nineteenth century for catering establishments and hotels where 'silver service' was taken to be a sign of quality.

Price bands

Sets of a dozen:
Wide rim Queen Anne, £20,000+.
Gadroon circular, £12,000–£15,000.
Shaped circular, £8,000–£10,000.
Victorian heavy quality, £4,000–£8,000.

19th-century, £2,600–£4,500.

Half-dozen less than half, singles £80–£400.

One of 24 dinner plates with shaped gadrooned rims engraved with contemporary armorials. Edward Wakelin. London 1753.
9¾ in (25 cm) diameter. 520 g each.

One of 12 George III dinner plates with reeded and foliate borders. Robert Cox. London 1766. 9½ in (24 cm) diameter.

Silver gilt dish with reeded borders overlaid with naturalistic leaves, engraved with armorials and foliate mantling. Paul Storr for Storr and Mortimer. London 1838.
10¾ in (27.5 cm) diameter. 595 g.

Teapots 1700–1730

China tea came into Europe as early as 1610 and crossed the Channel to England in about 1644, where it was considered at first as a medicine, and then as a useful addition to ale-making when, added to the traditional brew of hops and yeast, it made 'China Ale'.

By the turn of the century, two sorts of tea were in fairly widespread use, although still prohibitively expensive: Bohea and Hyson, or Black and Green. Both were apparently taken without milk or cream but well sweetened. Teapots and covered sugar bowls *en suite* are far more common than teapots and matching milk or cream jugs until far later in the century. Rare matching sets of tea and coffee pots were undoubtedly made as early as the Queen Anne period, and may cast some light on the small covered jugs, generally called milk jugs today, which were made to match contemporary tea-pots. It seems more likely, however, that these were in fact for strong black coffee, taken Turkish-style and well sweetened, since the surviving sets include a covered sugar bowl and not the type of small jug suitable for cream or milk.

In Scotland, tea-drinking caught on fast, and as early as 1729 a disconsolate Scot wrote that '... in lieu of a dram of good wholesome Scots spirits, there is now the tea-kettle put to the fire, the tea-table and silver and china equipage brought in ...'. Scottish tea-pots seem to have been of larger capacity than their English counterparts, and while the English soon added a tea urn to their equipage, in Scotland a tea kettle was a more standard piece of para-phernalia for serious tea drinkers.

Signs of authenticity

1. Britannia Standard marks 1697–*c*.1720.
2. Full set of hallmarks on base inside foot rim.
3. Rare but occasionally marked near top of body to one side of handle socket.
4. Spout cast in two halves, seamed vertically on join.
5. Punched strainer fillet soldered to interior of body.
6. Maker's mark and lion's head erased on lid 1697–*c*.1720 – with sterling lion passant guardant after that date.
7. Foot rim made separately and applied to body.
8. Silver pins securing ebony, fruitwood handle in socket.
9. Stand-away hinge soldered to upper handle socket and lid.
10. Finial cast separately and soldered to high domed lid.
11. Small capacity at this period – $4\frac{1}{2}$–6 in (11.5–15 cm) high including finial and domed lid.
12. Either full armorials or crest on body – rarer on lid.

Likely restoration and repair
13. Weakest points on body round spout, handle sockets – check for signs of splitting, cracking, leaks.
14. Foot rim replaced.
15. Signs of tampering, heavy soldering, round hinge – may have been replaced, restored.
16. Later engraved armorials – considerably reduces value.
17. Interior deliberately tinned, stained to conceal repairs.
18. No seaming visible down cast spout – entire piece may have been electroplated to conceal extensive repair, restoration.

Construction and materials

The bodies and high domed lids of early teapots were raised from a single sheet with no seams. Occasionally the lid may have been cast but this is rarely found. Spouts were cast in two halves vertically and soldered together with a brass/silver alloy. Pierced strainer fillets were soldered over the interior of the hole for the spout, which was also firmly soldered to the body. Handle sockets were made separately, and polished ebony or ebonised fruitwood handles were fitted into the socket and held in place with stout silver pins. Foot rims were also made separately and applied to the body. On octagonal-shaped teapots it is sometimes found that the lids are completely detachable and have no hinges, but generally lids were hinged until the shape of teapots changed to a more spherical shape around 1725–35.

Decoration

The only decoration to be found on early teapots is an engraved coat of arms or a crest, and this was by no means the rule. The cast spouts nearly always had an animalier head, sometimes hardly recognisable but derived from Chinese porcelain dragon-spouted pots. The spouts themselves are faceted or hexagonal until more spherical-shaped teapots were made, when spouts became straight, tapering from a generous diameter at the base.

Variations

The most delightful variation on the plain, pear-shaped teapot occurred from about 1710 to 1725, when for a short period the silversmiths embarked on octagonal and hexagonal shapes which were not repeated in later years. Octagonal teapots were usually of heavier weight, and sometimes have a line of double moulding around the body as well as on the rims of both body and lid. The shape was not easy to achieve with sheet metal, and sometimes the lids were cast, although this is uncommon. Spouts lost their animalier shape, and often had tiny little lids over the opening to keep in the heat. Foot rims were octagonal, and armorials are more common than on earlier plain, pear-shaped teapots.

Reproductions

So closely did Victorian copies of 'Queen Anne' teapots follow the originals in form that they might almost be called facsimiles. There are slight but obvious differences, however, which can soon be spotted – such as the shape of the foot rim, the rather more bun-shaped lid (usually without an applied rim), more button-shaped finials, and the proportions, which are just not quite perfect. Octagonal shapes were very seldom reproduced, since they are difficult to make with any degree of success.

'Queen Anne' teapot with a silver handle in Britannia Standard silver, of a type made at the turn of the century and in the 1920s. 6¼ in (16 cm) high.

Octagonal-shaped early Georgian teapot with high domed lid and standaway hinge engraved with contemporary armorials. London 1719. 6¼ in (16 cm) high.

Octagonal covered jug with spreading foot, engraved with contemporary initials just below the cast lip, and with a later crest on either side. c.1710. 5¼ in (13.5 cm) high.

Price bands

Queen Anne, £2,800–£4,000.
Octagonal, faceted,
£3,200–£5,000.

19th-century reproductions,
£390–£480.

Britannia Standard
reproductions, £480–£750.

119

Teapots 1730–1770

Signs of authenticity

1. Full set of hallmarks for sterling silver on underside of body inside foot rim.
2. Maker's mark and sterling lion passant guardant on lid, if hinged.
3. On detachable lids, full set may be struck.
4. Flush hinges and slightly convex lids, following spherical outline of body.
5. Foot rim cast and applied to body.
6. Spouts cast in two halves, seamed vertically.
7. Collar round base of spout on many examples to strengthen join.
8. Band of engraved decoration round top of body with design continuing on lid and often over flush hinge.
9. Rather heavy ebony or fruitwood handles pinned to handle sockets with silver pins.
10. On teapots with silver handles, ivory or bone collar to prevent heat being conducted round handle.

Likely restoration and repair
11. Flush hinges to lids damaged, repaired, restored. Examine hallmarks closely if decorative engraving breaks over the hinge, indicating repair or replacement.
12. Handle sockets weak point – likely area for repair.
13. Heavy soldering round spout base and join – cracks and splits repaired, restored.
14. Foot rims dented, beaten out or partly restored.
15. Tip of spout damaged, tampered with to conceal rebuilding, restoration, repair.
16. On teapots with detachable lids, examine hallmarks closely in case it is a 'marriage' from another piece, or a complete replacement.

By mid-century the price of tea had tumbled and Doctors of Physick had become alarmed at the effects of this 'deleterious produce' of China, which they classified together with gin and blamed for sapping the strength of England's toiling masses. The upper echelons of society were counselled to dilute this strong drug with cream, while the rest of the population was advised to drink beer, which was considered to be their proper beverage. But by the 1750s tea had taken the place of beer for a large proportion of the populace – not 'fine hyson tea, sweetened with refined sugar and softened with cream, but ... spring water, just coloured with a few leaves of the lowest price tea, sweetened with the brownest sugar'.

Although it cannot be said with certainty that the spherical or bullet-shaped teapot originated in Scotland, it was certainly more common there at an earlier period than in England. The Scottish method of making tea differed from the English in that they made or 'mashed' their tea in a tea kettle and then poured it into a teapot – possibly the reason that silver-handled teapots were made in Scotland and not in England, where boiling water was poured from a tea urn directly on to the tea leaves in the pot. Teapots with matching spherical cream jugs seem to have been made from about 1735 onwards.

Between about 1755 and 1770 there is a remarkable dearth of silver teapots, and while it cannot be proved with any accurate documentation, the cause would seem to be the meteoric rise in popularity for 'china' teapots, first in red stoneware from Staffordshire and then from the Worcester porcelain factory, which dominated the market throughout this period.

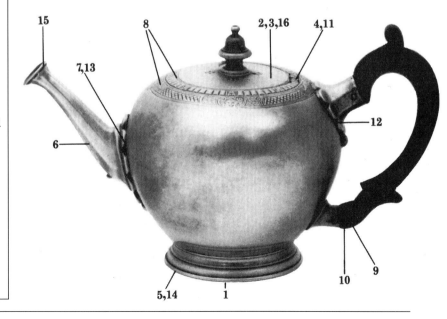

Construction and materials

Bullet-shaped teapots, which date from as early as the second decade of the eighteenth century, may be made in higher-standard Britannia silver, but they are very rare and mostly made by silversmiths of Huguenot descent. This is the most likely explanation of that particular shape becoming popular in Scotland before it was accepted in England – French links with Scotland were still very close at that time. It is more likely that teapots of this period will be dated after 1720 and have the sterling lion passant guardant.

Bodies were hammered up in a single piece without seams. Foot rims were cast and applied, and spouts were cast in two halves and seamed vertically. Handle sockets were soldered on to the body and wooden handles held in place with silver pins. The flush hinges are remarkable for their workmanship. Finials were either simple shapes in cast metal, or turned wooden finials with a silver shank joining them to the lid.

Decoration

On bullet-shaped teapots, bands of engraving encircled the rim of the body and continued over the flush hinge, with the pattern continuing over the lid, broken with a narrow border wholly in keeping with the engraved design. On the inverted pear-shaped teapot, decoration was florid and, where successful, fully rococo from leaf-wrapped spout to leaf-capped handle sockets. Finials were frequently in the shape of buds, acorns or, on Scottish examples, more decorative and often in the shape of a perching bird.

Reproductions

Bullet-shaped teapots more or less ceased to be popular after about 1745, but they continued to be made in Scotland for another 20 years. They were among the most common pieces to be made by 'duty dodgers' – a fact that has been used to advantage by some unscrupulous people in recent years. Duty was imposed between 1719 and 1758, during which period many silversmiths transposed marks from small pieces on which duty had been paid to larger pieces, thus evading a considerable amount of tax. This practice has resulted in marks being openly 'let in' at a far later date, and false claims as to the piece's antiquity being made.

Price bands

Bullet-shaped, £2,500–£3,200.
Rococo, £1,000–£1,800.
Drum, £850–£2,000.

Variations

For a brief period in the early 1750s silversmiths tried to design teapots to conform to the lines of other fashionable silver of the period. The inverted pear-shape with rococo decoration was only successful in the hands of a master craftsman, however, and many versions of this shape are strangely inelegant.

In Scotland this form of teapot was made in considerable quantities, of larger capacity than English versions, and often with extremely flamboyant finials in the shape of perching birds. Where the spouts were not wholeheartedly rococo with leaf-wrapped bases and scrolls, they were often cast with shallow flutes on the base, narrowing to a beaked shape at the tip. Scottish examples are more likely to have silver handles with ivory or bone insulating collars than English teapots of this form.

Below left *Bullet-shaped teapot with a straight spout and an engraved band round the upper body and lid, with a spool finial. London 1714. 3¾in (9.5cm) high.*

Centre *Inverted pear shape with leaf-wrapped spout and handle sockets, chased with rococo scrolls, with a cast bud finial. London 1750. 6in (15cm) high.*

Below *Another of the same shape, but made in the 19th century from an 18th-century body by John Emes, with cover, spout and foot by Lias Brothers. London 1877. 5¾in (14.5cm) high.*

Teapots 1770–1840

The famous Boston Tea Party of 1773 which foreshadowed the American War of Independence was caused by the enormous duty being levied on tea by the British Government. 'John sent the tea from o'er the sea with heavy duties rated; but whether hyson or bohea I've never heard it stated.' The infamous duty of 119 per cent which was levied on English tea drinkers coincided with the opening of the canal system and the flooding of home markets with creamware, porcelain and pottery teapots, now available to all and sundry instead of to the exclusive minority. The latter, preserving their superiority at all costs, began to return to silver teapots and tea services, and from the 1770s onwards there was a remarkable increase in the manufacture of tea ware in silver plate.

The first of the new wave of teapots were drum-shaped, handsome and of heavy gauge silver, but within the decade a lighter, oval shape took its place and continued to be the most popular form for the next 25 years. Sometimes decorated with bright cut engraving, sometimes with beaded rims, they were originally supplied with small stands to raise them off polished surfaces and prevent their flat bases from damaging glossy tables. By the 1790s the angular lines were softened into a curved boat shape with a swan-necked curving spout, standing on four small ball feet. In the last few years of the eighteenth century the first of the long line of half-reeded teapots were being made, also exaggerated into pronounced lobing and a more bulbous shape known as the half-melon.

By 1825, with new mass-production techniques of manufacture in full swing, teapots and tea services were heavily decorated with stamped embossed flutes, flowers and rococo revival motifs. Chinoiserie and japonaiserie decoration in chased all-over designs, sometimes mixed with elements from other, earlier periods was also a common feature.

Signs of authenticity

1. Full set of hallmarks on base or side of body, including sovereign's head duty mark from 1784.
2. Maker's mark, duty mark and lion passant guardant on lids.
3. On detachable cast finials, maker's mark and sterling lion passant guardant.
4. Reintroduction of flush hinges from c.1780.
5. On teapots with flat bases, good signs of wear through age and use.
6. Spouts, handle sockets no longer cast but made from sheet metal, seamed down the join.
7. Bright cut engraving from c.1785.
8. Armorials, crests, initials, monograms contemporary, with correct style, cartouche and design.

Likely restoration and repair

9. Bases damaged, dented, beaten out. May not be entirely watertight.
10. Handle sockets split down seam and resoldered, repaired, restored.
11. Spouts split, bent at tip, beaten out and cut down if damage is too bad to repair.
12. Armorials, crests, initials later engraved – reduces value.
13. Many teapots in last decade of eighteenth century of flimsy construction, thin gauge silver, reinforced with rim wires, mouth wires, and although by highly sought-after named makers should be viewed with critical eye for weaknesses, leaks, splitting and damage, repair, restoration.

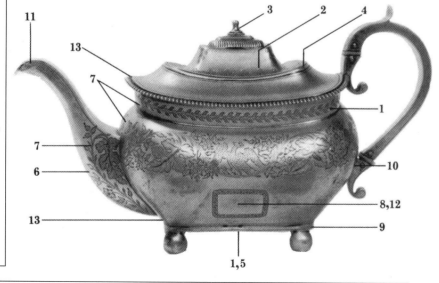

Construction and materials

The most desirable examples are the round drum-shaped teapots of heavy gauge silver, often made with ivory or bone handles and finials. From the 1780s, with the newly installed 'flatting mills' for rolling silver, teapots and tea services were made with much thinner gauge metal, beguilingly decorated with bright cut engraving which makes them look more costly than they are. Flush leaf hinges were made mechanically, handle sockets, sleeves and spouts were made from sheet silver seamed on the under-surfaces, and decorative beaded or reeded rim wires, mouth wires and foot rims were stamped and applied. From about 1810 onwards many better-quality teapots had silver handles with insulating collars, the first of which were cast in solid silver, but soon, like many other items, they were stamped out in two halves and seamed together, sometimes with a filling of lead solder to add weight to the piece.

Decoration
Once the surface of teapots began to be decorated, from c.1780–85 onwards, the variety became wider and wider. Adam-style bright cut engraving gave way to an extreme rococo revival style after the relatively simple lines of fluted and lobed shapes had had a brief popularity. Later in the nineteenth century not only were Chinese and Japanese motifs pressed into service but also Gothic, floral, and almost every shape and style imaginable. Among the finest and most restrained were the many 'Queen Anne' tea services, which are a welcome relief from the overburdened forms of the Victorian era.

Reproductions

Sterling silver versions of 'Queen Anne' tea ware, with neat acorn finials, are among the best-known reproductions – although in fact no tea services were ever made in the original plain shapes, only teapots. It is not unknown for wealthy families to have added to their original early-eighteenth-century teapots, commissioning other pieces to make up full tea services with derivative pieces from famous retail shops and large companies at a much later date. If these pieces ever come on the market divorced from their original teapots, they may present quite a problem to novice collectors.

Price bands

Oval, £650–£950.
Bright cut engraving, £780–£1,100.
Regency, £650–£1,500.
Melon, reeded, £380–£550.
Tea sets, £420 and upwards.
Fused plate, £280–£400.
Electroplate, from £140.

Variations

Tea and coffee services, many of which have been split up into their component parts, abound from the 1820s onwards. Also made from this period onwards are bachelors' tea sets of slightly smaller capacity than tea services, and cabaret sets complete with matching trays.

Both fused plate and electroplate teapots and tea services were made in considerable quantities, generally in matching sets complete with tea trays, from the late 1790s onwards, and in electroplate from the 1840s. Among the most popular designs were the half-reeded and lobed patterns, still to be encountered in smart tea rooms and hotels.

Victorian tea service with applied decorative rims, each piece standing on four small feet, with silver handles and ivory collars. c.1859.

Below *Compressed oval drum-shaped teapot with straight tapering spout and domed hinged lid. The body is decorated with bright cut engraving. London 1792. 5¾ in (14.5 cm) high.*

Coffee pots 1680–1740

1. Hallmarks of Britannia and lion's head erased 1697–c.1720.
2. Maker's mark, date letter, sterling and town mark – struck on base in rather random fashion, or near top of body to one side of handle in relatively straight line.
3. Spout cast in two halves and seamed vertically.
4. Body made in sheet, seamed down the back under the handle.
5. Handle sockets soldered to body, sometimes with circular reinforcing plate.
6. Handle secured by strong silver pins.
7. Stand-away hinge sometimes with removable pin to facilitate washing, cleaning of lid.
8. Lion's head erased and maker's mark struck on lid during Britannia Standard period 1697–c.1720.
9. Maker's mark and sterling lion passant guardant after that date.
10. Finials cast and soldered to lids.

Likely restoration and repair
11. Foot rims dented, battered, repaired with heavy solder on underside – sometimes restored, replaced.
12. Cracking, splitting, weakening round handle joints – extra reinforcing plate may have been added when repaired at later date.
13. Original handles split, broken and replaced – wood should be smooth to the touch.
14. Area round top of lid under finial tampered with – finial refixed, replaced.
15. Weak area round base originally soldered in, not raised from single sheet – check for splitting, leaks, heavy restoration inside.

When it was first introduced into England from Turkey and the Middle East, coffee was considered manly, potent and stimulating. Coffee beans were chewed on long journeys by the hardy explorers of the early seventeenth century, and John Evelyn records having seen coffee being drunk in Balliol College, Oxford in 1637. Indeed, the first English coffee house established in 1650 was The Angel in Oxford. London's first coffee house was opened two years later, in Cornhill in the City.

In 1663 coffee houses came under the same regulations as licenced premises selling alcohol, and by the end of the seventeenth century coffee was highly esteemed as a restorative for heavy drinkers.

Like tea, coffee was taken in a china dish. No silver coffee pots survive dating from before the Restoration of 1660 – the earliest known example is dated 1681. It is tall, tapering, with a sharply pointed domed lid – a common form in Turkey even today. Continental coffee pots were generally made with handles at right angles to the spout and early versions made in England by Huguenot silversmiths tend to follow this pattern.

By the time that coffee pots were being made in any quantity the fashion for cut card work had largely passed, but there are some examples, rare to find, with cut card work round the spout and handle sockets as well as on the domed covers.

Construction and materials

Simple cylindrical coffee pots, as well as the more adventurous octagonal form, were made from heavy gauge sheet silver soldered together with a brass/silver alloy, usually on the line of the handle. The circular base was then soldered into the resulting tapering cylinder shape. The foot rim was cast and applied separately, along with the spout, which, like early teapots, often had an animalier form and was softly faceted. Additional rim wires were applied to the top of the body and the base of the lid – sheet silver has not been subjected to repeated hammering and annealing and splits more easily. Some stand-away hinges had removable pins so that the lids could be properly cleaned, but this is more often found on chocolate pots than coffee pots.

Decoration

Virtually the only decoration on these early straight-sided coffee pots was an engraved armorial. Some spouts were leaf-wrapped, some simply faceted and some fluted or partly fluted. The shape of the lid changed from a high dome to a more flattened bun-shape with a single step, and then to an even more flattened pattern, while handle sockets developed a more elegant shape, changing from a plain sleeve to a scrolling shape towards the beginning of the 1730s.

Variations

Pots of identical shape and form, but with finials on hinged plates were intended for chocolate, which enjoyed a brief reign of public popularity at the beginning of the eighteenth century, when 'chocolate houses' were almost as common as coffee houses. It was not an easy drink to make, since chocolate was not defatted and eggs were essential to hold the coarsely grated untreated chocolate in suspension. The chocolate served in the 1720s was made with plain hot water to dissolve the grated chocolate, with a strong measure of brandy, sherry or port wine added to the brew. The hinged finial was to allow a whisk, similar to a swizzle stick, to be held in the pot and twirled to prevent the chocolate from separating and sinking to the bottom.

Coffee pot with ivory handle at right angles to the curved faceted spout with animalier head. London 1719. 9½ in (24 cm) high.

Tapered cylindrical shape with fluted spout. The armorials and rococo cartouche are contemporary. London 1740. 8½ in (21.5 cm) high.

Reproductions

There was a great vogue for copies of these delightfully plain coffee pots at several periods. In the early nineteenth century, made in pairs for coffee and hot milk, they were produced in fused plate, with handles at right angles to the straight spouts. And in the first decade of the twentieth century the well-established goldsmiths' and silversmiths' companies of Bond Street and Regent Street made reproductions for the American market as well as for wealthy clients – a vogue which repeated itself during the 1920s.

Reproduction coffee pot which mixes two styles: the early tapering body with a later leaf-wrapped spout with shell mouldings. A. & F. Parsons for Tessiers Ltd. London 1936. 8½ in (21.5 cm) high.

Price bands

Queen Anne, £3,800–£5,000.
Octagonal, faceted, £5,000–£8,000 +.
Early baluster, £850–£3,500.
Tapered cylindrical, £2,000–£3,800.

Fused plate, same patterns, £180–£450.

Reproductions, £300–£500 +.

Late engraved armorials can reduce value by as much as 50%.

Coffee pots 1740–1770

Signs of authenticity

1. Hallmarks struck near rim of body, to one side of handle. Occasionally may be struck on underside of base.
2. No sign of vertical seaming down body on good-quality coffee pots.
3. Spouts cast in two halves, soldered vertically.
4. Handle sockets cast and applied to body, often with small circular reinforcing plate.
5. Maker's mark and lion passant guardant struck on inside of lids.
6. Foot rims cast and applied – soldered to body with silver/brass alloy.
7. Cast finials also soldered neatly to lids.
8. Correct style, cartouche for contemporary armorials.

Likely restoration and repair
9. Foot rims dented, battered – beaten out, restored, sometimes completely replaced.
10. Plain pots later embossed, often with consequent weakening of silver, stretching, splitting. If design does not betray late origins, inner surface of pot may be better guide.
11. Signs of tampering, repairs, round base of spout. Spout removed, body repaired and spout replaced.
12. Spouts made by specialist spout makers – many to identical patterns. May be a 'marriage' from a badly damaged body of the same period.
13. On full-blown rococo decoration, cartouches vacant – check thickness of metal for signs of armorials removed.
14. Full armorials the general rule to c.1770 – if engraved with crest only, check authenticity to ensure that it has not been later engraved.

While pottery and porcelain captured the market for tea ware, coffee pots continued to be made in silver throughout the Georgian period, although it remained a drink for the gentry rather than the general populace. This was not because of the expense – coffee was made with a bare three ounces of ground coffee to a quart of water, and best Turkish coffee cost four shillings and sixpence a pound in the 1750s – it was the inconvenience which told against it.

The size of coffee pots seems to have changed very little over the years, although at the very beginning of the eighteenth century it is recorded that individual members of wealthy households had their own personal coffee pots which were almost certainly smaller. By mid-century it had become a breakfast drink for the gentry, much preferred to tea at that hour of the day.

By the 1740s, coffee pots had tucked-in bodies and had become more decorative and ornate. Spouts were leaf-wrapped, swirled, fluted or shell-shaped to balance scrolling socket handles, and elaborate rococo chasing and cartouches adorned the bodies. By the 1750s the bodies had become more baluster-shaped, with spreading foot and stepped domed lids, changing imperceptibly to a pear shape by the 1760s, with a slightly raised foot, often gadrooned.

Construction and materials

From the time that the first slightly curved, tuck-in bodies were made, coffee pots were hammered up on the sinking block and the raising stake from a single piece with no seams. Towards the very end of this period, however, thinner gauge coffee pots were made using the old method of a single sheet soldered vertically and then shaped over a raising stake. This method resulted in bodies that were far less springy and strong and more subject to cracking due to the difference in structure of metal which has not been repeatedly heated and annealed. On these pots, the base may be made as an integral part of the foot, and cracks may appear where it has been soldered and joined. There should be no seams on the lid, and finials and their reinforcing plates should be firmly and cleanly soldered with no signs of any joining on the inner surface.

Decoration

Plain-surfaced baluster- or pear-shaped coffee pots may have gadrooned rims to the top of the body and foot rims. The spouts are more beak-shaped and pointed, but the curve is still sharp and close to the body. Full-blown rococo decoration should be asymmetric and flowing right round the body. Any symmetry should be viewed with suspicion since it is characteristic of late-embossed Victorian work. Chinoiserie is rare, but enjoyed some popularity with Dublin silversmiths at this period.

Reproductions

Plain and decorated baluster-shaped coffee pots were made in fused plate from the end of the 1760s onwards. The interiors are tinned or, if the tinning has worn off, copper, since the bodies were always made of single-faced plate.

In sterling silver many fine Georgian forms have been beautifully reproduced by well-established goldsmiths and silversmiths. Recent reproductions do not, of course, have the sovereign's head duty mark included in the hallmarks – this was not struck after 1890.

Good reproduction of a mid-18th-century coffee pot with leaf-wrapped spout and spreading base. Mappin & Webb. London 1965. 11 in (28 cm) high.

Variations

Hot-water jugs of the same period which are found under a separate section on p. 94 might confuse those unfamiliar with the different forms, but they are quite distinct in having a lip as opposed to a spout, and their handles are often a simple strip of silver wrapped with cane. The Scots continued to drink chocolate from silver pots long after the English had ceased to make special chocolate pots. This may cause confusion because of the squatter baluster-shaped bodies decorated with sparse rococo chasing, until the detachable finial with a hole for the moliquet is taken into consideration, when all will become clear.

Early curved shape, with tuck-in body and plain spreading foot. The engraved armorials and formal cartouche are contemporary. London 1745. 9¾ in (25 cm) high.

Richly decorated coffee pot in full rococo taste, with a very decorative cast spout. Gabriel Sleath. 1739. 9½ in (24 cm) high.

Price bands

Georgian tuck-in base, £1,000–£2,500.
Rococo, £1,500–£4,000 + .
Baluster, £1,200–£2,800.

Fused plate, same patterns, £180–£500.

Electroplate, £50–£210.

Coffee pots 1770–1840

Signs of authenticity

1. Full set of hallmarks usually on outer side of foot rim or on underside of base.
2. Must include sovereign's head duty mark after 1784.
3. On fine examples, spouts cast in two halves and soldered together with vertical seam.
4. On more mass-produced examples, spouts stamped from sheet and brazed together.
5. Applied girdles of beaded or reeded wire round widest part of vase shape add strength as well as decoration.
6. Applied rim wires round mouth of vessel.
7. Finials cast and fixed to lids with threads and small nuts after c.1800.
8. Wooden finials not common much before c.1800.
9. Silver handles from c.1805 should have maker's mark, sterling lion and sovereign's head duty mark.

Likely restoration and repair
10. Weakest areas round base of body where it joins pedestal, base of spout and handle joins. Check carefully for signs of splitting, cracking and repair, restoration.
11. Areas which have been restored, repaired should show up when breathed on.
12. Signs of repairing, beaten-out denting visible on inside. Recent tinning, staining may conceal extensive repairs.
13. On fused plate, bases, lids stamped from two sheets of single-faced plate back-to-back. No raw copper core should be visible.
14. On fused plate, definite pinkish tinge, light weight, no decoration on surface – possibly poor-quality imported French plate c.1800–10.

It took some time for the breach between America and England to heal after the War of Independence – a period during which, incidentally, coffee became the national drink of the Americans, who were temporarily deprived of tea. By the end of the eighteenth century, however, coffee was being grown in America and in Latin America, and was readily available, roasted, ground and packaged, from tea and coffee merchants everywhere in the British Isles. For breakfast, coffee was served with hot milk; after dinner a richer, stronger blend was served black or with cream for the ladies.

The inevitable transformation of the shape of coffee pots into vase and urn forms took place from the end of the 1760s onwards, in line with other domestic silver. By the nineteenth century most coffee was percolated and then transferred to a silver coffee pot. Many coffee pots of this period are light in weight, with little embellishment, often made using mass-production techniques to the detriment of design and proportion. Many versions of the pedestal-footed coffee pot were made in pairs with a jug for hot milk – poured simultaneously by a servant – often made in fused plate, not only for private households but for hotels, restaurants and institutions.

Construction and materials

There can be little doubt about genuine good-quality pieces in early vase and urn shapes. The weight is still considerable, the finish and applied detail is finely made, and the pedestal bases are sufficiently large and heavy to make these pots practical and functional. Later, lighter-weight versions made from c.1790 onwards are often made in rolled silver plate with lids stamped out and not hammered up by hand. From about 1795 coffee pots were made as part of tea and coffee sets, with surface design, fluting, reeding and lobing to match teapots of the same period. While some of them are well balanced and well proportioned, others, particularly those made in fused plate, have feet which are too small in diameter for their light weight, and tend to be unsuitable for use because of their instability.

Decoration
Early Adam-style coffee pots of high quality may be elegantly embellished with typical swags and drapes, and engraved with initials or monograms within a wreath or medallion shape. Once coffee pots had become part of sets, the lower part of their bodies were often fluted, reeded or lobed in a half-melon design to match teapots. Beaded borders and girdles were popular between c.1775 and 1785, with the beading becoming less generous and more mechanical as the years went by. Handles often had a small flying scroll, in fact a thumbpiece, to help in lifting these rather awkward coffee pots.

Variations

At the very end of the eighteenth century a type of squat, lipped jug, often with an angular handle, made its appearance. Known as 'coffee biggins', they were fitted with an inner collar to which was attached a cotton bag to hold the grounds. Coffee biggins were made in silver plate, fused plate and also in tinned iron, and the shape was in many ways far more pleasing than the tall, compressed oval forms on pedestal feet. Many were lobed or reeded on the lower part of the body and on the lids, and their curving beak-shaped spouts were almost entirely enclosed, sometimes with a hinged flap, often an integral part of the spout.

Reproductions

Unwisely perhaps, many of the rather unstable forms from this period continued to be made in both fused plate and electroplate throughout the nineteenth century. The weight of the metal was often too light for them to be very stable, but they endured in one form or another, particularly in hotels, clubs and restaurants, right through to Edwardian times. The vase- or urn-shaped coffee pot from the beginning of this period was less often reproduced, although jugs with lips in this basic form continued to be made for many decades.

Price bands

Pedestal base, Adam-style, £800–£2,500.
Bright cut engraving, £450–£1,400.
Reeded, fluted, lobed, £360–£1,000.

Fused plate, same patterns, £150–£450.

Electroplate, £45–£200.

Coffee biggins, from £380.

Baluster coffee pot with gadrooned foot, engraved with contemporary armorials. Whipham & Wright. London 1761. 10½ in (27 cm) high.

Above *Early 19th-century coffee biggin with a curved lip, lobed base and corded borders. London 1813. 8¾ in (22 cm) high.*

Left *Baluster shape on a spreading foot just beginning to be shaped inwards with a low pedestal. London 1775. 11½ in (29 cm) high.*

Cream and milk jugs 1700–1750

There is no pictorial or documentary evidence that either milk or cream was added to tea or coffee in England much before the 1750s, when tea was blamed for a variety of nervous complaints as a result of its stimulant effect, and milk or cream was added to counteract the effects of tannin. In one isolated case, a painting by William Hogarth in the Tate Gallery of *The Strode Family* dated 1738, there is a small three-footed silver jug on a table where tea is being taken, but its contents remain a mystery. Other contemporary paintings of families taking tea show the full equipage including spoon trays, with the teaspoons left in the tea bowls instead of being placed neatly in saucers, but no small jug of any kind.

Many additional flavourings were added to tea, from spices and cinnamon to a traditional shot of whisky for the last cup in Scotland. What weighs against these small jugs being used for milk is the universal knowledge that fresh milk could and did frequently cause disease and death. On farms and in country houses where conditions in the dairy could be vouched for, fresh milk was drunk practically straight from the cow, but it was more common to skim it for its valuable cream and butter and drink whey or buttermilk, considered efficacious against minor complaints, and health-giving. In towns, however, milk was rarely, if ever, consumed unless boiled, and then generally made into a posset, curdled with wine or ale, or used in cooking. From the scanty evidence available, it would seem more likely that small silver jugs were used, like brandy saucepans, for a small measure of spirits to add to a regular beverage, rather than for milk or cream.

Signs of authenticity

1. Rare to find – Britannia hallmarks on small jugs before *c.*1720.
2. Full set of hallmarks struck on underside of base – occasionally on pitcher-shaped jugs, near top of body in roughly straight line.
3. No vertical seaming on body – jugs raised from single sheet.
4. Foot rims, handles, feet cast and applied.
5. Feet applied low on body with plain or trefid headings.
6. Small size: 3–4 in (7.5–10 cm).
7. Rare to find crests, armorials on such thin gauge silver – occasionally a crest is engraved on round-bellied examples of thicker gauge.
8. Hoof, trefid, pad feet most common at this period – scroll feet, paw feet of later date.

Likely restoration and repair
9. Joins of handles to bodies cracked, torn, repaired.
10. Lower joins similarly damaged – often with recently added small reinforcing plate.
11. Feet bent, damaged, pushed up into body – signs of soldering, patching, visible on inside of body as well as outside, round headings to feet.
12. Feet broken on angle, curve above terminals – repaired, restored.
13. Monogram, initials, crests engraved at later date.
14. On octagonal shapes, spouts, bodies split down ridges of shaping – check for hairline cracks, repairs.

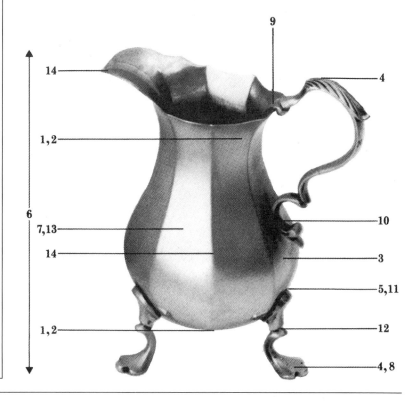

Construction and materials

In general, small jugs of this form from early dates were hammered up from sheet in a single piece, with the rims sometimes reinforced with a simple line of reeded wire. Foot rims were cast and applied, and on pitcher-shaped jugs the lip was made separately and soldered to the body, which was notched to receive it. Handles were cast, and so were the little feet on the three-footed forms. The lower terminal of the handle was sometimes attached to the body with a small reinforcing plate or disc, but this was by no means always the case, and such discs have often been added at a later date as part of a repair. Very rare, extremely ornate small jugs in rococo forms were cast and are of superb workmanship, but the chances of coming across such a piece is remote.

Decoration
Most of these jugs had very little added decoration, but from the 1730s onwards some far grander versions were made in cast silver with shapes derived from more classical origins, with elaborate cast feet and handles, engraved or flat chased with scrolls, shells and swirls.

Reproductions

A more elongated, baluster-shaped pitcher of small size was made in considerable quantities as part of 'Queen Anne' tea services from the Victorian period onwards. They should not be confused with the dumpy little early pitchers, and a very quick glance at the hallmarking will generally reveal a sovereign's head duty mark which places them well outside the period. Little three-footed plain silver jugs do not seem to have been much copied or reproduced, probably because their shape is none too practical, although some small jugs of similar shape were made during the Victorian period.

Small cream jug of 'Queen Anne' form, from a tea service made in Sheffield. 1886. 3¼ in (8 cm) high.

Variations

There is a further conundrum over covered bullet-shaped jugs made at about the same period as early bullet-shaped teapots. They quite often have silver handles, which indicates cold or tepid liquids, although they were also covered, probably for the purpose of keeping the heat in. However, spouted pots of this period in both silver and, slightly later in the eighteenth century, in porcelain, have been catalogued by contemporary hands as 'punch pots', which might provide a satisfactory explanation.

Above Superb early cast silver gilt cream jug, engraved and flat chased with shells and scrolls and rococo cartouche. John Pero, London 1735. 3¾ in (9.5 cm) high.

Price bands

Early baluster, £400–£1,000.
Sparrow-beak, £350–£1,200.
3-footed baluster, £200–£800 + .
Octagonal, faceted,
£1,200–£2,500 + .
Heavy cast rococo,
£500–£900 + .
Bullet, spherical,
£1,200–£2,200.

Reproductions, £60–£180.

Above Pitcher-shaped jug with 'sparrow-beak' spout and an applied cast handle, standing on a spreading foot. London 1736. 3 in (7.5 cm) high.

Left Small bullet-shaped covered jugs seem to have been more common in Scotland, though English examples are known. c.1735. 4 in (10 cm) high.

Cream and milk jugs 1750–1800

The resistance to milk and milk products was still strong in the second half of the eighteenth century – mainly for health reasons. Cream of any kind was in seasonal supply: during the summer flush, which gave rise to so many clotted and scalded cream dishes, the peasant's house cow produced rich milk with enough cream left over from butter-making to pour over fresh fruit. However, 'raw cream, undecocted, eaten with strawberries ... is a rural man's banquet. I have known such banquets hath put men in jeopardy of their lives' – a seventeenth-century condemnation which was still held to be true a century later. In some parts of England, in the West Country particularly, no one heeded such warnings, and small cream jugs assayed at Exeter are a testament to the rich cream from Devonshire and Cornwall.

Fashionable society of the day took the dangers of over-stimulating tea to heart after the 1750s and 'softened' their tea with milk, probably scalded, or with cream. This new fashion can be dated with some accuracy by the appearance, first in silver and then in pottery, of 'cow creamers' – charming little jugs made in the shape of cows whose curled tails provided the handles. High-footed baluster-shaped cream jugs survive in large numbers, many of them embossed and chased with rustic scenes, made in thin sheet silver with punch-beaded rims, dating from the 1760s onwards. Predictably, with the neo-classical fashions of the last quarter of the century, helmet-shaped cream jugs made their appearance, some with the high looping handle of other silverware on rounded or shaped pedestal feet, some with simple beaded rims on square plinth bases.

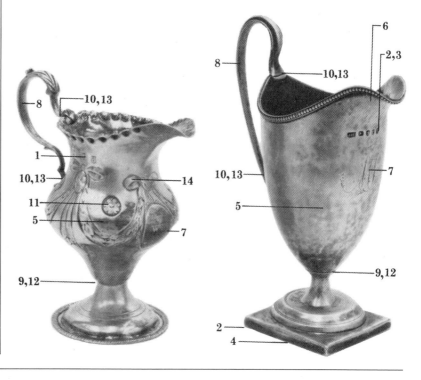

Construction and materials

Almost all small cream jugs of this period are made from thin gauge silver, the body in one piece raised without seams, and the base soldered on, sometimes with a thin line of moulding to conceal the join. Baluster-shaped jugs were not endowed with an extra mouth wire but simply punch-beaded, a fairly crude method of decoration since the reverse side shows as a series of pits and the raised beading effect is seen on the outer edge only. The same treatment was accorded to many lightweight helmet-shaped jugs, but the better-quality versions were reinforced and neatly finished with a beaded or reeded rim wire. On these there may be a line of applied beading or rat-tail down the handle as well.

Decoration
Fairly crude swags and punched flowerheads embellish many baluster-shaped cream jugs, and some, particularly Irish versions, often include little farmyard animals. Bright cut engraving will enhance the value, but only if it is still crisp and sharp, which is rare since these jugs came in for a great deal of use and wear. Flat-bottomed nineteenth-century cream jugs found on their own today are almost always from split-up tea and coffee services.

Reproductions

The makers of fused plate found that helmet-shaped cream jugs were an ideal form for both single- and double-faced plate, although with a little poetic licence they also made them in octagonal shapes, merging two totally different periods together in an entirely original product. Once tea and coffee services came within reach of their market, the plate makers turned out great numbers of matching services which included small jugs in as many shapes and designs as the silversmiths were making.

Victorian cream jug in Gothic revival taste, engraved with Gothic medieval motifs. London·1840. 4½in (11.5cm) high.

Variations

A small number of cream boats for use at table were made during the eighteenth century, and in general there is little to distinguish them from sauce boats except for their slightly smaller size. It is unlikely that the heavy, cast, rococo-style versions will be encountered except on very rare occasions, for they were few in number and have seldom survived – those that do exist are mainly in museums and private collections. The same could almost be said for cast silver 'cow creamers' made in the second half of the eighteenth century, which are rare and extremely expensive. From the 1790s a small quantity of cheap cow creamers were made in die-stamped sheet silver, but they were never as popular as their pottery counterparts. Flimsy and impractical, most of them have long since disintegrated.

Above Helmet-shaped jugs of this pattern were made in Scotland and Ireland, with a shaped base to the pedestal foot. This one is decorated with bright cut engraving and has a reeded rim. Dublin 1794. 5in (12.5cm) high.

Price bands

Late baluster £120–£500.
Plain or embossed, £100–£480.
Helmet, £100–£1,000.
Flat-based, £80–£300.

Victorian, from £50 upwards.

Left *Flat-bottomed cream jugs came into fashion at the very end of the 18th century and remained popular for the next fifty years. This one is decorated with a bright cut engraved wreath cartouche. Exeter c.1800. 3¼in (8cm) high.*

Tea caddies

A few rare tea canisters survive from the end of the seventeenth century, but as they became more widely used from the 1720s onwards, they were generally made in pairs, for Bohea and Hyson tea, or Black and Green, and are sometimes engraved with the initials 'B' and 'G'. Tea canisters were lead-lined and had small removable caps which were used as measures. The tops or bases slid off when they needed to be refilled. By the 1730s, still measuring only about 3–5 in in height, tea canisters were made in sets with sugar canisters, often boxed, and frequently with locks, since tea was still an extremely expensive commodity.

In the 1770s tea was imported via Malaya and Java, packed in miniature tea chests holding a 'kati' of tea – a measure of weight approximately equal to 1⅓ lb – and from that date the word 'caddy' began to replace the older term canister. At about this time the inevitable urn or vase shape came in, far taller and more capacious, measuring anything up to 9 in. By this time Souchon, Pekoe and Congou were among the 'black' teas – the green teas included 'Singlo', 'Twankay' and 'Gunpowder'. Silver drums with stave decoration imitated the miniature tea chests; some were heavily ornate, made in the shape of Chinese pagodas.

Indian tea was imported in the 1830s, followed by Ceylon in the 1870s, by which time it had become fashionable for the ladies to have double casket-shaped caddies holding one blend of China and one of Indian, often in ivory, veneered or Tunbridge ware with two zinc-lined containers.

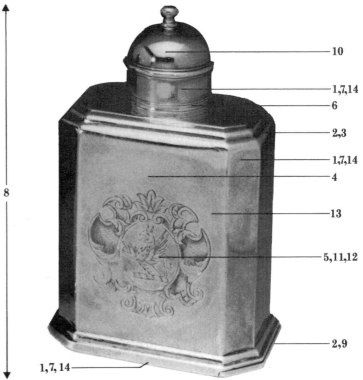

134

Construction and materials

It would be a rare and delightful acquisition – and an expensive one – to find the earliest form of tea canister with sliding base or top and removable cap made in Britannia Standard silver dating from before c.1720. Most tea canisters were made after that date, although such master silversmiths as Paul de Lamerie did continue to use the higher standard for extremely grand cast and chased sets, usually boxed in elaborately decorated caskets. Most tea canisters and caddies are made in sheet silver, embossed and chased – later, from about 1780 onwards, bands of bright cut engraving were used to decorate them. Finials are always cast and sometimes soldered, and in later examples may be fixed to the covers with threads and nuts. There is no hard-and-fast rule about hinges on lids, except that they are seldom found before c.1765.

Decoration
It is only to be expected that chinoiserie decoration was a popular motif for tea canisters and caddies, although this was another rare corner of the silversmith's output which favoured a full-blown rococo style during the mid-eighteenth century. Vase shapes and urn shapes are predictably decorated with swags, festoons, rams' heads and other Adam motifs. From the 1780s far simpler shapes such as the drum and the compressed oval were fashionable, decorated with bands of beading and then with bright cut engraving. During this period they were often fitted with locks.

Reproductions

Some excellent contemporary copies, particularly of simple drum shapes, square boxes and compressed oval tea caddies were made in fused plate, complete with bands of bright cut engraving, and lacking only the cast silver finials – more prosaic finials of turned wood, or bone, ivory or thin stamped silver were more common. Almost all of them were fitted with locks, although boxed pairs were also made, with the lock on the box and not on individual canisters.

Silver biscuit boxes were added to domestic silverware around the 1880s, some of them bearing a close resemblance to earlier designs of tea caddies, particularly those decorated with Victorian rococo revival or chinoiserie motifs. They should not be confused with their genuine earlier counterparts.

Variations

The grandest variations on a simple pair of tea canisters are the large boxed sets which held two canisters, a sugar bowl, half a dozen or more tea spoons, a pair of sugar tongs (or a sugar-sifting spoon, slightly later in period) and a mote spoon for skimming tea leaves from the surface of bowls and cups, with a sharp pointed end to the handle for clearing the spout of blocked leaves. Many of these sets have long since become scattered, their boxes damaged beyond repair, and all the individual items are collected today as separate pieces.

Price bands

Singles:
Queen Anne, early Georgian, £800–£1,200.
Rococo, £800–£3,000.
Drum, oval, square, £300–£1,000 + .
Vase-shaped, £300–£1,000.

Sets of three more than treble.

Far left *Queen Anne canister of plain, square shape engraved with a crest surmounted by a baron's coronet. The lock may have been added at a later date, and the lid hinged – the maker's mark is overstruck with another. London 1707. 4 in (10 cm) high.*

Left *Compressed drum-shaped tea caddy with beaded borders and an urn-shaped finial, fitted with lock and key. London 1785. 5¾ in (14.5 cm) high.*

Caddy spoons

There is a popular myth that caddy spoons were made in the very early days of tea-drinking in Britain, and were shaped like shells in imitation of the real shells packed in the small tea chests from China. There is, however, no proof that this is so – indeed early tea canisters had small cylindrical pull-off lids which seem to be well designed as measures, and the small openings would not have admitted the typical caddy spoon. Even the sumptuous early fitted shagreen cases containing one or two tea canisters and a full equipage do not seem to have included tea caddy spoons.

From the late 1760s, with sets of three urn-shaped or vase-shaped tea and sugar canisters, there was often a long-handled spoon which hooked over the handles, but it was usually pierced like a sugar-sifting spoon, and cannot really be called a caddy spoon, although in all likelihood such spoons may have been used for tea leaves, with which there was usually also a fair amount of dust.

The characteristic small short-handled caddy spoon seems to date from the 1770s, when tea began to be imported from Malaya and Java – and the word 'caddy' replaced the earlier 'canister'. This date also coincides with individual caddies fitted with locks. An enormous variety of shell and leaf shapes were made and there was also a rather inexplicable fashion for caddy spoons in the shape of jockey caps, some of which were made in very fine filigree silver by the Birmingham silversmiths from about 1800 onwards. Caddy spoons became a popular and profitable line of 'toys' or 'smalls' from Birmingham; from the 1790s onwards they were primarily die-stamped and produced at very reasonable prices.

Signs of authenticity

1. Minimum hallmarking of maker's mark and sterling lion passant guardant – on base of stem or back of bowl.
2. May be found without sovereign's head duty mark between 1784 and 1790, but exemption from duty withdrawn after that date.
3. When made by Birmingham and Sheffield, double duty mark found the year that duty was doubled, 1797.
4. No seams, joins between stem and bowl – stamped or raised from single piece.
5. Much less common, heavy cast caddy spoons.
6. Hallmarking often considerably worn through use.
7. Bright cut engraving in bowl of spoon, or on stem from *c.*1780.
8. Rare forms include bird's wing, shell with serpent handle, and jockey cap – particular attention should be paid to authenticity.

Likely restoration and repair
9. On shovel-shaped spoons, handle often made separately, in silver, mother-of-pearl or coral. May have broken at join and been repaired, restored, replaced.
10. Often given as gifts with initials, monograms engraved: later engraving lowers value.
11. Most popular patterns made in great quantities – extra value for those with rare, unusual shapes, engraving, decoration.
12. From *c.*1830 also made in fused plate with British Plate base metal.

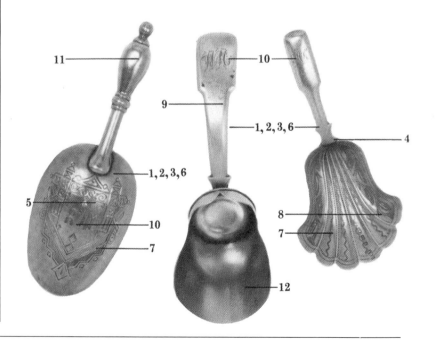

Construction and materials

Caddy spoons were almost without exception made in one piece, apart from those shovel-shaped versions which have either a hollow silver handle or a handle of bone, ivory, mother-of-pearl, coral or rarer materials such as agate. Occasionally they were cast and are of a heavier weight than those made in sheet metal, but in general they were die-stamped and hand-finished, with lines of reeding or feather-edging, or with stems conforming to sets of flatware. Others may have twining stems to leaf-shaped bowls, or bright cut engraving decorating bowls and flattened handles.

Decoration
There is a wide variety of themes, from those associated with leaves and tendrils to flower-embossed, shields, shells, and bright cut embellishment, although it is curious that chinoiserie patterns are remarkably rare. Nor do there seem to have been caddy spoons marked with the most popular blend names or countries of origin, even after tea was being grown and imported from India in the 1830s. Caddy spoons seem to have ignored their function in terms of their decoration.

Reproductions

From about 1830 heavyweight caddy spoons were made in fused plate on a white metal alloy known as British Plate. Earlier fused plate examples were not very practical because of the soft nature of the copper or copper/brass core, which bent easily, and was not very suitable for scooping. Caddy spoons continued to be made right through the nineteenth century and into the Edwardian period – they seem to have gone out of fashion during the last 50 years or so, but reproductions have certainly been made in recent years.

Price bands

Late 18th-century:
Heavy quality, £90–£150.
Filigree mint condition, £80–£200.
Shell, scallop, £50–£120.

19th-century:
Shovel, £40–£90.
Shell, scallop, £40–£120.
Leaf, £60–£120.

Fused plate, £25–£65.

Collector's market – rare examples as much as £300 + .

Variations

Occasionally one will come across silver gilt examples of caddy spoons with rare semi-precious handles, such as agate or coral. These variations tend to be the shovel-shaped patterns. Also rare to find are those with filigree work as part or all of the spoon – because of their delicate structure they have not endured as well as their more ordinary counterparts in die-stamped silver or those which were cast in solid metal.

Shovel, shell and leaf patterns were made extensively from the end of the 18th century to the beginning of the 19th century in London, Birmingham and Sheffield, 1780–1815. The design became more elaborate in the mid-19th century.

Apostle spoons 1500–1660

Signs of authenticity

1. Town mark in bowl of spoon.
2. Maker's mark, date letter and sterling lion passant guardant on back of stem.
3. Size about 7 in (18 cm).
4. Very concave sides to bowl.
5. Apostle finial cast separately and joined to stem with a V-joint on London-made spoons, with rare exceptions.
6. Finial joined to stem with lap-joint on provincial spoons almost invariably.
7. Steeply curving shape of bowl from base of stem.
8. No sign of joins between base of stem and bowl.
9. Nimbus or halo pierced like tiny cartwheel in very early examples.
10. Nimbus no longer pierced towards end of 16th century – solid disc with imprint of 'dove descending' symbolising Holy Spirit.
11. On provincial spoons, town mark in bowl often unidentifiable – may be maker's mark or badly struck town mark.

Likely restoration and repair
12. London mark of 'leopard's head' on stem with lap-jointed terminal – most unlikely to be authentic, more likely to be a 'marriage' of finial.
13. Marks struck just below finial joint – apostle figure added to plain slip-top spoon.
14. Any signs of tampering, seaming, joining between finial, stem and bowl – two spoons married up.
15. The rounder the shoulders of the bowl, the later the date – spoons of later periods may have been altered by hammering stem into hexagonal shape, casting up finial from an early example and applying with correct V-joint or lap joint.

Although not the earliest recorded spoon pattern, probably the best-known spoons are the apostle spoons, which were certainly being made from 1500 onwards, if not earlier. The first spoon pattern mentioned as it were by name was the 'maidenhead' spoon with the head of the Virgin Mary as a finial, which was bequeathed in a will of 1446. Apostle spoons were a traditional gift of godparents to a child at a christening. A full set numbers 13 and not 12, and such a rich gift might be given by wealthy godparents. At the very least, one, the child's patron saint, would be enough.

Full surviving sets of 13 are extremely rare from the sixteenth century – a complete complement of saints is as follows: St James the Less, St Bartholomew, St Peter, St Jude, St James the Greater, St Philip, The Saviour, St John, St Thomas, St Matthew, St Matthias, St Simon Zelotes and St Andrew. Not in fact apostles, but disciples. Some sets or part-sets surviving have St Paul in place of St Jude, and St Mark and St Luke instead of St Simon and St Matthias.

It seems that the tradition of giving them as christening gifts had virtually died out by the Restoration in 1660, although there is a single St James surviving with a date of 1665. It has been claimed that 'slip-top' or 'Puritan' spoons were no more than apostle spoons with their finials lopped off during the Commonwealth. But slip-top spoons have been recorded as early as 1500, with the added authentication of being marked with the date letter at the end of the handle.

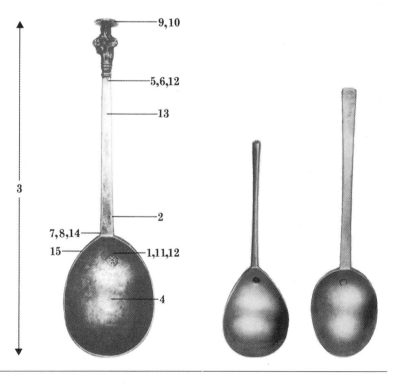

Construction and materials

London-made spoons have certain distinctions in construction: the finial bearing the apostle figure is joined to the shaft with a V-joint. On provincial apostle spoons the join is almost invariably a lap-joint – that is to say that the top of the stem and the base of the finial were cut away in two L-shapes which fitted together.

Spoons were made from a single piece of silver – one part being drawn out to form the stem and the remaining piece being hammered into a shaped lead die to form the bowl. Early spoons have hexagonal stems and the town mark is struck at the top of the bowl with a maker's mark, date letter and town mark at the base of the stem when made in London. Provincial spoons are less easy to identify – many of them have only a mark of some description in the bowl or at the base of the stem which might be either a town mark or a maker's mark.

Decoration

The saints can be identified by the symbolic objects which they hold – there may be some slight variations but the most recognisable and well documented are shown below. Occasionally the back of the bowl will be pricked with the initials of the owner – otherwise there is no other decoration.

Reproductions

Almost everyone has seen sets of so-called 'apostle spoons' varying from extremely expensive facsimiles to cheap and nasty versions with an anonymous robed figure identical on every spoon, stamped from silver, fused plate or electroplate, usually the size of teaspoons. There is little need to explain the difference. In recent years, however, some extremely deceptive copies of early spoons have filtered on to the market and although the source has now been discovered and dealt with, no one is entirely sure that all of these deliberately fraudulent early spoons have been traced and taken off the market.

Variations

The earliest silver spoons with cast finials are the rare 'maidenhead' spoons with a head of the Virgin Mary as a finial. The 'lion sejant' or seated lion finial was also contemporary with apostle spoons – a heraldic lion seated facing the front, occasionally with a shield between its paws. More well known are the seal top, made up to about 1660, with a flat disc terminal on which the owner's initials may be pricked, stamped or engraved. The more pronounced the vase shape beneath the disc, the later the spoon. The baluster top, similar in form but ending in a small ball or button, was also made from the late fifteenth century through to the early seventeenth century. Bowl shapes changed as the years progressed, from early, steeply sloping fig-shapes to more rounded and egg-shaped.

Facing page, left *St Matthew with a wallet. The bowl is struck with a cross surmounted by a crown – the town mark for Exeter. c.1640.*

Facing page, centre *Henry VIII slip top spoon with London mark for 1520.*

Facing page, right *Commonwealth Puritan spoon, struck with London mark for c.1655.*

Right *The 12 disciples and Jesus Christ in the centre, with their individual symbols which identify them.*

Price bands

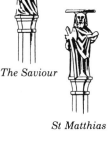

St James the Less St Bartholomew St Peter   St John   St Thomas   St Matthew

The Saviour

St Jude   St James the Greater   St Philip   St Matthias   St Simon Zelotes   St Andrew

Spoons 1660–1760

Signs of authenticity

1. Hallmarks still fairly sparse and random, but in general bowl ceased to be marked on the inside – two or more marks struck on base of stem.
2. From c.1680 four hallmarks generally on back of stem.
3. Britannia Standard marks 1697–c.1720.
4. Early trefid spoons with pronounced notches on terminal on a broadly rounded silhouette.
5. Simple, short V-moulding at junction of bowl and stem to c.1680.
6. Rat-tail with pronounced spine, sometimes beaded, from c.1680 below a rounded drop or button moulding.
7. From c.1690 rat-tail more rounded with steeper curve between bowl and stem.
8. From c.1690 terminals with exaggerated central lobe – known as 'dog's nose'.
9. Around same period bowl backs stamped with swirling decoration.
10. Owner's initials, device, engraved on back of terminal.

Likely restoration and repair
11. Initials, device engraved on front of spoon terminal – later addition.
12. Initials, dates pricked or engraved which do not accord with date letter, hallmarks – may mark a christening, wedding, rather than date of spoon.
13. Crests, armorials extremely rare before c.1700 – check that dates, style accord with date letters.
14. Plain rat-tailed spoons of later date converted by shaping plain rounded finial – easy to spot because authentic period spoons have terminals curving upward when bowl is face-up – later spoon terminals curve downward.

From the time of the Restoration of Charles II, Court banquets must have been, to the English, the richest, most elegant occasions in all the world. To the French, these splendid occasions were seen in quite another light. 'The English are not very dainty and the greatest lords' tables . . . are covered only with large dishes of meat. . . . They scarce ever make use of forks or ewers. . . .' Thus commented a Frenchman in 1663, when forks had been in use in Italy and France from the early sixteenth century.

From the Restoration onwards spoons became less an instrument to shovel food into the mouth and more an elegant piece of tableware. The stem now became broader and flatter, turning up slightly at the end, with a more egg-shaped bowl. The end of the stem was shaped into a 'hind's foot' or trefid with a central lobe and a notch at either side. The stem was joined to the bowl with a short V-joint which gradually elongated into a 'rat-tail', strengthening the join between bowl and stem.

Early Queen Anne spoons, now made in two sizes and called 'table spoons' and 'dessert spoons', had less pronounced notches than the trefid pattern and were more curved, with a pronounced central lobe, known as 'dog's-nose' pattern. The ends of the stems curved backwards, and not forwards. By the time George I succeeded to the throne, spoons were made with matching three-pronged forks, in the first known flatware pattern, which was appropriately called 'Hanoverian'.

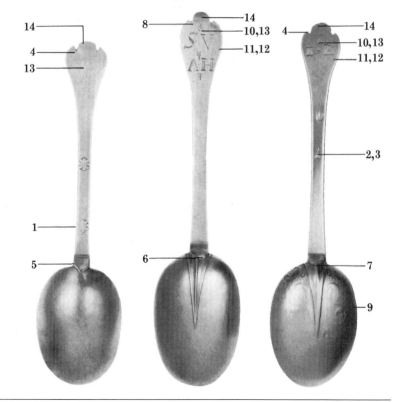

Construction and materials

From about 1660 to 1740, most spoons are of remarkably heavy gauge silver, quite unlike the thinner gauge later in the century. Spoons were made in one piece, with the bowl hammered into a lead die after the handle or stem had been roughly shaped, which accounts for the slight variations in thickness and shape until around 1700.

From this date onwards, regular sets of a dozen spoons were made, each cast in a mould, and then finished and planished by hand. From about 1710 the shaping on the terminal disappeared, leaving a smoothly rounded end, with a slight central ridge and a small turn-over, almost as though the 'dog's-nose' lobe had been doubled over.

Forks, made in matching sets with spoons as a regular accompaniment from about 1730, in general had three prongs until about 1760.

Decoration
Some of the earliest examples of decorated bowl-backs are like leaves with the 'rat-tail' as the central stalk, but these soon became more elaborate and are often found with swirls and scrolling decoration, known as 'fancy back' or 'lace back'. The shell pattern does not seem to have been made much before about 1740, but from that date onwards a shell in some form or another became a regular pattern for bowl-backs, eventually formalised in the 'King's pattern'.

Reproductions

The perfectly plain, sleek and functional Hanoverian pattern has been made almost continuously ever since it was first devised, although from about 1760 onwards forks were made with four prongs and not three. It has been made not only in sterling silver, but also in fused plate from about 1780 onwards, and with a core of white metal alloy from about 1830 onwards. During the Napoleonic Wars, flatware from Sheffield was also made on a variety of base metals, close-plated with silver.

Price bands

Trefid, £150–£350.
Dog's-nose, £110–£280.

Decorated, gilt, £300–£600.

Sets of knife, fork and spoon, £1,000–£2,000 +.

Teaspoons, £50–£200.

Variations

Tea spoons or coffee spoons, identical and interchangeable, were first made in England at the beginning of this period, with a trefid or 'dog's-nose' type of terminal, often more decoratively finished than table or dessert spoons. Very few sets of six have survived intact, and those which have are generally to be found as part of full tea equipages in cases. They were seldom marked with more than a maker's mark and the sterling lion, and were often originally silver gilt. Because of their small size and absence of hallmarks, they are inevitably prey to forgery.

Below right Silver gilt trefid teaspoon with the stem engraved with scrolling foliage and a ribbed rat-tail bowl decorated with an acanthus leaf. c.1690.

Facing page, left 17th-century trefid spoon, probably West Country. c.1690.

Facing page, centre Charles II 'dog's nose' spoon with ribbed rat-tail. c.1675.

Facing page, right William & Mary trefid spoon with lace back bowl and ribbed rat-tail. London 1691.

Right William & Mary 'dog's nose' silver gilt spoon and fork with arabesques and foliage decorating the stems. London 1694.

Centre right Queen Anne Hanoverian pattern table spoon with rat-tail bowl and terminal engraved with crests. London 1716/26.

Flatware 1760–1830

Signs of authenticity

1. Hallmarked from base of stem towards terminal – four marks until 1784.
2. After 1784, sovereign's head duty mark must also be struck.
3. Marks usually struck nearer terminal, no longer at 'bottom end' of stem.
4. Single, commemorative spoons with decorated bowl backs made until *c.*1770 with upward-curving terminals when spoon is laid face up. Initials, devices also on the backs of the stems.
5. On sets of flatware from *c.*1760, crests engraved on terminals, as a general rule on the front, which now curves downward when laid face upwards.
6. Hanoverian spoons with bowl rim lower than stem in silhouette.
7. Old English pattern, bowls tip slightly upwards when face upwards.
8. Beaded edge ending in line with stem-ending above bowl on both spoons and forks.

Likely restoration and repair
9. 'Fancy back' spoons with terminals curving backwards – decorated at later date.
10. Sets of six or 12 spoons and forks may have one or more genuine replacements with later dates – added after loss during one ownership.
11. Beaded edge punched at later date – often continues too far towards bowl of spoon, round shoulder of fork.
12. Crests engraved at later date – considerably reduces value.
13. Thin gauge flatware from *c.*1780 onwards may result in badly worn spoons, tines of forks, subsequently filed down.

There seems to be no particular reason why the English changed their customary manner of setting places at the table at the beginning of George III's reign, but from about 1760 onwards, unlike Continental countries, the English adopted the place settings we still use today, with spoons and forks facing upwards, not face-down on the table. At about the same time, it was noted, the French reintroduced rich pastries and sweets – a custom which the English had never really dropped, although they called them 'puddings'.

Knives with pistol-grip handles joined spoons and forks from about 1725–30 onwards, and from about 1760 onwards sets of special dessert services, very grand, often silver gilt, were also part of full place settings on banqueting tables. The 'Old English' pattern, similar to the 'Hanoverian' pattern except that the terminals of the spoons turned backwards while the forks still turned forwards, was decorated with a feather edge, then a beaded edge and, by the 1780s, in common with many other items of domestic silverware, with bright cut engraving. The gauge by this time had become in some cases extremely thin – Hester Bateman made a great deal of flatware light enough to be within the housekeeping budgets of the middle-class families she supplied. In too many surviving pieces the gauge has become too thin to keep its value in spite of her maker's mark.

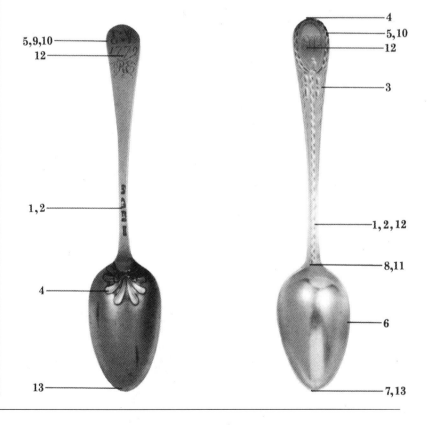

Construction and materials

Spoons continued to be made in a traditional manner, more often than not by specialist makers, up until about 1780, when die-sinking techniques began to revolutionise the making of flatware. The gauge of metal became much thinner, the size of place settings became standardised, and once the great cutlery-manufacturing town of Sheffield began to make flatware, mass-production techniques became more and more common.

The fused plate makers began to make knife-handles from stamped patterns, and then by the beginning of the nineteenth century, close-plated flatware and then fused plate on a alloy of nickel, zinc and copper. Electro-plating came in around 1840, and quickly ousted the more costly fused plate.

Decoration

Single spoons with 'fancy back' or 'lace back' patterns continued to be made and, more often than not, individually engraved up to the 1780s. When bright cut engraving became fashionable, feather-edged and bright cut stems to spoons and forks gave an added glitter to the table. Bright cut flatware may have an oval left vacant for initials or crests – up to that date the only added decoration on Hanoverian and Old English patterns were family crests, engraved on the front of the ends of stems.

Variations

From about 1800 onwards, a wide variety of flatware patterns were made, many of them with small 'shoulders' at the bottom of the stem. From about 1820 the fiddle pattern became popular, followed by a fiddle and thread pattern with a single line of reeding deeply incised round the border. After that came fiddle, thread and shell, with a die-stamped shell on the face of the terminal. From this period onwards, die-struck patterns proliferated, many of whose names give clues to their dates – 'Consort', 'Albert', 'Queen's' pattern. Canteens of silver in heavy mahogany boxes were introduced at the beginning of the Victorian period, which marked the addition of soup spoons to place settings.

Facing page, left Georgian 'fancy back' spoon with a shell back – variations of this pattern were popular between 1758 and 1778.

Facing page, right Georgian Old English pattern spoon with bright cut engraved feather edge by Hester Bateman. London 1787.

Right Ornate 19th-century presentation christening set with cast and gilt silver handles.

Far right Three pieces from a grand silver gilt Coburg pattern dessert service by William and Mary Chawner, London 1827/34, which included two-pronged serving forks, a serving spoon with a fluted bowl and an ice-serving spoon.

Reproductions

The Victorians had a quirky, ephemeral taste for first one period and then another, during which brief time they made handsome reproductions of earlier styles. Among them was the return to the romantic and medieval, with corresponding full canteens of three-pronged forks, spoons, ladles and even fish slices in a 'dog's-nose' pattern.

With Old English beaded edge and feather edge they were less successful, as the beading is often too large and not delicate enough, apart from continuing down the shoulders of the fork which makes it very uncomfortable to eat with. Quickest check – five hallmarks on the back indicate 1784–1890.

Price bands

Spoons:
Lace-back, £30–£150.
Rat-tail, early, £30–£80.

Set of six early Hanoverian spoons and forks, £800–£1,500.

Flatware canteens, £1,200–£15,000 +, depending on period, weight, number of pieces.

143

Nips and tongs

Sugar nips and tongs seem to have become part of the tea equipage from about 1720 onwards, when they were first included in the magnificent boxed sets of tea caddies and bowls. From the early nineteenth century they were often made as presentation pieces in velvet-lined leather cases, but it is extremely rare to find them still with their individual boxes.

There is a tendency today to call nips and tongs decorated with vine leaves and grapes 'grape scissors', but it is more probable that this particular design was kept for use when adding sugar to wine – a common custom which lasted well into the nineteenth century. There are, indeed, proper grape scissors as well, with blunt blades for delicately cutting off a few grapes from the stalk.

3. *George II sugar nips with bright cut engraving and scalloped shell grips and the initials 'S.B.' engraved on the hinge box. Possibly by Richard Mills. c.1758. £120–£190.*

1. *Plain early George II sugar nips with a crest engraved in the centre of the hinge box. c.1735. £220–£350.*

2. *George II sugar nips with scallop shell grips, possibly by George Smith. c.1750. £180–£275.*

4. *George II scroll-handled sugar nips with hinge box and quatrefoil design. c.1755. £220–£350.*

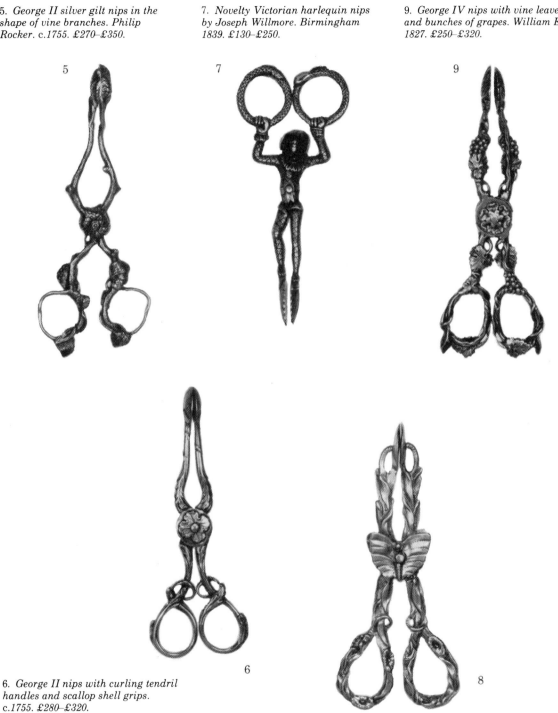

5. George II silver gilt nips in the shape of vine branches. Philip Rocker. c.1755. £270–£350.

7. Novelty Victorian harlequin nips by Joseph Willmore. Birmingham 1839. £130–£250.

9. George IV nips with vine leaves and bunches of grapes. William Eley. 1827. £250–£320.

6. George II nips with curling tendril handles and scallop shell grips. c.1755. £280–£320.

8. Victorian butterfly nips by Joseph Willmore. Birmingham 1840. £130–£220.

Boxes and vinaigrettes

The three most common types of small silver box are nutmeg graters, snuff boxes and vinaigrettes. Nutmeg graters are generally hinged at the top and bottom, with a grater lid inside and space for a nutmeg to be kept, which often means they have domed lids, or are rounded or vase shaped, and between 2 and 3½ in (5.5 and 9 cm) long. Larger boxes, generally 3 to 5 in (7.5 to 12.5 cm) long, were used for 'rapee' or 'carotte' – a knob of solid snuff which was grated as required. Snuff in powder form was kept in small pocket boxes which were made in gold until the middle of the eighteenth century, after which they were part of the Birmingham 'toy' manufacturers' stock in trade.

Vinaigrettes were made from about 1775 onwards, but most found at reasonable prices today are from the nineteenth century. They are distinguished from ordinary small pocket boxes for pills, patches and potions by their inner, decoratively pierced lids. A small scrap of sponge was soaked in aromatic oils or scents, and the piercing in the lid allowed the perfume to escape. Vinaigrettes frequently have a small ring attached, for they were often hung around the neck.

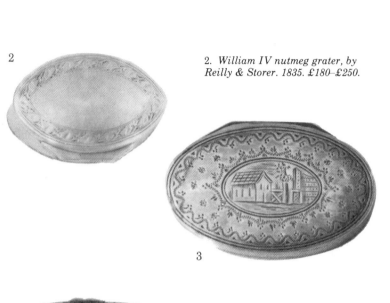

2. *William IV nutmeg grater, by Reilly & Storer. 1835. £180–£250.*

3. *George III silver snuff box by Samuel Pemberton. Birmingham 1818. £120–£180.*

4. *George III silver gilt snuff box with beaded decoration by Joseph Taylor. Birmingham 1814. £280–£400.*

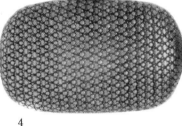

5. *Vinaigrette engraved with a rural scene by the highly collectable Nathaniel Mills. Birmingham 1842. £200–£300.*

6. *Vinaigrette with arabesque decoration and a crest in the centre. Frederick Marson. Birmingham 1857. £120–£300.*

1. *George III nutmeg grater, probably by Samuel Bellingham. 1809. £300–£450.*

7

7. *Vinaigrette with C-scroll decoration. Francis Clark. Birmingham 1842. £120–£250.*

8

9

10

8, 9, 10. *Vinaigrettes in the shape of a purse – a very popular design made in Birmingham from the end of the 18th century to 1850 and later. £40–£160.*

11. *Oblong engine-turned toothpick case by Thomas Shaw. Birmingham 1838. £125–£250.*

11

12. *George III vinaigrette with a Greek key border, possibly by Samuel Pemberton. Birmingham 1804. £125–£175.*

12

13

13. *Visiting card case, die-stamped with a view of Windsor Castle. Taylor & Perry. Birmingham 1842. £180–£350.*

14. *Visiting card case, die-stamped with a view of the Scott Memorial, Edinburgh. Joseph Taylor. Birmingham 1844. £180–£350.*

14

Collectables

By the beginning of the nineteenth century all manner of things were being made in silver, from the purely practical to the decorative and delightful. There are livery buttons and bo'suns' whistles, little silver-cased notebooks and dangerous babies' teething rattles, as well as practical vesta cases which were made in an almost unlimited variety of shapes from about 1870 onwards.

3. *Silver clay pipe holder for keeping the pipe safe from breakage when not in use. Late 18th century. £65–£115.*

1. *Silver bo'sun's whistle with Royal Navy anchor, decorated with leaves. Birmingham. 1873. £20–£65.*

4. *Victorian vinaigrette for a gentleman, in the shape of a military horn or trumpet. c.1873. £100–£180.*

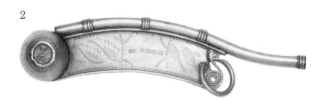

2. *Slightly larger and more elaborate, a bo'sun's whistle with a wirework scrolled loop. Birmingham 1871. £25–£80.*

7

7. *Vinaigrette with C-scroll decoration. Francis Clark. Birmingham 1842. £120–£250.*

8

9

8, 9, 10. *Vinaigrettes in the shape of a purse – a very popular design made in Birmingham from the end of the 18th century to 1850 and later. £40–£160.*

10

11. *Oblong engine-turned toothpick case by Thomas Shaw. Birmingham 1838. £125–£250.*

11

12. *George III vinaigrette with a Greek key border, possibly by Samuel Pemberton. Birmingham 1804. £125–£175.*

12

13

13. *Visiting card case, die-stamped with a view of Windsor Castle. Taylor & Perry. Birmingham 1842. £180–£350.*

14. *Visiting card case, die-stamped with a view of the Scott Memorial, Edinburgh. Joseph Taylor. Birmingham 1844. £180–£350.*

14

Collectables

By the beginning of the nineteenth century all manner of things were being made in silver, from the purely practical to the decorative and delightful. There are livery buttons and bo'suns' whistles, little silver-cased notebooks and dangerous babies' teething rattles, as well as practical vesta cases which were made in an almost unlimited variety of shapes from about 1870 onwards.

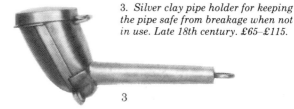

3. *Silver clay pipe holder for keeping the pipe safe from breakage when not in use. Late 18th century. £65–£115.*

1

1. *Silver bo'sun's whistle with Royal Navy anchor, decorated with leaves. Birmingham. 1873. £20–£65.*

4. *Victorian vinaigrette for a gentleman, in the shape of a military horn or trumpet. c.1873. £100–£180.*

2

2. *Slightly larger and more elaborate, a bo'sun's whistle with a wirework scrolled loop. Birmingham 1871. £25–£80.*

4

5

5. *Silver note case engraved with an early steam-and-sail ship, the* Bernina. c.1881. £80–£150.

8

6

6. *Victorian vesta box in the shape of a boot – the sulphur-headed matches were struck on the sole. Birmingham. c.1800. £120–£280.*

8. *A fine 18th-century scent bottle with a hinged silver lid decorated with a coronet and a monogram, with a cut star patterned bottle. £120–£300.*

9. *An amusing Victorian plain tear-shaped scent bottle with a hinged lid in the shape of an owl's head. c.1870. £80–£150.*

7

7. *Baby's rattle with silver bells and a whistle, with a coral teether. They were made from the early 18th century onwards, but most surviving examples date from the 19th century. £180–£250.*

9

Left *An early George III coffee pot decorated with chinoiserie. London 1764.* Right *A hot milk jug beautifully made to match. London 1932.*

Glossary

Acanthus Scrolled leaves of classical origin used as decorative motif for silverware – embossed, chased and applied.

Adam style Neo-classical style popularised by Robert Adam and his brothers, and fashionable *c.*1765–1790.

Alloy In silver, the composite metal resulting from the addition of small amounts of copper to pure silver, to produce sterling silver.

Alms dish Large dish often associated with the church for dispensing food, money to the poor.

Andiron Fire dog.

Animalier Of animal form, resembling an animal.

Anneal The heating of metal repeatedly while working it to keep it malleable.

Annulet Small ring-shaped decoration.

Anthemion Formalised flower-head based on the honeysuckle.

Applied Not part of the integral shape, but ornament, decoration, made separately and added.

Arabesque Of Moorish, Arab origins, pattern of twining leaves and tendrils, used as a border pattern in the late sixteenth and early seventeenth centuries and in pierced work of the eighteenth century.

Argyll Spouted pot made from the mid-eighteenth century with an inner jacket which, filled with hot water or a heated iron, kept gravy hot at table.

Armada jug Wine ewer, claret jug made from *c.*1860 onwards with long slender neck, scrolling handle and pedestal foot, often in silver-mounted cut glass.

Armorials Coats of arms represented in full.

Assay The testing and proving of precious metals to verify that they contain only the legal proportion of base metal alloy. The Assay Office strikes the relevant marks as proof that it has been tested.

Associated A term often found to denote part of a composite set of silverware of which part is correct in design but not originally made with it – e.g. teapot and associated stand.

Asymmetrical Not symmetric – a design that flows, rather than balancing up equally on either side.

Auricular Resembling the curves and lobes of an ear.

Avoirdupois British measurement, scale of weights.

Baluster Slender form swelling out to a pear shape, on stems of candlesticks, wine glasses, wine cups, made from the end of the sixteenth century, but particularly during the early eighteenth century when the baluster form is found also in coffee pots, tankards and jugs.

Baroque A rich and florid style originating during the Renaissance, particularly favoured in England during the seventeenth century.

Bayonet fitting A method of joining covers to bases, particularly of casters, with small lugs twisting into slots, as a light bulb fitting.

Beading Repetitive pattern like a string of beads, sometimes graduated down a spine, more commonly as a border, cast and applied, or simply punched into edges and rims.

Acanthus leaf.

Anthemion and husk.

Argyll.

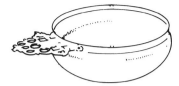

Wine taster.

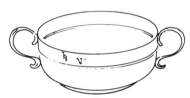

Bleeding bowl.

Capstan salt.

Bezel The groove or flange round a rim.

Bifurcated Forked or split – divided in two.

Biggin A late-eighteenth-century patent coffee pot with a cotton sleeve to hold the coffee grounds.

Billet Thumbpiece of a tankard or flagon. Also an old word for ingot.

Bleeding bowl A small shallow dish or cup with two ring handles – a contentious issue. Many of these are classified as wine tasters.

Blind A cover, usually of a caster, which is identical to its companions but which has not been pierced.

Boss Rounded or raised, as in 'embossing'. Also the term for the slightly domed centre of alms dishes etc.

Bougie box A container for a taper, like a string box, with a hole through which the taper was drawn.

Bound and reeded A border pattern. Also for a short time a pattern for flatware and cutlery.

Bright cut An engraving technique much used in the late eighteenth century and early nineteenth century, using tools which produced a brilliant faceted effect.

Britannia metal A pewter-like alloy developed in the 1770s as an alternative to pewter but without the dangerous lead content. From *c.*1840 it was used extensively as a base for electroplating, generally stamped 'E.P.B.M.', standing for ElectroPlated Britannia Metal.

Britannia Standard Higher standard of silver content for wrought plate, not coinage, obligatory 1697–1720 and marked with a lion's head erased and a figure of Britannia, in place of the lion passant guardant and the leopard's head of sterling silver.

British plate A silver-coloured nickel alloy, sometimes also known as German silver, used from *c.*1830 as a base for fused plate.

Bullet An almost spherical shape.

Bullion Gold and silver before it has been made up.

Calyx The cupped leaves enfolding a bud.

Campana An exaggerated vase shape, with a pronounced waist.

Camp canteen Set of travelling cutlery, forks, spoons and accoutrements.

Candelabrum (pl. candelabra) A standing branched candlestick.

Canteen Matched set of flatware, generally boxed or cased.

Capstan Finial, foot, salt. Shaped like a dockside capstan, with a more pronounced curve than a spool.

Carolean The period spanned by the reign of Charles II, 1660–85, who signed his name 'Carolus Rex' and generally including the brief rule of James II and the Interregnum, to 1689. Erroneously used sometimes for the reign of Charles I, which is generally known as Stuart.

Cartouche The decorative frame or surround to a coat of arms.

Caryatid Originally in classical architecture, stone or carved female figures, revived and used extensively during the Renaissance, and subsequently in England as a decorative motif up to the late seventeenth century. Revived during the neo-classical period of the eighteenth century and again with the Gothic revival of the nineteenth century.

Cast Shaped or made by pouring molten metal into a cast or mould, made of wood, plaster, metal, or by the 'lost wax' process.

Caster Container for condiments, spices and sugar, with pierced cover for sprinkling.

Casting bottle Small decorative container for scents and perfumes, swung on a chain in the same manner as a church censer.

Caudle cup Two-handled covered drinking cup, sometimes also with a stand or saucer, for drinking warm spiced milk.

Chairback Type of tankard thumbpiece of specific pattern.

Chalice A wine cup with a shallow bowl on a stem.

Chandelier A many-branched hanging light.

Charger A large circular dish, generally with a wide flat rim and shallow centre, for serving meats.

Chased, chasing Decoration raised in relief on the surface of the metal without cutting any away. A series of punches and tools push and coax the metal into patterns, sometimes so finely that it can almost be mistaken for engraving. *See also* Flat chasing, Embossed chasing.

Chinoiserie Decoration in the Chinese style, drawn from merchandise reaching Europe from the Far East. There were three waves of popularity for chinoiserie – in the latter part of the seventeenth century, the mid-eighteenth century and the early nineteenth century.

Cire perdu See Lost wax.

Chippendale Thomas. Furniture maker and designer of the mid-eighteenth century whose name has been given to a type of border for salvers and waiters, also known as 'piecrust'. 'Chinese Chippendale' is a term sometimes used to describe a 'cracked ice' trellis-like pierced border of trays, coasters in the second half of the eighteenth century.

Close plating Originally used by cutlers to protect steel knives from staining and rusting, a method of applying a layer of silver foil to steel with a flux of tin. A slightly different method is known as 'French plating'.

Collet foot A foot with a collar.

Commonwealth The period between 1649 and 1660 when England was ruled by the Lord Protector, Oliver Cromwell.

Comport A fruit or dessert dish raised on a single foot.

Corded Resembling twisted string.

Corinthian The capital of a column which is formed of stylised acanthus leaves.

C-scroll A pattern, a shape of handles, based on the letter C.

Cut card work A simple form of applied decoration using sheet silver cut in leaf shapes, fleur-de-lys or trefoil, generally soldered round the base of a bowl or cup

Chinoiserie.

Caudle cup.

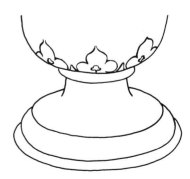

Cut card work.

Cymric silver.

Dog's nose terminals.

like a calyx. Most frequently found between c.1680 and 1710. Also used after that date as a decorative stregthening round handle sockets, spouts, and as a base for finials, generally in the first years of the eighteenth century.

Cutlery Tableware, household articles with blades for cutting, including scissors.

Cymric Derived from Celtic designs – a term used at the end of the nineteenth century and the beginning of the twentieth.

Diaper Repetitive pattern of diamonds, trellis or lozenges.

Die-sinking A mechanical method of hammering sheet metal into a cast or mould to make feet, finials etc. in two halves which were then soldered together and filled with a lead/ tin alloy.

Die-stamping A method of raising patterns in relief by mechanical means, using a steel die and a drop hammer.

Dished, dishing Slightly shaped with a concave curve.

Dog's nose Shape of a spoon terminal with a pronounced central lobe, a later version of the trefid spoon, made from c.1690 onwards.

Double-faced plate Fused plate with both sides coated with silver.

Douter A form of snuffer with two flat blades at the end of scissor-like arms.

Dredger Used today as an alternative term for 'caster'. 'Dredge' was a spiced sugar in the Middle Ages.

Drip pan A flange to catch the wax from a dripping candle.

Duty dodging Prevalent between 1720 and 1758 when duty was imposed on wrought plate according to its weight. The practice of removing the hallmarks from a small piece of assayed plate and inserting them into a much larger piece, thereby only paying duty on the small item.

Duty mark The sovereign's head, struck on all silverware with a few exemptions for small ware from 1784 to 1890.

dwt Shortened form of 'pennyweight'.

Ecuelle A shallow bowl and cover with two flat handles, up to about 6 in (15.5 cm) in diameter, and more common in France than in England, where the few surviving examples seem generally to have been made by Huguenot silversmiths around the end of the seventeenth century and the beginning of the eighteenth century.

Edict of Nantes An act of 1598 which gave full civil rights to the Protestant Huguenots in Catholic France. It was constantly flouted and, after years of religious persecution, the Huguenot cities were denied self-government by Cardinal Richelieu in 1629. In 1685 Louis XIV revoked the Edict, and Huguenots were forced to flee the country.

Electroplate Base metal alloy of copper or nickel coated with a thin layer of silver by electrolysis, using pure silver as opposed to sterling silver which is used in the manufacture of fused plate.

Electrotype An electrolytic process in which deposits of pure silver are built up in a cast or mould in order to produce a facsimile.

Embossing The technique of producing raised decoration by working the metal from the back or reverse surface. Fairly simple shapes such as domes and lobes were raised in this manner, and then given detail and definition by repoussé chasing from the back, or chasing on the surface.

Engraving Incised decoration on the surface of the metal, using tools which cut into the surface at varying depths and thicknesses of stroke – a specialist skill seldom carried out by silversmiths for work of any importance.

Epergne An elaborate table centrepiece which became the *pièce de résistance* for eighteenth-century silversmiths, often consisting of a decorative frame supporting arms for candles as well as small dishes for desserts, fruit and sweetmeats.

Etui A small fitted box containing a variety of small objects, from bodkins, needles and pins, to toothpicks, tweezers, pens and ink bottles, ingeniously made.

Ewer A large and sumptuous jug, accompanied by an imposing basin, originally for rinsing hands and fingers at table before the use of forks.

Extinguisher Shaped like a dunce's cap, most commonly found together with a chamberstick, for putting out a candle. Also made on long slender poles and used for extinguishing candles in a chandelier or hanging light.

Faceted A shape with many faces, polygonal in section.

Fancy back Spoons with decoration on the back of the bowl.

Fashioning Working up – the old term used by silversmiths for making an article in silver. The cost of a commission was always by weight of metal plus the cost of fashioning.

Feather edge Chased or bright cut sloping lines, generally used to describe a flatware pattern of 1770–90.

Festoon A delicate, looping garland of fruit or flowers.

Filigree Very fine openwork in silver wire, such as caddy spoons, or as decorative panels.

Filled *See* Loaded.

Finial The topmost ornament on a piece of silverware except, strictly speaking, on the cover of a cup, when it is called a knop. Also the ends of spoons which are cast, such as baluster, seal or apostle figures.

Fire gilding *See* Gilding.

Flat chasing Impressed decoration on the surface of silver which produces a similar effect to engraving without cutting any of the metal away. It is not as sharp as engraving and, unlike engraving, it can be seen in a blurred form on the reverse side. Cast silver was often 'chased up' to achieve immaculate detail and definition.

Flatware All tableware without a cutting edge.

Fluting Parallel concave grooves, running vertically, swirled or curved which, apart from being decorative, also added strength to flat surfaces of sheet silver.

Fly-punching Mechanical method of piercing fused plate by using hardened steel punches.

Classical ewer.

Extinguisher cap.

A melon fluted teapot with an acorn finial, engraved with a crest. Paul Storr. London 1837.

Flying scroll An upward-scrolling handle joined to the body at the base of the scroll only.

Foliate Decoration consisting of leaves, foliage, or in leaf shapes.

Foot rim The base on which a vessel stands.

Fret Repetitive pattern of right angles, often known as Greek key pattern.

Fretwork Pierced decorative band or edge cut with a fretsaw.

Fused plate Sterling silver fused to base metal alloy, generally called 'Sheffield Plate' – misleadingly, because much of the early production was from Birmingham.

Gadroon Repetitive pattern of slanting lobes, originally derived from the knuckles of a clenched fist.

Gauge The thickness of metal.

Gilding The application of a thin layer of gold to silver. An amalgam of mercury and gold leaf with the consistency of thick clay was spread over the part to be gilded and then heated over a charcoal fire, causing the mercury to evaporate, leaving a film of gold which was then burnished. Mercury fumes were extremely toxic and once the process of electrogilding had been developed in the mid-nineteenth century, fire gilding with mercury was prohibited by law.

Girdle A narrow band encircling a vessel or object.

Gold plating Electrogilding technique which is similar to the process of electroplating with silver.

Greek key pattern *See* Fret.

Guilloche Repetitive pattern consisting of two interlaced ribbons or bands enclosing a circle, sometimes containing a rosette or quatrefoil motif.

Hallmark The mark struck by the Assay Office in proof that a piece of gold or silver contains no more than the legal amount of alloy.

Hanoverian Denotes the period spanned by the reign of the first two ruling monarchs of the House of Hanover, George I, 1714–27, and George II, 1727–60.

Hanoverian pattern A flatware pattern made *c*.1714–75 and revived frequently since that time.

Heraldry The art or science of blazoning armorial bearings and settling the rights of persons entitled to bear arms.

Hind's foot A more elegant term for 'dog's nose' finials on spoons, from the French *pied de biche*.

Hollow ware Vessels, jugs, pots, tankards and any article raised, spun, turned or cast in a hollow shape.

Hoof foot A foot shaped like a hoof, popular in the first half of the eighteenth century.

Huguenot French Protestant, many of whom fled to England as a result of religious persecution after the Revocation of the Edict of Nantes.

Husk Bell-shaped decorative motif derived from a corn husk, particularly popular during the neo-classical period in the eighteenth century.

Imperial measure System of measures imposed in 1826 to bring all measures of ale, wine etc into conformity.

Hanoverian.

Albert.

Albany.

Bright vine.

Coburg.

Chased vine.

King's husk.

King's pattern.

Faceted baluster stem.

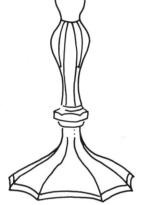

Faceted inverted baluster.

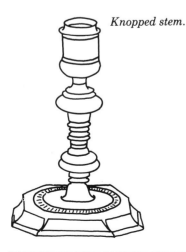

Knopped stem.

'Improved' Decorated at a later date, generally during the nineteenth century.

Incised Cut into, as distinct from impressed or applied.

Incuse Technical difference in method of stamping, in which the image was impressed more deeply into the metal than the surrounding outline of the whole face of the punch.

Inkstandish Ink pots, pounce pots, quill pen holders in a fitted dish – seventeenth- and eighteenth-century term for an inkstand.

Inverted baluster Literally, a baluster shape upside down with the swelling at the top, tapering to a slender shape below.

Jacobean The period spanned by the reign of James I of England, 1603–25. Used loosely to include the Commonwealth.

Japonaiserie Design based loosely on Japanese forms and decorative styles.

Judaica Silver particularly related to the Hebrew and Jewish faith.

Knop A knob as an integral part of a stem of a candlestick, cup, goblet, sometimes treated differently, sometimes conforming in shape with the stem. Also the finial of a cup, and the end of a spoon when cast.

Lace back A particular version of a fancy back spoon.

Lanceolate Shaped like a spearhead or lance, often used to describe a stiff leaf design.

Lap joint A joint formed by cutting away the two ends to form L-shapes.

Lattice A criss-cross pattern of diamonds.

Loaded Term describing items of sheet silver and fused plate which are then filled with pitch or other substances for stability and solidity.

Lobe, lobing Repetitive decoration of tear-shaped domes, rather like a large version of gadrooning.

Lost wax An ancient technique of achieving crisp, finely detailed cast work by modelling an original in wax and taking a mould from it. The wax was then melted, leaving its crisp impression in the mould. Molten metal could then be poured into the mould through small channels.

Lozenge A diamond shape.

Maidenhead spoon One of the earliest forms of spoon with a cast finial in the shape of a woman's head, presumed to be the Virgin Mary, although without a halo, dating from the fourteenth century.

Mantling The plumes or drapery falling either side of the helmet in a coat of arms.

'Marriage' The joining of two parts from different items to form an apparent whole.

Marrow scoop An implement with a deep groove, used for extracting the marrow from bones at table, at first combined with a spoon at the other end, from the last decade of the seventeenth century. In the eighteenth century, more often a separate implement, often with a different-sized scoop at either end.

Mask Head of a lion, ram, bird or human derived from the masks of classical Greek theatre. Used as a decorative motif in almost every period, but particularly during the neo-classical period in the eighteenth century.

Matt, matting A distinct non-shiny surface achieved by using an implement with a tiny circular punch – used to produce a heightened effect, as a background to raised decoration, or as a decoration on its own.

Mazarine A flat dish liner pierced with decorative patterns, used as a drainer or strainer on which a fish or joint of meat was placed, on a large dish.

Milling, milled edge An edge ground like the sides of a minted coin.

Moliquet, molinet A whisk, usually of wood, used to froth up chocolate and prevent it settling at the bottom of a chocolate pot. The moliquet fitted into a small covered hole in the lid.

Mote spoon A small spoon with a decoratively pierced bowl and a spike or point at the end of the stem, for skimming tea leaves off and spiking the perforations at the base of a teapot spout when they became clogged.

Moulding A decorative rim or strip, either applied or cast.

Mount Decorative silver forming part of an object made in a different material.

Mouth wire The strengthening wire applied to beakers, mugs, tankards, round the mouth of the vessel to give added protection from denting, buckling.

Nef Extremely grand and ornate vessel for containing salt, generally Continental in origin, and performing a similar function as a standing salt. Nefs were revived during the romantic movement of the nineteenth century.

Nimbus A halo.

Nozzle The part of a candlestick into which the candle fits.

Octafoil With eight sides of unconforming shape and length.

Octagonal Eight-sided with eight equal straight sides.

Old English pattern The first matching pattern for table services of flatware and cutlery.

Pale The stake of a fence, sometimes upright, sometimes slanting.

Palladian Related to, or influenced by the drawings and designs of Antonio Palladio 1518–80, who revived classical Roman architecture and proportions.

Palmate Shaped like the palm of a hand, not like a palm leaf.

Parcel gilt A corruption of 'partially gilded'.

Paten A shallow dish used to hold the wafer bread at a Communion service.

Patera (*pl* paterae) Small circular or oval disc-shaped ornament, derived from classical origins, particularly fashionable during the Regency period.

Pedestal foot A foot joined to a vessel by a support which is more substantial than a stem.

Peg tankard A form of tankard originating in Scandinavia and found mostly made in the North of England, in York, Hull and Edinburgh, in the late seventeenth century. The tankard usually rests on three or four cast feet, and the level of ale is marked off by pegs inside the pot, presumably so that no drinker in a communal bout should exceed his ration.

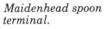

Maidenhead spoon terminal.

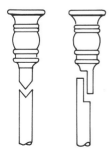

Left *V joint*. Right *lap joint*.

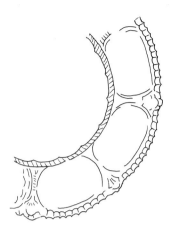

Crimped piecrust edge.

Chippendale piecrust edge.

Pennyweight The smallest measure of Troy weight, usually written as dwt.

Piecrust Generally taken to describe a forward and reverse curve border popularised by Thomas Chippendale on his 'piecrust' tables. The earlier Stuart version is simply a crimped wire, as though pinched between finger and thumb.

Pied de biche See Hind's foot.

Piercing, pierced Openwork decoration done with great precision with extremely sharp chisels until about 1760, after which it was done with a saw similar to a fretsaw, sometimes known as fretwork. Towards the end of the eighteenth century piercing was done mechanically, with a fly press, using cutting tools and punches.

Pistol grip Shape of knife handles in the eighteenth century, with swelling curved ends like a pistol butt.

Planishing One of the final processes in the making of wrought plate, using a broad-faced hammer with a convex curve to smooth and polish plain surfaces.

Plate The old, traditional word for silver and gold. Not to be confused with 'fused plate' (or 'Sheffield plate'), a term which led to the erroneous but generally held belief that 'plate' was 'plated'.

Plate makers Manufacturers of fused plate. In the trade, makers of sterling silver wrought plate are also known as plate makers.

Plinth The square base at the bottom of a column.

Pottle Old measure for two quarts of ale.

Pounce pot A small container with a perforated lid or cover for sprinkling paper with finely powdered gum sandarac, a sort of pumice, which made the surface smooth and non-absorbent.

Pricked Simple form of engraving done with a needle point, most commonly found as initials or dates.

Provenance The history, vouched for with sound evidence, of a piece of silverware or an antique.

Provincial Silver made and hallmarked by Assay Offices other than London, and excepting Scottish and Irish silver.

Punched Simple decorative motifs stamped or embossed on early silver.

Putti Small cherubs – a word inherited from Renaissance Italy.

Quatrefoil With four leaves or lobes.

Quaich A Scottish two-handled shallow bowl, about the same size and shape as a French *ecuelle* but without a cover.

Ram's-horn Twisting shape, most common on tankard thumb-pieces, which are also known as 'corkscrew'.

Rat-tail The slender, tapering spine on the back of a spoon bowl, from the end of the seventeenth century.

Raising stake A cast iron, anvil-like stake on which hollow ware is raised after being initially shaped in the sinking block.

Reeding Lines of parallel convex decoration, like the

Pounce pot.

surface of a bunch of reeds. A more decorative version, used on rims of plates and flatware in the mid-eighteenth century, was bound with ribbons and known as 'bound and reeded'.

Regency Strictly speaking, the period during which George, Prince of Wales was Prince Regent from 1811 to 1820, but generally covering the wider span of 1800–30.

Renaissance The revival or rebirth of classical disciplines in the arts in Italy from the end of the fourteenth century to the middle of the seventeenth century.

Repoussé The combined technique of embossing on the back and adding detail and definition by chasing on the front surface.

Restoration The return of Charles II to the throne of England after the Commonwealth in 1660.

Revocation of the Edict of Nantes *See* Edict of Nantes.

Rim wire The strengthening wire round the edge of a plate, bowl or dish.

Rocaille Stony, rocky seabed landscape with seaweed, coral, shells and scrolls, on which the French rococo style was based.

Rococo Asymmetric swirling design introduced by Juste Aurèle Meissonier in France in the 1730s.

Saltire A diagonal cross, like the cross of St Andrew.

Sconce The candle socket of a candlestick. Also a candle holder with one or more arms and a backplate, known as a wall sconce.

Seal top An early pattern of spoon with a truncated baluster finial.

Shagreen Originally the untanned skin of an ass, dyed green, sometimes red or black and, rarely, blue. Used for scabbards, and to cover a multitude of small boxes. Replaced in the 1760s by shark-skin, almost always dyed green.

Sheffield plate *See* Fused plate.

Shoulder The widest part of an item or object.

Shoulder knop The knop on the stem of a candlestick almost directly below the sconce.

Silver gilt Silver which has been wholly or partly covered with gilding.

Single-faced plate Fused plate with a coating of silver on one side only.

Sinking block A wooden block with a dish-shaped hollow in the centre, into which sheet silver was hammered before being further shaped on the raising stake into hollow ware.

Slip lock Bayonet fitting.

Slip top Spoon with no finial or shaped terminal. The stem is cut in a sharp diagonal wedge shape from front to back.

Sovereign's head Duty mark struck 1784–1890 to show that duty had been paid at the time of assay.

Soy frame A frame to hold small bottles of sauce, like a cruet frame. A soy frame could hold anything from two to six or more bottles, often of cut glass with silver mounts.

S-scroll Handle of a cup or vessel based on the letter S.

Rococo candlestick.

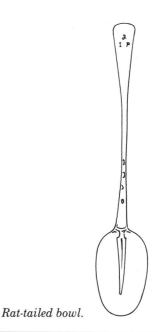

Rat-tailed bowl.

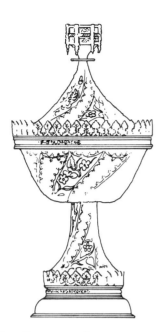

Standing cup and cover.

Strapwork.

Stamping Decoration in relief produced by hammering the metal into or over a die bearing the reverse relief. Used at an early period for narrow borders and mouldings, and by the end of the seventeenth century for decorative spoon-bowls and stems. In the second half of the eighteenth century mechanical die-stamping was introduced and used extensively on fused plate and sheet silver.

Standing cup An important piece of display plate, particularly from the Renaissance onwards, when it was a measure of wealth for the owner and of skill for the goldsmith and silversmith.

Standing salt The Great Salt was of equal importance with the Standing Cup from the Middle Ages until the end of the Tudor period. Elaborate, often set with gemstones or of silver gilt or parcel gilt and rock crystal, they are among the finest examples of the craft of goldsmithing.

Stave A lathe of wood forming part of a cask or barrel.

Sterling The standard of purity for silver alloyed with copper laid down by statute before 1300 and adhered to, with brief exceptions, to this day. Sterling silver is 92.5 parts pure silver to 7.5 parts copper.

Strapwork Interlacing straps or bands of ornament, engraved as border decoration on sixteenth-century Communion cups, beakers and wine cups, often combined with simple flowers and leaves. From the end of the seventeenth century, strapwork ornament was cast and applied in a more elaborate form, on two-handled cups and covers, tankards and bowls. This form of strapwork appears to have been brought to England by Huguenot craftsmen, and should not be confused with cut card work, which produces a simpler effect with cut patterns of sheet silver, not cast.

Strawberry dish A name given to shallow fluted dessert dishes.

Struck More authoritative than 'marked' or 'stamped', a term still used for coinage – a seal or device carried on gold and silver by law.

Stuart The period during which England was ruled by monarchs of the Stuart line – generally speaking from 1603, when James I became king, to 1689, when William of Orange succeeded to the throne.

Sucket fork A two- or three-pronged fork with a long slender handle for spiking such delicacies as ginger and other confectionery from their jars – sucket forks were often made with a spoon at the other end of the handle.

Supporter The figures on either side of a shield – viz. the Lion and Unicorn. Only persons included in the rank of nobility are entitled to supporters.

Swag A heavier version of a festoon, often cast or chased, hanging, looped or draped, bunches of fruit, flowers and leaves.

Swage block A pair of hinged jaws, the lower cut with a pattern in relief, the upper with the pattern correspondingly sunk, about 1 in (2.5 cm) wide and 8–10 in (20–25 cm) long. The jaws were covered in leather to protect the surface of the metal and closed over the edge of sheet silver or fused plate, impressing the pattern when the jaws were struck or pressed tightly together. Lengths of decorative edging were made by repeating the process on the next length or, using curved swage blocks, borders round all manner of plates, dishes, trays etc. were stamped with a repeating pattern. The device was invented in 1762 and was superseded by die-stamping in the 1780s.

Tallow Suet and hard animal fat used for making candles.

Taper stand An upright plain stem, often threaded, on which a scissor-like device of flat blades holds the end of a taper which is coiled round the stem.

Tastevin A wine taster.

Tazza A wide, shallow bowl standing on a single central foot or stem originating in the sixteenth century in England, used either as a shallow drinking vessel or as part of church plate, possibly a font cup or Communion cup. Today the word is extended to cover any ornamental shallow dish on a single foot.

Tea table, tea board A term used in the eighteenth century to denote a tea tray, which sometimes fitted into a wooden stand, like a small table.

Terminal The ends of all or part of a piece of silverware, such as the end of a spoon without a finial, or the ends of a handle or spout.

Thread One or two lines of reeding.

Tine A prong of a fork.

Tinning, tinned A necessary finishing process for insides of hollow ware in single-faced fused plate, covering the interior copper surface with a flux of tin which gave it a silvery appearance and prevented the copper from interacting with acid-based liquids.

Touch Originally the test by touchstone to discover the purity of metal before it was struck with the hallmark of the Assay Office. Through usage, associated with the marks, came to mean the marks themselves.

Touchstone A black slatey basanite or basalt on which gold and silver were tested.

Town mark The identification of the town or city of an Assay Office.

Toy Small pieces of all kinds, not necessarily miniatures or children's toys, but all manner of trinkets, boxes and small articles and implements.

Trefid, trifid Divided into three.

Trefoil Having three leaves or lobes.

Trencher salt Individual small dishes for salt, taking their name from the depression in one corner of a wooden platter.

Triton A sea god, usually helmeted with a trident and fish-tail.

Troy weight A system of weights and measures used for precious metals and stones.

Tudor The period during which England was ruled by members of the House of Tudor, from Henry VII in 1485 to Elizabeth I, who was succeeded by the first Stuart monarch, James I (of England, VI of Scotland), in 1603.

Tumbler cup A round-bottomed drinking vessel without seams, with extra weight in its base to allow it to return to an upright position if knocked or jogged.

Vacant A cartouche which has no coat of arms in the centre.

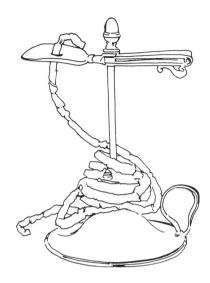

Taper stand.

Triton handle.

Wrythen knop.

Vinaigrette A small box, generally in silver, with a gilt interior, and an inner, pierced lid, for holding a small scrap of sponge soaked in penetrating aromatic vinegar – like a smelling bottle of later years – generally dating from the 1770s onwards.

Vitruvian scroll Repetitive pattern of rather angular, stylised wave forms.

V-joint A joint formed by a shaped notch which receives a shaft cut in the shape of an arrowhead.

Volute Spiral, curled, scrolling.

Voyder In the Middle Ages, a dish into which all the scraps of food from the table were scraped, later used to refer to an early form of tray. Generally accompanied by a voyding knife, with a broad spatulate blade.

Waiter Today the term is generally used to describe any salver measuring less than about 9 in (23 cm) in diameter, although in the eighteenth century it was more common usage than 'salver'.

Wall sconce One or more candle arms fixed to a backplate and secured to the wall.

Wax jack The word 'jack' simply meant an instrument or device in the sixteenth century. Thus a wax jack is a device for holding a taper, also known as a taper stand.

Wine taster A shallow dish or bowl between 3 and $5\frac{1}{2}$ in (7.5 and 14 cm) in diameter, with outward-sloping sides and domed base – an English pattern until the mid-eighteenth century. Continental wine tasters generally have one or possibly two simple ring handles, curved sides and bowl bases.

Wrought plate General term for all silverware and gold which has been handmade.

Wrythen knop A spiral swirled ball finial of a spoon dating mainly from the late fifteenth and early sixteenth centuries.

Wyvern A mythical beast, said to have originated in Wales, with a body like a dragon, two front feet, and a curled serpent's tail.

Sheffield Plate epergne.

Weights and Measures

The old traditional measure for silver was Troy weight, and there are many references to this scale in books and catalogues. It differs from standard avoirdupois weight and uses some different units. Today, since decimalisation, the gram is widely used as a unit of measurement.

Troy weight
24 grains = 1 pennyweight (dwt)
20 pennyweight = 1 ounce Troy
12 ounces Troy = 1 one pound Troy

Conversion
1 pennyweight = 1.555 g
1 ounce Troy = 31.1 g
1 pound Troy = 373.2 g

1 ounce Troy = 1.097 ounces avoirdupois.

The weight of an article is the weight of the alloy and not of the silver alone. Sterling silver is 92.5 per cent pure silver. Britannia Standard silver is 95.8 per cent pure silver.

Measures for ale, wine and dry measures were all slightly different until the imposition of the Imperial measure in 1826, which was a slightly larger measure than previously. An old pint of ale was $16\frac{2}{3}$ fl oz, whereas an Imperial pint is 20 fl oz. This measure helps in determining some tankard periods and dates.

Principal Silversmiths

Craftsmen Working in England from the Seventeenth Century to the Nineteenth Century

The craft of the goldsmith and silversmith was often a family tradition, and more than one member of the same name is found in the lists of makers' marks entered at the Goldsmiths' Hall. The dates given are those of the working years of silversmiths, not their dates of birth and death.

Abercrombie (Abercromby), Robert. 1731–43. Specialist salver maker.

Angell, Joseph. 1811–24. He and his son John, 1824–c.1850, are best known for teaware.

Barnard, Edward. 1791–95. A senior member of this family of silversmiths, which includes Thomas Barnard, 1784–96.

Barnard, Edward. 1808–29. In partnership with Rebecca Emes, formed the prestigious firm of **Emes & Barnard**. John Emes also worked for the firm which in 1829 became Messrs Barnard. Specialist makers of centrepieces, candelabra and grand cups as well as less important pieces.

Bateman, Hester. Recorded as entered to the Goldsmiths' Company in 1761. From 1773 to 1789 made flatware, spoons, forks, domestic silver of good quality. The business became Hester Bateman & Co. from 1790 to 1793.

Bateman, Jonathan and Peter. Hester's two sons who took over the business when Hester retired in 1790. Jonathan died in 1791 and his widow Anne registered with Peter from 1791 to 1796. Their son William joined the firm in 1800. Anne Bateman retired in 1805 and a new mark was struck for Peter and William Bateman.

Bateman, Peter and William. 1805–15. See above.

Bateman, William. 1815–39, after his father died. After 1839 the business passed to William Bateman II.

Boulton, Matthew. Took over his father's business at the Birmingham Soho Factory in 1759, taking into partnership John Fothergill, silversmith and jeweller, in 1762. Maker's marks for **Boulton and Fothergill** 1762–82. Executed many commissions for Robert Adam, as well as pioneering fused plate from c.1765 onwards. Fothergill died in 1782. Matthew Boulton was first to register at the new Birmingham Assay Office in 1773, having previously had work assayed at Chester or London. From 1781 to 1809 the firm was known as **Matthew Boulton & Plate Co.**

Boulton, Matthew Robinson. Succeeded to his father's firm in 1809, when it was called **M. R. Boulton** until 1834. From 1834 to 1843 it was know as the **Soho Plate Company.**

Cafe (Case), John. 1740–57. Specialist maker of candlesticks, chambersticks, snuffers and trays.

Cafe (Case), William. John's brother, who took over the business 1757–75, when he went bankrupt.

Chawner, Henry. 1790–96. In partnership with John Emes 1796–1808. One of a convoluted family which included William Chawner, who was in partnership with George Heming 1773–81; William Chawner, 1759–73; and Thomas Chawner 1759–99. Thomas and William Chawner were in partnership 1759–68.

Coker, Ebenezer (Ebonezer). 1738–81. Maker of important wares and one of the few English silversmiths to make in the rococo manner, particularly candlesticks, but also salvers and other important pieces.

Crespin, Paul. 1720–25. Of Huguenot origins, made sumptuous work, almost as great an influence on English silver as Paul de Lamerie.

Crespin, Paul. His son, who entered the business in 1740 and continued the same high style, including work of great richness and splendour – soup tureens, serving dishes and massive plate, including a considerable amount of rococo design.

de Lamerie, Paul. 1712–51. Family originated in the Netherlands. Apprenticed to Pierre Platel in London, and became one of the most influential silversmiths of the period, and one of the few genuine exponents of the rococo style in England.

Elkington & Co., Birmingham. Makers of fine silver in the 19th century on a commercial scale, notably with the use of the two processes of electrotyping and electroplating.

Emes, John. One of a traditional silversmithing family dating back to 1702 when the name was first entered. In partnership with Henry Chawner 1796–1808.

Emes, Rebecca. In partnership with Edward Barnard, as **Emes & Barnard**. 1808–29. See under separate entries.

Farrell, Edward Cornelius. 1813–35. Produced much fine silver and silver gilt based on early styles, particularly in the Carolean manner and designs based on 17th-century Dutch patterns.

Flaxman, John. b.1755–d.1826. Much influenced by classical Greek and Roman styles, his designs were made by **Rundell, Bridge & Rundell**, for whom he made massive pieces, some of which were later made in facsimile using the technique of electrotyping.

Fogelberg, Andrew. 1773–c.1800. Revived the use of portrait medallions in the classical manner for which his work is specially known during the Adam period. Master to Paul Storr who was one of his apprentices.

Fox, Charles. 1822–40. One of a family of talented silversmiths, including his father, Charles Fox I, who made many individually designed pieces of original tableware and accessories.

Fox, George. Another of the same family, working c.1860–1900 making original and unusual domestic ware.

Garrard, Robert. 1792–1802. In partnership with another dynasty, the Wakelins. John Wakelin & Robert Garrard 1792–1805. This firm includes a short period of Robert Garrard II, who took over his father's business in 1802–21. From 1818 to 1853 the firm was known as **Garrard & Bros (late Wakelin & Garrard)**.

Gould, James. 1722–37. Fine specialist candlestick maker.

Gould, William. 1732–57. Son of James, also a specialist candlestick maker. A John Gould entered his mark in 1773.

Harache (Harrache), Pierre. 1675–1700. Huguenot silversmith working in London who, together with his son, introduced the technique of cast silver candlesticks to England. His son, also Pierre, but anglicised to Peter, worked with him 1689–1705 and was succeeded by Peter Harache Jnr 1714–17.

Heming (Hemming), Thomas. *c.*1760–73. Leading silversmith of his day, and in partnership with William Chawner 1773–81.

Hennell, David. 1736–58. One of a dynasty of silversmiths which continues to this day. His son, Robert, worked with him 1763–97.

Hennell, Robert. 1769–91. Grandson of David Hennell. After the death of his grandfather, in 1778, he worked with his father, and then with both his sons, David Hennell II and Samuel, before his death in 1811. Another Robert Hennell, descendant of the original founder, was working until 1868. The firm is still in existence today.

Hunt, John Samuel. Took over the prestigious firm of **Storr & Mortimer** in 1838 after the death of Paul Storr. On the death of John Hunt in 1868 the firm became **Hunt & Roskell (late Storr & Mortimer)**.

Meissonnier, Juste Aurèle. Born in Turin in 1695, he worked in Paris and at the French court, and provided the seminal influence for the rococo style in silver and the decorative arts. He died in 1750.

Pitts, William. 1781–1800. Early exponent of Carolean revival design, whose interpretations were more formal than those of Edward Cornelius Farrell who worked in the same genre a decade or so later.

Platel, Pierre. 1699–1716. One of the great early Huguenot silversmiths working in England, influencing both design and technique indelibly. One of his many talented apprentices from Huguenot stock was Paul de Lamerie.

Pyne, Benjamin. 1693–1727. One of the traditional English silversmiths of the period who continued to work in his own style despite the overwhelming influence of the Huguenots at that period. His death is recorded in 1720, though his mark continued for another seven years – perhaps another case of a son of the same name entering the business. His maker's mark was entered from 1693 to 1696, and in 1697, and again from 1700 to 1727.

Rolles, Philip. Huguenot goldsmith and silversmith who registered his mark 1675–77, 1701–20 and again in 1727.

Rollos, Philip. Executed grand commissions, working at almost the same period as the above, 1701–22.

Rundell, Bridge. *c.*1780–1802. Philip Rundell and John Bridge who formed the most prestigious goldsmiths' and silversmiths' company of the Regency period, catering to rich and aristocratic families, creating massive plate and using designers and craftsmen who were names in their own right, among them John Flaxman and Paul Storr. In 1805–39 the company was renamed **Rundell, Bridge & Rundell.**

Schofield (Scofield), John. 1776–96. Prolific maker of a wide variety of decorative ware and tableware, for some reason undervalued despite his high-quality workmanship and design.

Smith, Benjamin. 1802–18. Birmingham silversmith who worked originally for Matthew Boulton. Went to London with fellow silversmith Digby Scott and set up in partnership, making fine-quality design and workmanship, much of it for **Rundell, Bridge & Rundell.**

Storr, Paul. 1792–1838. Regarded today as one of the greatest silversmiths, he worked on his own, in partnership with John Mortimer as **Storr & Mortimer**, and in association with **Rundell, Bridge & Rundell**, making richly decorated heavy quality important pieces. On his death in 1838 his company, Storr & Mortimer, became **Hunt & Roskell** (see entry).

Van Vianen, Christian. 1598–1666. Early influence on pre-Restoration silver, highly original and today might almost be mistaken for designs of a far more modern date. Came to England *c.*1630 probably at the invitation of Charles I, but left before the beginning of the Commonwealth in 1649. Developed a sinuous line known as 'auricular' because of its derivation from the convolutions of the human ear. Very little of his work survived the Civil War.

Wakelin, Edward. 1747–66. Member of a family of silversmiths, he made fine and grand tableware, much of it in association with Georges Wickes, with whom he worked from 1747.

Wakelin & Garrard. 1792–1805. John Wakelin and Robert Garrard.

Wickes, George. 1721–61. Appointed goldsmith to the Prince of Wales, the future George III, in 1735. Sumptuous silver, more in the English tradition than the French.

Willaume, David. 1674–1712. Of Huguenot origins, worked in London making pieces of deceptively simple design but remarkably high quality craftsmanship.

Willaume, David II. *c.*1706–46. Worked with his father (see above) and until recently the continuance of a David Willaume was thought to be that of his father, but in fact David II continued the business after his father's death in 1712.

Wood, Samuel. 1733–46. Skilled craftsman and specialist maker of casters and dredgers. A second Samuel Wood entered his mark in 1773.

Bibliography

Bannister, Judith. *English Silver*. London 1965.

Bannister, Judith. *The Country Life Collector's Pocket Book of Silver*. Country Life Books (Hamlyn Publishing Group) 1982.

Bradbury, Frederick. *Bradbury's Book of Hallmarks and Old Sheffield Plate Makers' Marks. 1743–1860*. Pocket Edition. Sheffield 1979.

Bradbury, Frederick. *A History of Old Sheffield Plate*. London 1912. Reprinted Sheffield 1968.

Clayton, Michael. *The Collector's Dictionary of Silver and Gold of Great Britain and North America*. Antique Collectors' Club 1971.

Cripps, Wilfred Joseph. *Old English Plate*. John Murray, London 1901. Reprinted by E.P. Publishing Ltd, East Ardsley, Wakefield, Yorks 1977.

Culme, John. *Nineteenth-century Silver*. London 1977.

Glanville, Phillippa. *Silver in England*. Unwin, Hyman, Holmes & Meyer, London 1987.

Grimwade, Arthur. *London Goldsmiths 1697–1837. Their Marks & Their Lives*. London 1976.

Grimwade, Arthur. *Rococo Silver. 1727–1765*. Faber & Faber 1975.

Hughes, G. Bernard. *Antique Sheffield Plate*. Batsfords, London 1970.

Hayward, J. F. *Huguenot Silver in England. 1688–1727*. Faber & Faber 1959.

Inglis, Brand. *The Arthur Negus Guide to British Silver*. Hamlyn Publishing Group Ltd 1980.

Jackson, Sir Charles J. *English Goldsmiths and Their Marks*. London 1921.

Luddington, John. *Starting to Collect Silver*. Antique Collectors' Club 1984.

Oman, Charles. *English Engraved Silver. 1150–1900*. Faber & Faber 1978.

Oman, Charles. *Caroline Silver. 1625–1688*. Faber & Faber 1978.

Rowe, Robert. *Adam Silver*. Faber & Faber 1965.

Wardle, Patricia. *Victorian Silver and Silver-Plate*. London 1963.

Waldron, Peter. *The Price Guide to Antique Silver*. Antique Collectors' Club 1982.

Index